Nikon® D3100™
FOR
DUMMIES®

by Julie Adair King

WILEY

John Wiley & Sons, Inc.

Nikon® D3100™ For Dummies®

Published by
John Wiley & Sons, Inc.
111 River Street
Hoboken, NJ 07030-5774

www.wiley.com

Copyright © 2011 by John Wiley & Sons, Inc., Hoboken, New Jersey

Published by John Wiley & Sons, Inc., Hoboken, New Jersey

Published simultaneously in Canada

For general information on our other products and services, please contact our Customer Care Department within the U.S. at 877-762-2974, outside the U.S. at 317-572-3993, or fax 317-572-4002.

For technical support, please visit www.wiley.com/techsupport.

Wiley publishes in a variety of print and electronic formats and by print-on-demand. Some material included with standard print versions of this book may not be included in e-books or in print-on-demand. If this book refers to media such as a CD or DVD that is not included in the version you purchased, you may download this material at http://booksupport.wiley.com. For more information about Wiley products, visit www.wiley.com.

Library of Congress Control Number: 2010941211

ISBN 978-1-118-00472-2 (pbk); ISBN 978-1-118-02595-6 (ebk); ISBN 978-1-118-02596-3 (ebk); ISBN 978-1-118-02597-0 (ebk)

Manufactured in the United States of America

10 9 8 7 6

WILEY

About the Author

Julie Adair King is the author of many books about digital photography and imaging, including the best-selling *Digital Photography For Dummies.* Her most recent titles include a series of *For Dummies* guides to popular digital SLR cameras, including the *Canon EOS Rebel T2i/550D, T1i/500D, XSi/450D, XS/1000D,* and *XTi/400D,* and *Nikon D5000, D3000, D300s, D90, D60,* and *D40/D40x.* Other works include *Digital Photography Before & After Makeovers, Digital Photo Projects For Dummies, Julie King's Everyday Photoshop For Photographers, Julie King's Everyday Photoshop Elements,* and *Shoot Like a Pro!: Digital Photography Techniques.* When not writing, King teaches digital photography at such locations as the Palm Beach Photographic Centre. A graduate of Purdue University, she resides in Indianapolis, Indiana.

Author's Acknowledgments

I am deeply grateful for the chance to work once again with the wonderful publishing team at John Wiley and Sons. Kim Darosett, Jennifer Webb, Steve Hayes, Jen Riggs, and Katie Crocker are just some of the talented editors and designers who helped make this book possible. And finally, I am also indebted to technical editor Dave Hall, without whose insights and expertise this book would not have been the same.

Publisher's Acknowledgments

We're proud of this book; please send us your comments at http://dummies.custhelp.com. For other comments, please contact our Customer Care Department within the U.S. at 877-762-2974, outside the U.S. at 317-572-3993, or fax 317-572-4002.

Some of the people who helped bring this book to market include the following:

Acquisitions and Editorial

Project Editor: Kim Darosett

Executive Editor: Steven Hayes

Copy Editor: Jennifer Riggs

Technical Editor: David Hall

Editorial Manager: Leah Cameron

Editorial Assistant: Amanda Graham

Sr. Editorial Assistant: Cherie Case

Cartoons: Rich Tennant
(www.the5thwave.com)

Composition Services

Project Coordinator: Katherine Crocker

Layout and Graphics: Samantha K. Cherolis

Proofreaders: Susan Hobbs, Jessica Kramer

Indexer: Sherry Massey

Publishing and Editorial for Technology Dummies

Richard Swadley, Vice President and Executive Group Publisher

Andy Cummings, Vice President and Publisher

Mary Bednarek, Executive Acquisitions Director

Mary C. Corder, Editorial Director

Publishing for Consumer Dummies

Kathleen Nebenhaus, Vice President and Executive Publisher

Composition Services

Debbie Stailey, Director of Composition Services

Contents at a Glance

Table of Contents

Introduction

*O*nce upon a time, making the move from a point-and-shoot digital camera to an SLR model required boatloads of cash and the willingness to cart around a bulky, heavy piece of equipment. All that changed a few years ago when Nikon introduced the D40, a digital SLR that offered a compact size *and* an equally compact price.

With the D3100, Nikon proves once again that you don't have to give an arm and a leg — or strain your back and neck — to enjoy dSLR photography. Yet despite its diminutive size, the D3100 doesn't skimp on power or performance, offering a great set of features to help you take your photography to the next level.

In fact, the D3100 offers so *many* features that sorting them all out can be more than a little confusing, especially if you're new to digital photography, SLR photography, or both. For starters, you may not even be sure what SLR means or how it affects your picture taking, let alone have a clue as to all the other techie terms you encounter in your camera manual — *resolution, aperture, white balance,* and so on. And if you're like many people, you may be so overwhelmed by all the controls on your camera that you haven't yet ventured beyond fully automatic picture-taking mode. Which is a shame because it's sort of like buying a Porsche 911 and never heading out for the open road.

Therein lies the point of *Nikon D3100 For Dummies*. Through this book, you can discover not just what each bell and whistle on your camera does, but also when, where, why, and how to put it to best use. Unlike many photography books, this one doesn't require any previous knowledge of photography or digital imaging to make sense of things, either. In classic *For Dummies* style, everything is explained in easy-to-understand language, with lots of illustrations to help clear up any confusion.

In short, what you have in your hands is the paperback version of an in-depth photography workshop tailored specifically to your Nikon picture-taking powerhouse.

A Quick Look at What's Ahead

This book is organized into four parts, each devoted to a different aspect of using your camera. Although chapters flow in a sequence that's designed to take you from absolute beginner to experienced user, I've also tried to make each chapter as self-standing as possible so that you can explore the topics that interest you in any order you please.

Here's a brief preview of what you can find in each part of the book:

- ✔ **Part I: Fast Track to Super Snaps:** Part I contains four chapters to help you get up and running. Chapter 1 offers a tour of the external controls on your camera, shows you how to navigate camera menus to access internal options, and walks you through initial camera setup. Chapter 2 explains basic picture-taking options, such as shutter-release mode and image quality settings, and Chapter 3 shows you how to use the camera's fully automatic exposure modes. Chapter 4 explains the ins and outs of using *Live View,* the feature that lets you compose pictures on the monitor, and also covers movie recording.

- ✔ **Part II: Working with Picture Files:** This part offers two chapters, both dedicated to after-the-shot topics. Chapter 5 explains how to review your pictures on the camera monitor, delete unwanted images, and protect your favorites from accidental erasure. Chapter 6 guides you through the process of downloading pictures to your computer, preparing photos for printing, and sharing images online.

- ✔ **Part III: Taking Creative Control:** Chapters in this part help you unleash the full creative power of your camera by moving into the advanced shooting modes (P, S, A, and M). Chapter 7 covers the critical topic of exposure, and Chapter 8 explains how to manipulate focus and color. Chapter 9 summarizes all the techniques explained in earlier chapters, providing a quick-reference guide to the camera settings and shooting strategies that produce the best results for portraits, action shots, landscape scenes, and close-ups.

- ✔ **Part IV: The Part of Tens:** In famous *For Dummies* tradition, the book concludes with two "top ten" lists containing additional bits of information and advice. Chapter 10 covers features found on the camera's Retouch menu, including tools that enable you to crop your photo, adjust color and exposure, and make other picture adjustments right in the camera. Chapter 11 wraps up the book by detailing some camera features that, while not found on most "Top Ten Reasons I Bought My Nikon D3100" lists, are nonetheless interesting, useful on occasion, or a bit of both.

Icons and Other Stuff to Note

If this isn't your first *For Dummies* book, you may be familiar with the large, round icons that decorate its margins. If not, here's your very own icon-decoder ring:

A Tip icon flags information that will save you time, effort, money, or some other valuable resource, including your sanity. Tips also point out techniques that help you get the best results from specific camera features.

When you see this icon, look alive. It indicates a potential danger zone that can result in much wailing and teeth-gnashing if ignored. In other words, this is stuff that you really don't want to learn the hard way.

Lots of information in this book is of a technical nature — digital photography is a technical animal, after all. But if I present a detail that is useful mainly for impressing your technology-geek friends, I mark it with this icon.

I apply this icon either to introduce information that is especially worth storing in your brain's long-term memory or to remind you of a fact that may have been displaced from that memory by some other pressing fact.

Additionally, I need to point out three details that will help you use this book:

- **Other margin art:** Replicas of some of your camera's buttons and onscreen symbols also appear in the margins of some paragraphs. I include these to provide a quick reminder of the appearance of the button or feature being discussed.

- **Software menu commands:** In sections that cover software, a series of words connected by an arrow indicates commands that you choose from the program menus. For example, if a step tells you to "Choose File⇨Convert Files," click the File menu to unfurl it and then click the Convert Files command on the menu.

- **Camera firmware:** *Firmware* is the internal software that controls many of your camera's operations. The D3100 firmware consists of parts called A, B, and L. At the time this book was written, both A and B were version 1.00, and L was version 1.002.

   Occasionally, Nikon releases firmware updates, and it's a good idea to check out the Nikon Web site (www.nikon.com) periodically to find out whether any updates are available. (Chapter 1 tells you how to determine which firmware version your camera is running.) Firmware updates typically don't carry major feature changes — they're mostly used to solve technical glitches in existing features — but if you do download an update, be sure to read the accompanying description of what it accomplishes so that you can adapt my instructions as necessary.

eCheat Sheet

As a little added bonus, you can find an electronic version of the famous *For Dummies* Cheat Sheet at www.dummies.com/cheatsheet/nikond3100. The Cheat Sheet contains a quick-reference guide to all the buttons, dials, switches, and exposure modes on your D3100. Log on, print it, and tuck it in your camera bag for times when you don't want to carry this book with you.

Practice, Be Patient, and Have Fun!

To wrap up this preamble, I want to stress that if you initially think that digital photography is too confusing or too technical for you, you're in very good company. *Everyone* finds this stuff a little mind-boggling at first. So take it slowly, experimenting with just one or two new camera settings or techniques at first. Then, each time you go on a photo outing, make it a point to add one or two more shooting skills to your repertoire.

I know that it's hard to believe when you're just starting out, but it really won't be long before everything starts to come together. With some time, patience, and practice, you'll soon wield your camera like a pro, dialing in the necessary settings to capture your creative vision almost instinctively.

So without further ado, I invite you to grab your camera, a cup of whatever it is you prefer to sip while you read, and start exploring the rest of this book. Your D3100 is the perfect partner for your photographic journey, and I thank you for allowing me, through this book, to serve as your tour guide.

Part I
Fast Track to Super Snaps

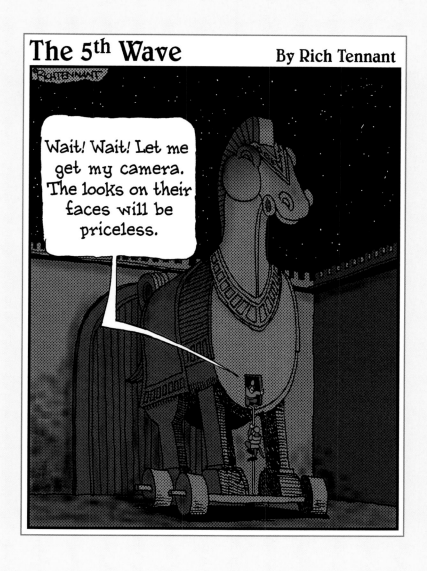

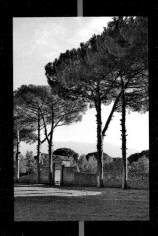

In this part . . .

Making sense of all the controls on your
D3100 isn't something you can do in an
afternoon — heck, in a week, or maybe even a
month. But that doesn't mean that you can't take
great pictures today. By using your camera's
point-and-shoot automatic modes, you can capture terrific images with very little effort. All you
do is compose the scene, and the camera takes
care of almost everything else.

This part shows you how to take best advantage
of your camera's automatic features and also
addresses some basic setup steps, such as adjusting the viewfinder to your eyesight and getting
familiar with the camera menus, buttons, and
other controls. In addition, chapters in this part
explain how to obtain the very best picture quality, whether you shoot in an automatic or manual
mode, and how to use your camera's Live View
and movie-making features.

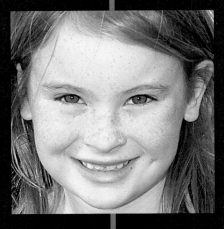

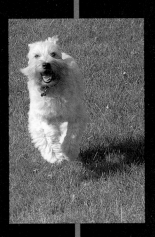

Getting the Lay of the Land

I still remember the day that I bought my first single-lens reflex (SLR) film camera. I was excited to finally move up from my one-button point-and-shoot camera, but I was a little anxious, too. My new pride and joy sported several unfamiliar buttons and dials, and the explanations in the camera manual clearly were written for someone with an engineering degree. And then there was the whole business of attaching the lens to the camera, an entirely new task for me. I saved up my pennies a long time for that camera — what if my inexperience caused me to damage the thing before I even shot my first pictures?

You may be feeling similarly insecure if your Nikon D3100 is your first SLR, although some of the buttons on the camera back may look familiar if you've previously used a digital point-and-shoot camera. If your D3100 is both your first SLR and first digital camera, you may be doubly intimidated.

Trust me, though, that your camera isn't nearly as complicated as its exterior makes it appear. With a little practice and the help of this chapter, which introduces you to each external control, you can become as comfortable with your camera's buttons and dials as you are with the ones on your car's dashboard. This chapter also guides you through the process of mounting and using an SLR lens, working with memory cards, navigating your camera's menus, and customizing basic camera operations.

Getting Comfortable with Your Lens

One of the biggest differences between a point-and-shoot camera and an SLR camera is the lens. With an SLR, you can swap out lenses to suit different photographic needs, going from a *macro lens,* which enables you to shoot extreme close-ups, to a *telephoto lens,* which lets you photograph subjects from a distance, for example. In addition, an SLR lens has a movable focusing ring that lets you focus manually instead of relying on the camera's autofocus mechanism.

Of course, those added capabilities mean that you need a little information to take full advantage of your lens. To that end, the next several sections explain the process of attaching, removing, and using this critical part of your camera.

Attaching a lens

Your camera can autofocus only with a type of lens that carries the specification *AF-S.* (Well, technically speaking, the camera can autofocus with *AF-I* lenses also. But because those are high-end, very expensive lenses that are no longer made, this is the only mention of AF-I lenses in this book.) You can use other types of lenses, as long as they're compatible with the camera's lens mount, but you have to focus manually.

Whatever lens you choose, follow these steps to attach it to the camera body:

1. **Turn the camera off and remove the cap that covers the lens mount on the front of the camera.**

2. **Remove the cap that covers the back of the lens.**

3. **Hold the lens in front of the camera so that the little white dot on the lens aligns with the matching dot on the camera body.**

Official photography lingo uses the term *mounting index* instead of *little white dot.* Either way, you can see the markings in question in Figure 1-1.

Note that the figure (and others in this book) shows the D3100 with its so-called *kit lens* — the 18–55mm AF-S Vibration Reduction (VR) zoom lens that Nikon sells as a unit with the body. If you buy a lens from a manufacturer other than Nikon, your dot may be red or some other color, so check the lens instruction manual.

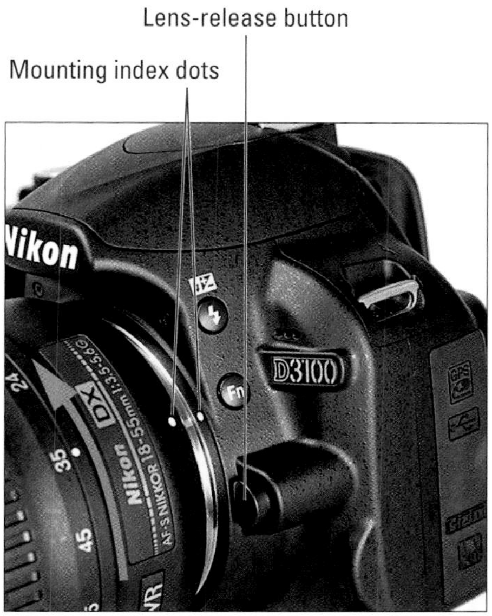

Lens-release button

Mounting index dots

Figure 1-1: When attaching the lens, align the index markers as shown here.

4. **Keeping the dots aligned, position the lens on the camera's lens mount, as shown in Figure 1-1.**

   When you do so, grip the lens by its back collar, not the movable, forward end of the lens barrel.

5. **Turn the lens in a counterclockwise direction until the lens clicks into place.**

   To put it another way, turn the lens toward the side of the camera that sports the shutter button, as indicated by the red arrow in the figure.

6. **On a lens that has an aperture ring, set and lock the ring so the aperture is set at the highest f-stop number.**

   Check your lens manual to find out whether your lens sports an aperture ring and how to adjust it. (The D3100 kit lens doesn't.) To find out more about apertures and f-stops, see Chapter 7.

Even though the D3100 is equipped with a dust reduction system, always attach (or switch) lenses in a clean environment to reduce the risk of getting dust, dirt, and other contaminants inside the camera or lens. Changing lenses on a sandy beach, for example, isn't a good idea. For added safety, point the camera body slightly down when performing this maneuver; doing so helps prevent any flotsam in the air from being drawn into the camera by gravity.

Removing a lens

To detach a lens from the camera body, take these steps:

1. **Turn off the camera and then locate the lens-release button, labeled in Figure 1-1.**

2. **Press the lens-release button while turning the lens clockwise (toward the button) until the mounting index on the lens is aligned with the index on the camera body.**

   The mounting indexes are the little guide dots labeled in Figure 1-1. When the dots line up, the lens detaches from the mount.

3. **Place the rear protective cap onto the back of the lens.**

   If you aren't putting another lens on the camera, cover the lens mount with the protective cap that came with your camera, too.

Setting the focus mode (auto or manual)

Again, the option to switch between autofocusing and manual focusing depends on matching the D3100 with a fully compatible lens, as I explain in the earlier section, "Attaching a lens." With the kit lens, as well as with other AF-S lenses, you can enjoy autofocusing as well as manual focusing.

The AF stands for *autofocus*, as you may have guessed. The S stands for *silent wave*, a Nikon autofocus technology.

For times when you attach a lens that doesn't support autofocusing or the autofocus system has trouble locking on your subject, you can focus manually by twisting a focusing ring on the lens barrel. The placement and appearance of the focusing ring depend on the lens; Figure 1-2 shows you the one on the kit lens.

To focus manually with the kit lens, take these steps:

1. **Set the focus mode switch on the lens to the M (manual) position.**

   Figure 1-2 gives you a look at the switch.

2. **While looking through the viewfinder, twist the focusing ring to adjust focus.**

   If you have trouble focusing, you may be too close to your subject; every lens has a minimum focusing distance. You may also need to adjust the viewfinder to accommodate your eyesight; you can get help with the process a few paragraphs from here.

Focal length indicator

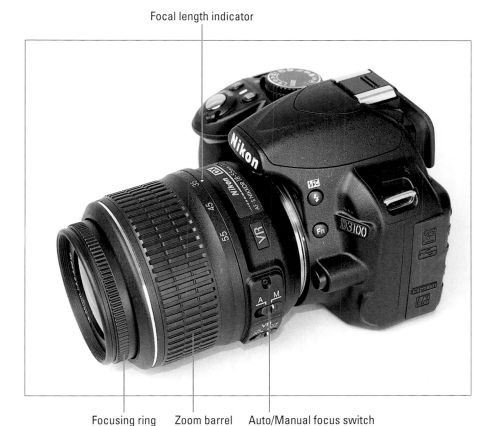

Focusing ring   Zoom barrel   Auto/Manual focus switch

Figure 1-2: On the 18–55mm kit lens, the manual-focusing ring is set near the front of the lens, as shown here.

If you use a lens other than the kit lens, check the lens instruction guide for details about focusing manually; your lens may or may not have a switch similar to the one on the kit lens. Also see the Chapter 8 section related to the Focus mode option on the Shooting menu, which should be set to MF for manual focusing. (With the kit lens and some other lenses, the camera automatically chooses the MF setting for you.)

By the way, even when you focus manually, the camera provides some feedback to help you determine whether focus is set correctly. Look in the Chapter 8 section that's devoted to manual focusing for details.

Zooming in and out

If you bought a zoom lens, it has a movable zoom barrel. The location of the zoom barrel on the D3100 kit lens is shown in Figure 1-2. To zoom in or out, just rotate that zoom barrel.

The numbers on the zoom barrel, by the way, represent *focal lengths.* I explain focal lengths in Chapter 8. In the meantime, just note that when the lens is mounted on the camera, the number that's aligned with the lens mounting index (the white dot) represents the current focal length. In Figure 1-2, for example, the focal length is 35mm.

Using a VR (Vibration Reduction) lens

If you purchased the D3100 kit — the body-and-lens combination put together by Nikon — your lens offers *Vibration Reduction.* On Nikon lenses, this feature is indicated by the initials *VR* in the lens name.

Vibration Reduction attempts to compensate for small amounts of camera shake that are common when photographers handhold their cameras and use a slow shutter speed, a lens with a long focal length, or both. That camera movement during the exposure can produce blurry images. Although Vibration Reduction can't work miracles, it enables most people to capture sharper handheld shots in many situations than they otherwise could.

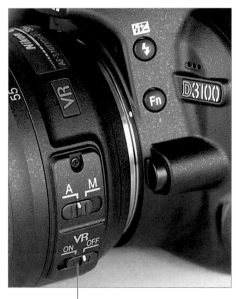

Here's what you need to know about taking best advantage of this feature with your D3100:

- ✐ **Turn Vibration Reduction on or off by using the VR switch, labeled in Figure 1-3.** The switch is located on the lens, directly underneath the Auto/ Manual focus switch.

Vibration Reduction switch

Figure 1-3: Turn off Vibration Reduction when you use a tripod.

- ✐ **Vibration Reduction is initiated when you depress the shutter button halfway (which also initiates autofocus and expo- sure metering).** If you pay close attention, the image in the viewfinder may appear to be a little blurry immediately after you take the picture. That's a normal result of the vibration-reduction operation and doesn't indicate a problem with your camera or focus.

✔ **With the kit lens, turn Vibration Reduction off when you mount the camera on a tripod.** When you use a tripod, Vibration Reduction can have detrimental effects because the system may try to adjust for movement that isn't actually occurring. This recommendation assumes that the tripod is "locked down" so that the camera is immovable.

✔ **For other lenses, check the lens manual to find out whether your lens offers a similar feature.** On non-Nikon lenses, it may go by another name: *image stabilization, optical stabilization, anti-shake, vibration compensation,* and so on. In some cases, the manufacturers may recommend that you leave the system turned on or select a special setting when you use a tripod or *pan* the camera (move it horizontally or vertically as you take the picture). For the kit lens, however, you don't need to disable Vibration Reduction when panning.

Chapter 8 offers more tips on achieving blur-free photos, and it also explains focal length and its impact on your pictures. See Chapter 7 for an explanation of shutter speed.

Adjusting the Viewfinder Focus

Tucked behind the right side of the rubber eyepiece that surrounds the viewfinder is a tiny dial that enables you to adjust the focus of your viewfinder to accommodate your eyesight. Figure 1-4 offers a close-up look at the dial, which is officially known as the *diopter adjustment control.*

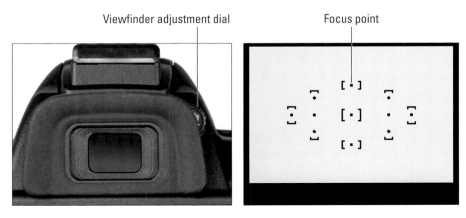

Figure 1-4: Use the diopter adjustment control to set the viewfinder focus for your eyesight.

If you don't take this step, scenes that appear out of focus through the viewfinder may actually be sharply focused through the lens, and vice versa. Here's how to make the necessary adjustment:

1. **Remove the lens cap from the front of the lens.**

2. **Look through the viewfinder and concentrate on the little black marks clustered around the center portion of the screen.**

   The marks represent the camera's autofocusing points, which you can read more about in Chapters 3 and 8. I labeled one of the points in Figure 1-4.

3. **Rotate the dial until the viewfinder marks appear to be in focus.**

The Nikon manual warns you not to poke yourself in the eye as you perform this maneuver. This warning seems so obvious that I laugh every time I read it — which makes me feel doubly stupid the next time I poke myself in the eye as I perform this maneuver.

Working with Memory Cards

Instead of recording images on film, digital cameras store pictures on *memory cards*. Your D3100 uses a specific type of memory card — an *SD card* (for *Secure Digital*).

Most SD cards sold today carry the designation SDHC (for *High Capacity*) or SDXC (for *eXtended Capacity*), depending on how many gigabytes (GB) of data they hold. SDHC cards hold from 4GB to 32GB of data; the SDXC moniker is assigned to cards with capacities greater than 32GB. You also can use an Eye-Fi SD card, which enables you to send pictures to your computer over a wireless network. (Because of space limitations, I don't cover Eye-Fi connectivity in this book; if you want more information about these cards, you can find it online at www.eye.fi.)

Safeguarding your memory cards — and the images you store on them — requires just a few precautions:

✓ **Inserting a card:** First, be sure that the camera is turned off. Then put the card in the card slot with the label facing the back of the camera, as shown in Figure 1-5. Push the card into the slot until it clicks into place; the memory card access light (labeled in Figure 1-5) blinks for a second to let you know the card is inserted properly.

✓ **Formatting a card:** The first time you use a new memory card or insert a card that's been used in other devices (such as an MP3 player), you should *format* it. Formatting ensures that the card is properly prepared to record your pictures.

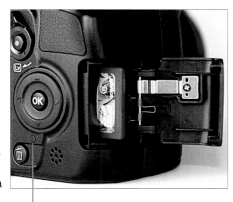

Formatting erases *everything* on your memory card. So before formatting, be sure that you have copied any pictures or other data to your computer.

Memory card access light

To format a memory card, choose the Format Memory Card command from the Setup menu. The upcoming section "Ordering from Camera Menus" explains how to work with menus. When you select the command, you're informed that all images will be deleted, and you're asked to confirm your decision to format the card. Highlight Yes and press OK to go forward.

Figure 1-5: Insert the card with the label facing the camera back.

If you insert a memory card and see *For* in the viewfinder, you must format the card before you can do anything else. You also see a message requesting formatting on the camera monitor.

Some computer programs enable you to format cards as well, but it's not a good idea to go that route. Your camera is better equipped to optimally format cards.

✓ **Removing a card:** After making sure that the memory card access light is off, indicating that the camera has finished recording your most recent photo, turn off the camera. Open the memory card door, as shown in Figure 1-5. Depress the memory card slightly until you hear a little click and then let go. The card pops halfway out of the slot, enabling you to grab it by the tail and remove it.

If you turn on the camera when no card is installed, the symbol [-E-] blinks in the lower-right corner of the viewfinder. If the Shooting Information screen is displayed on the monitor, that screen also nudges you to insert a memory card. If you do have a card in the camera and you get these messages, try taking it out and reinserting it.

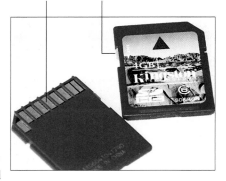

Don't touch! Lock switch

Figure 1-6: Avoid touching the gold contacts on the card.

✔ **Handling cards:** Don't touch the gold contacts on the back of the card. (See the left card in Figure 1-6.) When cards aren't in use, store them in the protective cases they came in or in a memory card wallet. Keep cards away from extreme heat and cold as well.

✔ **Locking cards:** The tiny switch on the side of the card, labeled *lock switch* in Figure 1-6, enables you to lock your card, which prevents any data from being erased or recorded to the card. Press the switch toward the bottom of the card to lock the card contents; press it toward the top of the card to unlock the data. (If you insert a locked card into the camera, you see a message on the monitor alerting you to the fact, and the symbol [d blinks in the viewfinder.)

You also can protect individual images on a card from accidental erasure by using the camera's Protect feature, which I cover in Chapter 5.

Do you need high-speed memory cards?

Memory cards are categorized not just by their storage capacity, but also by their data-transfer speed. SD cards (the type used by your D3100) fall into one of four *speed classes:* Class 2, Class 4, Class 6, and Class 10, with the number indicating the minimum number of *megabytes* (units of computer data) that can be transferred per second. A Class 2 card, for example, has a minimum transfer speed of 2 megabytes, or MB, per second. Of course, with the speed increase comes a price increase, which leads to the question: Do you really have a need for speed?

The answer is "maybe." If you shoot a lot of movies with the D3100, I recommend a Class 6 or 10 card, as does Nikon — the faster data-transfer rate helps ensure smooth movie-recording and playback performance. For still photography, users who shoot at the highest resolution or prefer the Raw (NEF) file format

may also gain from high-speed cards; both options increase file size and, thus, the time needed to store the picture on the card. (See Chapter 2 for details.)

As for picture downloading, how long it takes files to shuffle from card to computer depends not just on card speed, but also on the capabilities of your computer and, if you use a memory card reader to download files, on the speed of that device. (Chapter 6 covers the file-downloading process.)

Long story short, if you want to push your camera to its performance limits, a high-speed card is worth the expense, especially for video recording. But if you're primarily interested in still photography or you already own slower-speed cards, try using them first — you may find that they're more than adequate for most shooting scenarios.

One side note on the issue of memory cards and file storage: Given that memory cards are getting cheaper and larger in capacity, you may be tempted to pick up an 8GB (gigabyte) or 16GB card thinking you can store a gazillion images on one card and not worry about running out of room. But memory cards are mechanical devices that are subject to failure, and if a large card fails, you lose lots of images. And putting aside the potential for card failure, it's darned easy to misplace those little guys. So I carry several 4GB SD cards in my camera bag instead of relying on one ginormous card. Although I hate to lose any images, I'd rather lose 4GB worth of pictures than 8 or 16GB.

Exploring External Camera Controls

Scattered across your camera's exterior are buttons, dials, and switches that you use to change picture-taking settings, review and edit your photos, and perform various other operations. In later chapters, I discuss all your camera's functions in detail and provide the exact steps to follow to access them. This section provides just a basic road map to the external controls plus a quick introduction to each.

 One note before you move on: Many of the buttons perform multiple functions and so have multiple "official" names. The AE-L/AF-L button, for example, is also known as the Protect button. In the camera manual, Nikon's instructions refer to these multi-tasking buttons by the name that's relevant for the current function. I think that's a little confusing, so I always refer to each button by the first moniker you see in the lists here. In addition, when I reference a button, its picture appears in the margin to further clarify things. (The exceptions are the Menu and OK buttons — I don't show these because they are such frequent players in the camera's operation and so would appear way too many times on the page.)

Topside controls

Your virtual tour begins with the bird's-eye view shown in Figure 1-7. There are a number of controls of note here:

- **On/Off switch and shutter button:** Okay, I'm pretty sure you already figured out this combo button. But check out Chapter 3 to discover the proper shutter-button-pressing technique — you'd be surprised how many people mess up their pictures because they press that button incorrectly.

 - **Exposure Compensation button:** This button activates a feature that enables you to tweak exposure when working in three of your camera's autoexposure modes: programmed autoexposure, aperture-priority autoexposure, and shutter-priority autoexposure, represented by the letters P, S, and A on the Mode dial. Chapter 7 explains. In manual exposure (M) mode, you press this button while rotating the Command dial to adjust the aperture setting.

⌐ **Info button:** Press this button to display the Shooting Information screen on the camera monitor. The screen not only enables you to easily view the current picture-taking settings but also is the pathway to the Quick Settings screen, through which you can adjust some settings more quickly than by using the camera menus. See the upcoming section "Monitoring Shooting Settings" for details. To turn off the screen, press the Info button again.

You also can display the screen by pressing the Information Edit button (described in the next section) or by pressing the shutter button halfway and releasing it. I find these methods easier, so I use the Info button only when I want to turn off the screen.

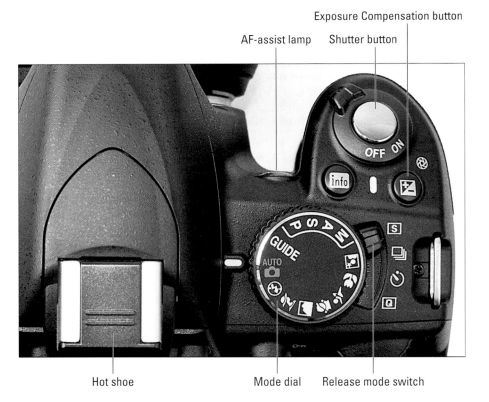

Figure 1-7: The tiny pictures on the Mode dial represent the automatic exposure modes known as Scene modes.

✓ **Mode dial:** With this dial, labeled in Figure 1-7, you set the camera to fully automatic, semi-automatic, or manual photography mode. Choosing the Guide setting brings up the guided menu display, which helps newcomers get acquainted with the camera. The little pictographs represent Scene modes, which are automatic settings geared to specific types of photos: action shots, portraits, landscapes, and so on. (You may hear these referred to in some quarters as *Digital Vari-Program* modes, which is the term Nikon used for past camera models.) Chapter 3 details the Scene and Auto modes; Chapter 7 explains the P, S, A, and M modes; and the section "Using the guided menus," later in this chapter, introduces you to that feature, which you can explore a bit more in Chapter 3.

✓ **Release mode switch:** This control enables you to quickly choose from four shutter-release modes: Single Frame, Continuous, Self-Timer, and Quiet Shutter. Chapter 2 discusses these options.

✓ **AF-assist lamp:** In dim lighting, the camera may emit a beam of light from this lamp when you use autofocusing. The light helps the camera find its focusing target. If you're shooting in a setting where the light is distracting or otherwise annoying, you can disable it via the AF-assist option on the Shooting menu.

The AF-assist lamp also shoots out light when you use red-eye reduction flash and the Self-Timer shutter-release mode, both covered in Chapter 2. You can't disable the lamp for these two functions. On the flip side, there are some situations in which the lamp is automatically disabled: It doesn't light in Live View mode or during movie recording, for example.

✓ **Flash hot shoe:** A *hot shoe* is a connection for attaching an external flash head. When not in use, the contacts on the shoe are protected by a little black cover, as shown in Figure 1-7; remove the cover to attach your flash. Chapters 2 and 7 discuss flash photography.

Back-of-the-body controls

Traveling over the top of the camera to its back side, as shown in Figure 1-8, you encounter the following controls:

✓ **Command dial:** After you activate certain camera features, you rotate this dial, labeled in Figure 1-8, to select a specific setting. For example, to choose an f-stop when shooting in aperture-priority (A) mode, you rotate the Command dial. And in manual exposure (M) mode, you change the f-stop by rotating the dial while pressing the Exposure Compensation button. (Chapter 7 explains apertures and f-stops.)

✓ **Live View switch:** As its name implies, this switch turns the Live View feature on and off. As soon as you turn on Live View, the scene in front of the lens appears on the monitor, and you no longer can see anything through the viewfinder. You then can compose a still photo using the monitor or begin recording a movie. Turn off Live View to return to normal, through-the-viewfinder still photography. Chapter 4 details Live View photography and movie recording.

✔ **Movie-record button:** After shifting to Live View mode, press this red button to start recording a movie using the default recording settings. (See Chapter 4 to find out how to adjust the settings.) Press again to stop recording.

✔ **AE-L/AF-L/Protect button:** Pressing this button initiates autoexposure lock (AE-L) and autofocus lock (AF-L). Chapter 7 explains autoexposure lock; Chapter 8 talks about autofocus lock.

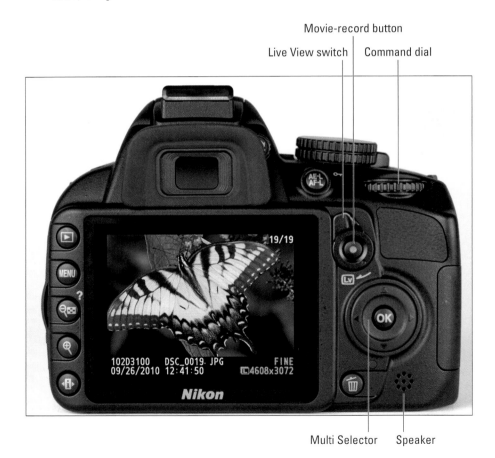

Figure 1-8: Use the Multi Selector to navigate menus and access certain other camera options.

In playback mode, pressing the button activates the Protect feature, which locks the picture file — hence the little key symbol that appears to the right of the button — so that it isn't erased if you use the picture-delete functions. See Chapter 5 for details. (The picture *is* erased if you format the memory card, however.)

You can adjust the performance of the button as it relates to locking focus and exposure, too. Instructions in this book assume that you stick with the default setting, but if you want to explore your options, see Chapter 11.

✔ **Multi Selector/OK button:** This dual-natured control, labeled in Figure 1-8, plays a role in many camera functions. You press the outer edges of the Multi Selector left, right, up, or down to navigate camera menus and access certain other options. At the center of the control is OK, which you press to finalize a menu selection or other camera adjustment.

✔ **Delete button:** Sporting a trash can icon, the universal symbol for delete, this button enables you to erase pictures from your memory card. Chapter 5 has specifics.

✔ **Playback button:** Press this button to switch the camera into picture review mode. Chapter 5 details the features available to you in this mode.

✔ **Menu button:** Press this button to access menus of camera options. See the section "Ordering from Camera Menus," later in this chapter, for details on navigating menus.

✔ **Zoom Out/Thumbnail/Help button:** This button has a number of functions, but the most important ones are

    • *Display help screens:* You can press this button to display helpful information about certain menu options. See "Displaying Help Screens," later in this chapter, for details.

    • *Adjust the image display during playback:* In playback mode, pressing the button enables you display multiple image thumbnails on the screen and reduce the magnification of the currently displayed photo. See Chapter 5 for a complete rundown of picture playback options.

✔ **Zoom In:** In playback mode, pressing this button magnifies the currently displayed image and also reduces the number of thumbnails displayed at a time. Note the plus sign in the middle of the magnifying glass — plus for zoom in. Like the Zoom Out button, this one also serves a few minor roles that I explain in later chapters.

✔ **Information Edit button:** With this button — which I hereby designate as simply the Info Edit button to save space — you can display the Shooting Information screen and then shift to the Quick Settings screen, where you can access and adjust some shooting settings more quickly than by using menus or other techniques. See the upcoming section "Using the Quick Settings Screen" for details.

✔ **Speaker:** When you play movies that contain sound, the audio comes wafting through the cluster of little holes labeled Speaker in Figure 1-8.

Front-left buttons

On the front-left side of the camera body, as shown in Figure 1-9, you find the following controls:

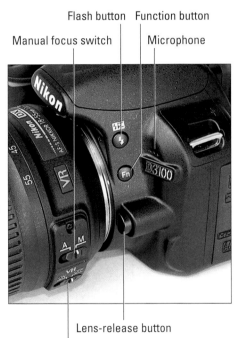

Flash button   Function button

Manual focus switch   Microphone

Lens-release button

Vibration Reduction switch

✔ **Flash/Flash compensation:** In the advanced exposure modes (P, S, A, and M), pressing this button pops up the camera's built-in flash. (In other modes, the camera decides whether the flash is needed.) By holding the button down and rotating the Command dial, you can adjust the Flash mode (normal, red-eye reduction, and so on). In advanced exposure modes, you also can adjust the flash power by pressing the button while simultaneously pressing the Exposure Compensation button and rotating the Command dial. See Chapter 2 for an introduction to flash; check out Chapter 7 for the detailed story.

Figure 1-9: Press the Flash button to pop up the built-in flash.

✔ **Function (Fn) button:** By default, this button gives you fast access to the ISO Sensitivity setting, which you can explore in Chapter 7. If you don't use that feature often, you can use the button to perform one of three other operations. Chapter 11 provides the details on changing the button's purpose. (***Note:*** All instructions in this book assume that you haven't changed the function.)

✔ **Lens-release button:** Press this button before removing the lens from your camera. See the first part of this chapter for help with mounting and removing lenses.

✔ **Lens switches:** As detailed in the first part of this chapter, use the A/M switch to set the kit lens to automatic or manual focusing. The VR switch turns the Vibration Reduction feature on and off.

✔ **Microphone:** The three little holes just above the silver D3100 label lead to the camera's internal microphone. See Chapter 4 to find out how to disable the microphone if you want to record silent movies.

Hidden connections

Hidden under little cover on the left side of the camera, you find the following four connection ports, labeled in Figure 1-10:

✔ **Accessory terminal:** You can plug in the optional Nikon MC-DC2 remote shutter-release cable or GP-1 GPS unit here. I don't cover these optional accessories in this book, but the manual that comes with the devices can get you up and running.

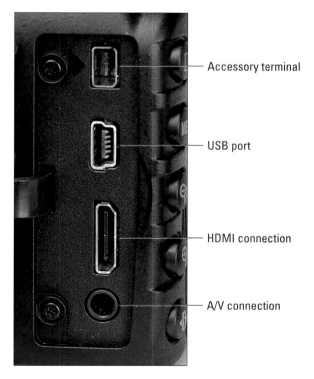

— Accessory terminal

— USB port

— HDMI connection

— A/V connection

Figure 1-10: Open the cover on the side of the camera to reveal these connections.

✔ **USB port:** You can connect your camera to your computer through this port, using a Nikon UC-E4 USB cable. As explained in Chapter 6, this connection gives you one way to transfer pictures from your memory card to the computer. The cable doesn't come with the camera as it did with earlier Nikon dSLR models; my guess is that Nikon figures that most people download pictures by using the memory- card readers that are now standard on most computers. If you want to go old school, it'll cost you: The cable sells for about $35. You can buy a good card reader that accepts multiple types of cards for less, so my advice is to forget about the cable. However, if you have other Nikon digital cameras that did ship with this cable, you can use it with your D3100.

✔ **HDMI and A/V jacks:** Through these jacks, you can connect your camera to a television so that you can share your pictures with a whole roomful of people. As with the USB cable, you need to pony up the cash for either cable, as neither ships with the camera. For HD playback, you need a Type C mini-pin HD cable; prices start at about $20. For regular (standard definition) playback, Nikon sells the EG-D2 Audio Video Cable, available for around $13. Chapter 5 offers more details on television playback.

If you turn the camera over, you find a tripod socket, which enables you to mount the camera on a tripod that uses a ¼-inch screw, plus the battery chamber.

Ordering from Camera Menus

Pressing the Menu button on your camera gives you access to a whole slew of options in addition to those you control via the external buttons and dials. But what type of menu screens you see depends on the setting of the Mode dial:

✔ **Guide:** Pressing the Menu button when the Mode dial is set to Guide brings up the first screen of the guided menus, which provide a simple, walk-me-through-it approach to using the camera.

✔ **All other settings:** Pressing the Menu button when the Mode dial is set to any option except Guide brings up the normal, text-based menus.

The next two sections provide an overview of using both types of menus. But for reasons you can discover in the following discussion, the rest of this book pretty much ignores the guided menus and relies on the regular menus to get things done — a choice that I suggest you make as well.

Using the guided menus

The guided menus work much like interactive menus you encounter in other areas of your life — on cell phones, bank machines, grocery-store self-checkout kiosks, and the like — except that instead of pressing buttons on the screen, you use the Multi Selector and OK button to make your menu selections. And thankfully, your camera also doesn't nag you to hurry up and "please place the item in the bagging area!" every three seconds.

With that rant about the modern grocery-store experience out of my system, here's how to use the guided menus:

1. **Set the Mode dial to Guide, as shown on the left in Figure 1-11.**

   You see the initial guided menu screen, shown on the right in the figure. You're offered three categories of options: Shoot, View/Delete, and Set Up.

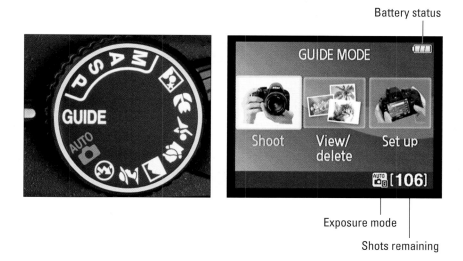

Figure 1-11: Set the Mode dial to Guide to use the guided menus.

The items labeled in the figure, which appear on all the guided menu screens, tell you the following information:

- *Battery status*: A full icon like the one in Figure 1-11 says you're good to go. If the little battery symbol appears only half full or less, it's time to dig out your battery charger.

- *Exposure mode:* Even though the Guide option is on the Mode dial, it's not an exposure mode per se — rather, it's a menu-based way for you to access the actual exposure modes. Through the guided menus, you can access any exposure mode except programmed autoexposure (P) and manual exposure (M). The symbol in the lower-right corner of the guided menu screen tells you which exposure mode is selected. In Figure 1-11, the symbol shows that the Auto exposure mode is selected. The G tells you that you're in Guide mode, in case you forget.

- *Shots remaining*: The other value in the lower-right corner shows you the number of shots you can fit in the remaining space on your memory card.

2. **Press the Multi Selector right or left to highlight the category you want to choose.**

   (Remember, the Multi Selector is the big four-way rocker switch that has the OK button in the middle.) Here's a quick preview of what each category enables you to do:

   - *Shoot:* Select this icon to select options that walk you through the process of choosing basic picture-taking options and shooting pictures.

   - *View/Delete:* Select this category to access picture-playback functions and erase pictures from your memory card.

   - *Set Up:* Choose this icon to access camera setup options — things like setting the date and time, adjusting monitor brightness, and so on.

   This category also contains two options that make a big impact on picture quality: Image Size and Image Quality. They really belong with the rest of the picture settings in the Shoot category, as they're organized in the regular menus. At any rate, check out Chapter 2 for help choosing the right settings. ***Note:*** For these two settings and some others, your settings apply only while you shoot in Guide mode.

3. **Press OK.**

   You see a screen that lists available options in the category you chose. The left screen in Figure 1-12 shows the first screen that appears if you select Shoot in Step 2, for example.

4. **Highlight the option that interests you and press OK to display the next screen of information and instructions.**

   For example, if you highlight Easy Operation, as in Figure 1-12, and press OK, you see the second screen in the figure. There, you can make another choice and press OK again to move to the next screen.

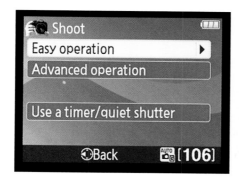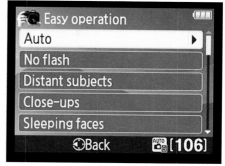

Figure 1-12: Use the Multi Selector to highlight an option and press OK to move to the next step.

If you see a right-pointing arrow next to a highlighted option, you can display the next screen by pressing the Multi Selector right instead of pressing OK, if you prefer.

From this point on, keep highlighting options and pressing OK to move forward. For the Shoot category, you ultimately reach a screen that looks like the one on the left in Figure 1-13, telling you which exposure mode the camera is using and inviting you to either start shooting or select More Settings to advance to another round of picture-taking options. If you've had enough of playing around with options, press OK. You then see a final menu screen, shown on the right in Figure 1-13, where you can tell the camera whether you want to shoot using the viewfinder, switch to Live View, or record a movie. Highlight your choice and press OK. If you select viewfinder shooting, you then see the Shooting Information screen, described later in this chapter. Otherwise, the camera initiates Live View, which enables you to frame the scene using the monitor (also the first step in shooting a movie). Chapter 4 details Live View still photography as well as movie recording.

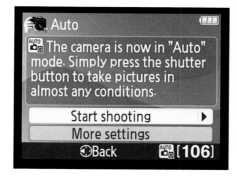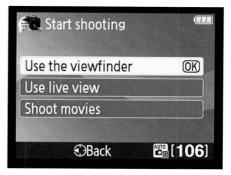

Figure 1-13: These two screens appear at the end of the Shoot section of the guided menu.

As you explore the guided menus, you also can take advantage of these menu-navigation tricks:

- **Return to the previous screen.** If you see a Back symbol at the bottom of the screen, you can press the Multi Selector left to go back one screen. The first screen in Figure 1-14 shows you what the Back symbol looks like.

- **Exit a screen without making changes.** Don't see a Back icon? Look instead for a little "turnaround" arrow like the one labeled Exit symbol on the right screen in Figure 1-14. Highlight that symbol and press OK to exit the current screen.

- **Display more help.** If you see a little question mark like the one labeled Help symbol in Figure 1-14, press and hold the Zoom Out button to display a help screen with more information. This help system is also available when you're not using Guide mode; see the upcoming section "Displaying Help Screens" for details.

- **Return to the main guided menu screen.** Press the Menu button to jump from any screen to the initial guided menu screen, shown on the right in Figure 1-11.

- **Exit the guided menus.** If you're on the final shooting screen (shown on the right in Figure 1-13), press OK. You also can depart from your guide at any time by pressing the shutter button halfway and releasing it. The Shooting Information screen then appears on the monitor; see the "Monitoring Shooting Settings" section later in this chapter.

Although I appreciate the idea of the guided menus, I opted to largely ignore them in this book and instead show you how to perform different camera operations through the regular menus, which you can investigate in the next section. Here's why:

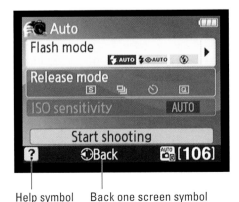
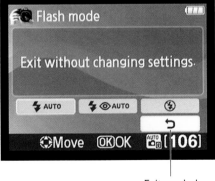

Help symbol   Back one screen symbol   Exit symbol

Figure 1-14: These symbols remind you of some additional guided menu features.

✓ You can't access all your camera's features through the guided menus. For example, you can't control white balance, a color-related setting discussed in Chapter 8, through the guided menus. Instead, you have to wait until you reach the final Shoot menu screen and exit the guided menus to make adjustments.

✓ In many cases, using the guided menus actually makes things more difficult. For example, if you select the Easy Operation choice on the Shoot menu, you're presented with a list of possible picture types. (See Figure 1-12.) Suppose that you select No Flash. The camera then simply engages the Auto Flash Off exposure mode — which you could do yourself simply by turning the Mode dial to the No Flash symbol. (Chapter 3 introduces you to this exposure mode.)

✓ Some choices Nikon made for the arrangement of the guided menus set you up for confusion down the line. Remember my tip in the preceding steps about the Image Size and Image Quality options found in the Set Up section of the guided menus? Well, in the regular menus, those options live on the Shooting menu, not on the Setup menu. So if you get used to selecting those options in one place when you use guided menus, you have to learn a whole new organization when you move on to the regular menus.

Additionally, when you adjust certain settings, including Image Size and Image Quality, your changes apply *only* in Guide mode. So when you return to another shooting mode, you have to adjust those settings again.

✓ After you get past the initial guided menu screens, some options you encounter aren't any less confusing than they are when you access them through the main menus. In some cases, you can display a help screen by pressing the Zoom Out button (the one with the question mark symbol), but you can get the same help when using regular menus, too.

Don't get me wrong: If you like the guided menus, by all means, take advantage of them. But my guess is that you don't need any more help from me to do so. So with the exception of Chapter 3, which provides some details about one cool option available when you select Advanced Operation from the Shoot menu, I limit future discussions to the regular menus so that I have more room to help you explore the camera's more advanced features.

Ordering off the main menus

To display the regular (non-guided) menus, set the Mode dial to any setting but Guide and then press the Menu button. You then see a screen similar to the one shown in Figure 1-15. The icons along the left side of the screen represent the available menus. (Table 1-1 labels the icons and includes a brief description of the goodies found on each menu.) In the menu screens, the icon that's highlighted or appears in color is the active menu; options on that menu automatically appear to the right. In the figure, the Shooting menu is active, for example.

Table 1-1		D3100 Menus
Symbol	*Open This Menu . . .*	*To Access These Functions*
▶	Playback	Viewing, deleting, and protecting pictures
●	Shooting	Basic photography settings
☒	Setup	Additional basic camera operations
☑	Retouch	Built-in photo retouching options
☰	Recent Settings	Your 20 most recently used menu options

I explain all the important menu options elsewhere in the book; for now, just familiarize yourself with the process of navigating menus and selecting options therein. The Multi Selector, as shown in Figure 1-8, is the key to the game. You press the edges of the Multi Selector to navigate up, down, left, and right through the menus.

In this book, the instruction "Press the Multi Selector left" simply means to press the left edge of the control. "Press the Multi Selector right" means to press the right edge, and so on.

Menu icons

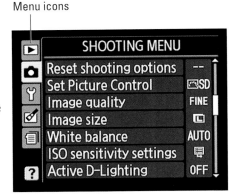

Figure 1-15: Highlight a menu in the left column to display its contents.

Here's a bit more detail about the process of navigating menus:

✓ **To select a different menu:** Press the Multi Selector left to jump to the column containing the menu icons. Then press up or down to highlight the menu you want to display. Finally, press right to jump over to the options on the menu.

✓ **To select and adjust a function on the current menu:** Again, use the Multi Selector to scroll up or down the list of options to highlight the feature you want to adjust and then press OK. Settings available for the selected item then appear. For example, if you select the Image Quality item from the Shooting menu, as shown on the left in Figure 1-16, and press OK, the available Image Quality options appear, as shown on the right in the figure. Repeat the old up-and-down scroll routine until the choice you prefer is highlighted. Then press OK to return to the previous screen.

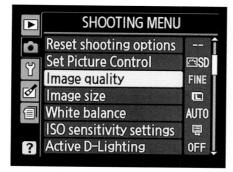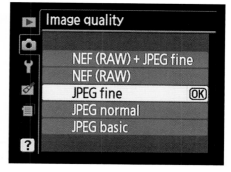

Figure 1-16: Select the option you prefer and press OK again to return to the active menu.

In some cases, you may see a right-pointing arrowhead instead of the OK symbol next to an option. That's your cue to press the Multi Selector right to display a submenu or other list of options (Although, most of the time, you also can just press the OK button if you prefer.)

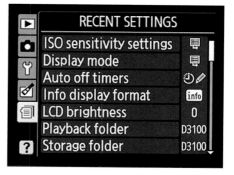

TIP

✔ **To quickly access your 20 most recent menu items:** The Recent Settings menu, as shown in Figure 1-17, provides a list of the 20 menu items you ordered most recently. So if you want to adjust those

Figure 1-17: The Recent Settings menu offers quick access to the last 20 menu options you selected.

settings, you don't have to wade through all the other menus looking for them — just head to this menu instead. You can remove an item from the menu by highlighting it and pressing the Delete (trash can) button twice.

Monitoring Shooting Settings

Your D3100 gives you the following ways to monitor the most critical picture-taking settings.

✔ **Shooting Information display:** If your eyesight is like mine, reading the tiny type in the viewfinder is a tad difficult. Fortunately, you also can press the Info Edit button to display the Shooting Information screen on the monitor. As shown in Figure 1-18, the Shooting Information screen — which I hereby dub the Shooting Info screen to save space in this book — displays the current shooting settings at a size that's a little easier on the eyes and also provides more detailed data than the viewfinder. If you rotate the camera to compose a *portrait* shot (the image is taller than it is wide), the Shooting Info display rotates as well.

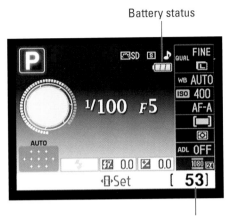

Battery status

Shots remaining

Figure 1-18: Press the Info or Edit Info button to view picture-taking settings on the monitor.

In this book, I show the screen with the black-and-white color scheme you see in Figure 1-18, instead of the default colors, which feature white text on a greenish background and don't reproduce as well in print. To find out how to change the color scheme, see the section "Customizing Your Camera: Setup Menu Options" later in this chapter.

To display the Shooting Info screen, you also can just press the shutter button halfway and release it (my favorite tactic) or press the Info button (top of the camera, near the shutter button). Press the Info button again to turn off the display.

✔ **Viewfinder:** You can view some camera settings in the viewfinder as well. For example, the data in Figure 1-19 shows the current shutter speed, f-stop, ISO setting, and number of shots remaining. The exact viewfinder information that appears depends on what action you're currently undertaking.

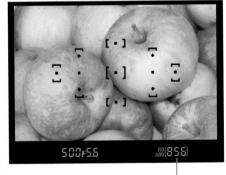

Shots remaining

Figure 1-19: You also can view some camera information at the bottom of the viewfinder.

If what you see in Figures 1-18 and 1-19 looks like a big confusing mess, don't worry. Many of the settings relate to options that won't mean anything to you until you make your way through later chapters and explore the advanced exposure modes. But do make note of the following two key points of data that are helpful even when you shoot in the fully automatic modes:

- ✔ **Battery status indicator:** A full battery icon like the one in Figure 1-18 shows that the battery is fully charged; if the icon appears empty, look for your battery charger.

  Your viewfinder also displays a tiny low-battery icon when things get to the dangerous point. The icon appears just to the right of center in the settings strip at the bottom of the viewfinder. If the icon blinks, the battery is totally kaput, and shutter release is disabled.

- ✔ **Shots remaining:** Labeled in Figures 1-18 and 1-19, this value indicates how many additional pictures you can store on the current memory card. If the number exceeds 999, the value is presented a little differently. The initial K appears above the value to indicate that the first value represents the picture count in thousands. For example, 1.0K means that you can store 1,000 more pictures (*K* being a universally accepted symbol indicating 1,000 units). The number is then rounded down to the nearest hundred. So if the card has room for, say, 1,230 more pictures, the value reads 1.2K.

Using the Quick Settings Screen

After you press the Info Edit or Info button to display the Shooting Info screen, as shown on the left in Figure 1-20, press the Info Edit button to toggle to a second screen, the Quick Settings display. Shown on the right in the figure, the Quick Settings display does just what its name implies: It enables you to adjust many picture-taking settings faster than you can by digging through camera menus.

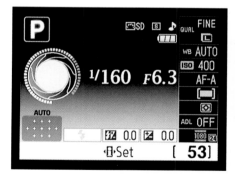
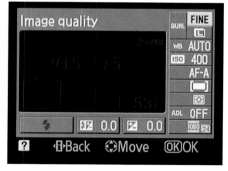

Figure 1-20: Press the Info Edit button to shift from the Shooting Info screen (left) to the Quick Settings display (right).

Note the little symbol at the center of the bottom of the Shooting Info screen, by the way: The little *i* and the word Set remind you to press the Info Edit button to get to the Quick Settings display.

After you see the Quick Settings display, follow these steps to adjust the available options:

1. **Use the Multi Selector to highlight the setting you want to change.**

   The available settings are represented by the icons along the right side and bottom of the screen. A little label appears at the top of the screen to tell you the name of the selected setting. For example, in Figure 1-20, the Image Quality setting is selected.

2. **Press OK to jump to a screen that contains the available settings for the selected option.**

   For example, Figure 1-21 shows the available Image Quality options.

3. **Use the Multi Selector to highlight your choice and then press OK.**

   You return to the Quick Settings display.

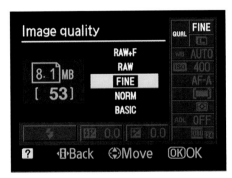

Figure 1-21: Highlight the setting you want to use and press OK to return to the Quick Settings screen.

To exit the Quick Settings display and return to the Shooting Info screen, press the Info Edit button again, or press the shutter button halfway and release it. Or if you're done adjusting settings, just go ahead and take your next picture.

Displaying Help Screens

If you see a small question mark in the lower-left corner of a menu, press and hold the Zoom Out button — note the question-mark label above the button — to display information about the current shooting mode or selected menu option. For example, Figure 1-22 shows the help screen associated with the Image Quality setting. If you need to scroll the screen to view all the help text, keep the button depressed and scroll by using the Multi Selector. Release the button to close the information screen.

A blinking question mark in the viewfinder or Shooting Info screen indicates that the camera wants to alert you to a problem. Again, press the Zoom Out button to see what solution the camera suggests.

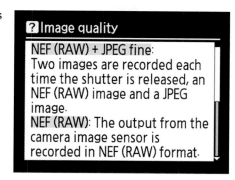

Figure 1-22: Press and hold the Zoom Out button to display onscreen help.

Customizing Your Camera: Setup Menu Options

Your camera offers scads of options for customizing its performance. Later chapters explain settings related to actual picture taking, such as those that affect flash behavior and autofocusing. The rest of this chapter details options found on the Setup menu, which relate to the basic camera interface and operation.

To access the Setup menu, first set the Mode dial on top of the camera to any setting except Guide. Press the Menu button to display the regular menus. The Setup menu is the one marked with the little wrench icon, as shown in Figure 1-23.

Figure 1-23 shows just the first screen of menu options; the menu actually contains four screens of settings. Press the Multi Selector up and down to scroll through the menu.

Here's what you can accomplish with the first seven options, as shown in Figure 1-23:

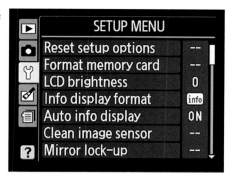

Figure 1-23: Visit the Setup menu to customize your camera's basic appearance and operation.

✔ **Reset Setup Options:** You can use this option to restore all the Setup menu options to their default settings. Before you do, though, see the last section of this chapter for some important details.

✔ **Format Memory Card:** You can use this command to format your memory card, which wipes all data off the card and ensures that it's properly set up to record pictures. See the earlier section "Working with Memory Cards" for more details about formatting.

✔ **LCD Brightness:** This option enables you to make the camera monitor brighter or darker, as shown in Figure 1-24. If you take this step, keep in mind that what you see on the display may not be an accurate rendition of the actual exposure of your image. Crank up the monitor brightness, for example, and an underexposed photo may look just fine. So I recommend that you keep the brightness at the default setting (0).

✔ **Info Display Format:** You can use this command to customize the appearance of the Shooting Info screen. You can choose from two styles, Classic and Graphic, and for each style, you can select from three color schemes. Figure 1-25 shows you a couple possible variations. The one on the left shows the default style, Graphic Green; the one on the right illustrates the Classic Blue style.

In this book, I use the Graphic Black color scheme because it makes the settings data easier to see in figures.

✔ **Auto Info Display:** When this option is set to On, as it is by default, the Shooting Info screen appears when you press the shutter button halfway and release it. And, if you disable Image Review (an option covered in Chapter 5), the screen also appears after you take a picture. Turn off the Auto Info Display option, and the screen appears briefly when you first turn on the camera, but after that, you must press the Info button or the Info Edit button to display it. Instructions in this book assume that you stick with the default setting (On).

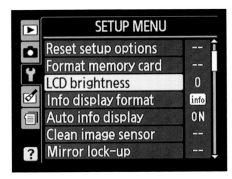
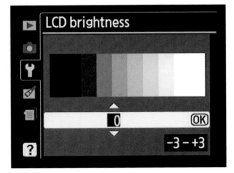

Figure 1-24: If you adjust the monitor brightness, you may not be able to accurately judge exposure during playback.

Graphic Green style   Classic Blue style

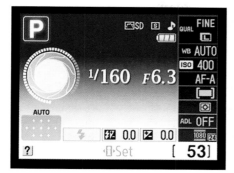
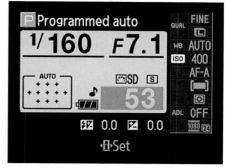

Figure 1-25: Change the appearance of the Shooting Info screen through the Info Display Format option.

✔ **Clean Image Sensor:** Your D3100 is set up at the factory to perform an internal cleaning routine each time you turn the camera on or off. This cleaning system is designed to keep the image sensor — that's the part of the camera that actually captures the image — free of dust and dirt.

By choosing the Clean Image Sensor menu item, you can perform a cleaning at any time, however. Just choose the menu item, press OK, select Clean Now, and press OK again. (Nikon recommends that you set the camera on a solid surface, base down, when you perform the cleaning.) Don't try to perform the cleaning several times in a row, by the way — if you do, the camera will temporarily disable the function to protect itself.

The other option available through the Clean Image Sensor item, called Clean At, enables you to specify whether you want the camera to change from the default setting (cleaning at startup and shutdown) to clean only at startup, only at shutdown, or never. I suggest that you stick with the default, however.

✔ **Mirror Lock-Up:** This feature is necessary when cleaning the camera interior — an operation that I don't recommend that you tackle yourself because you can easily damage the camera if you don't know what you're doing. And if you've used mirror lock-up on a film camera to avoid camera shake when shooting long-exposure images, note that in this case, mirror lock-up is provided for cleaning purposes only. You can't take pictures on the D3100 while the mirror lock-up option is enabled.

To get to the next seven customization options, use the Multi Selector to scroll to the second screen of the Setup menu, as shown in Figure 1-26:

✓ **Video Mode:** This option is related to viewing your images on a television, a topic I cover in Chapter 5. Select NTSC if you live in North America or other countries that adhere to the NTSC video standard; select PAL for playback in areas that follow that code of video conduct.

✓ **HDMI:** This setting relates to options involved with connecting your camera to an HDMI (high-def) device; again, check out Chapter 5 for details.

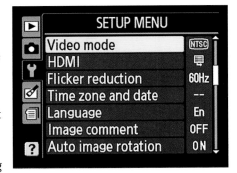

Figure 1-26: Use the Multi Selector to scroll to this second screen of the menu.

✓ **Flicker Reduction:** If you notice flickering or color banding on the monitor when Live View is enabled, changing this setting may help alleviate the problem. See Chapter 4 for details.

✓ **Time Zone and Date:** When you turn on your camera for the very first time, it automatically displays this option and asks you to set the current date and time. Keeping the date and time accurate is important because that information is recorded as part of the image file. In your photo browser, you can then see when you shot an image and, equally handy, search for images by the date they were taken.

✓ **Language:** You're asked to specify a language along with the date and time when you fire up your camera for the first time. Your choice determines the language of text on the camera monitor. Screens in this book display the English language, but I find it entertaining on occasion to hand my camera to a friend after changing the language to, say, Swedish. I'm a real yokester, yah?

✓ **Image Comment:** See Chapter 11 to find out how to use this feature, which enables you to add text comments into a picture file. You then can read that information in Nikon ViewNX 2, the software that shipped with your camera. (The text doesn't actually appear on the image itself.)

✓ **Auto Image Rotation:** When enabled, this feature records the camera orientation (horizontal or vertical) as part of the picture file information. This enables the camera to automatically rotate the picture to its proper orientation, and the auto-rotating also occurs when you browse your image thumbnails in ViewNX 2 and other photo programs that can read the orientation date. See Chapter 5 for more about this option and rotating pictures during playback.

Scrolling to the third screen of the Setup menu, as shown in Figure 1-27, brings you to the following additional setup options:

✔ **Dust Off Ref Photo:** This specialty feature enables you to record an image that serves as a point of reference for the automatic dust-removal filter available in Nikon Capture NX 2. I don't cover this accessory software, which must be purchased separately, in this book.

✔ **Auto Off Timers:** To help save battery power, your camera automatically shuts off the monitor, exposure meter, and viewfinder display if you don't perform any camera operations for a period of time. Through the Auto Off Timers menu option, you can specify how long you want the camera to wait before taking that step.

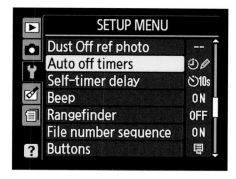

Figure 1-27: Through the Auto Off Timers option, you can adjust the timing of automatic shutdown of the monitor, viewfinder, and exposure meter.

After selecting the option, press OK to display the screen shown on the left in Figure 1-28. Here, you can select from three prefab timing settings, Short, Normal, and Long, which produce the following shut-off intervals:

- *Short:* For picture playback and menus, the monitor shuts off after 8 seconds; for image review, 4 seconds; and during Live View shooting, 30 seconds. The exposure meter turns off after 4 seconds.

- *Normal:* This setting also uses a 30-second delay for Live View shutoff but increases the playback/menu display to 12 seconds and the exposure meter shutoff to 8 seconds. It's the default option.

- *Long:* Auto shutdown occurs after 20 seconds for playback, menu display, and image review. The meter cuts out at 1 minute; the Live View display at 3 minutes.

If none of those settings works well for you, choose Custom, which displays the screen shown on the right in Figure 1-28. You then can customize the shut-off timing for playback and menu display, image review, Live View, and metering independently. If you go this route, be sure to highlight Done, as shown in the figure, and press OK after changing the settings. Otherwise, your changes don't "stick."

✔ **Self-Timer Delay:** This setting comes into play when you take pictures using the Self-Timer Release mode, covered in Chapter 2. Your choice determines how long the camera waits to record the picture after you press the shutter button.

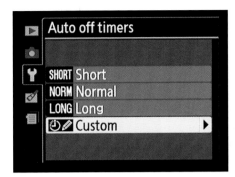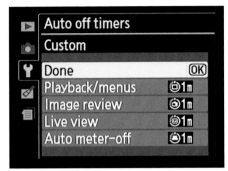

Figure 1-28: Select Custom to adjust shutoff delay timing for individual items.

✔ **Beep:** By default, your camera beeps at you after certain operations, such as after it sets focus when you shoot in autofocus mode. If you're doing top-secret surveillance work and need the camera to hush up, set this option to Off. On the Shooting Info display, a little musical note icon appears near the top-right corner of the screen when the beep is enabled. Turn off the beep, and the icon appears in a circle with a slash through it.

✔ **Rangefinder:** In some exposure modes, you can choose to swap out the normal exposure meter for a *rangefinder,* which is another type of meter that can come in handy when you use manual focus. See Chapter 8 for details.

✔ **File Number Sequence:** This option controls how the camera names your picture files. When the option is set to Off, as it is by default, the camera restarts file numbering at 0001 every time you format your memory card or insert a new memory card. Numbering is also restarted if you create custom folders (an advanced option covered in Chapter 11).

Needless to say, this setup can cause problems over time, creating a scenario where you wind up with multiple images that have the same filename — not on the current memory card, but when you download images to your computer. So I strongly encourage you to set the option to On, as shown in Figure 1-27. Note that when you get to picture number 9999, file numbering is still reset to 0001, however. The camera automatically creates a new folder to hold for your next 9999 images.

As for the Reset option, it enables you to assign the first file number (which ends in 0001) to the next picture you shoot. Then the camera behaves as if you selected the On setting.

Should you be a really, really prolific shooter and snap enough pictures to reach image 9999 in folder 999, the camera will refuse to take another photo until you choose that Reset option and either format the memory card or insert a brand new one.

✏ **Buttons:** Through this Setup menu item, you can change the function of the Function (Fn) button and the AE-L/AF-L button. You can also specify whether you want a half-press of the shutter button to lock focus only, as it does by default, or lock focus and exposure together. For now, leave all three options alone so that the instructions you find in this book work the way they should. When you're ready to go further, Chapter 11 shows you how to customize the button functions.

Continue scrolling through the menu to uncover the final Setup menu options, as shown in Figure 1-29 and presented for your consideration in the following list:

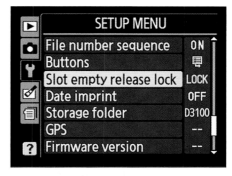

SETUP MENU

File number sequence	ON
Buttons	
Slot empty release lock	LOCK
Date imprint	OFF
Storage folder	D3100
GPS	--
Firmware version	--

✏ **Slot Empty Release Lock:** This cryptically named feature determines whether the camera lets you take a picture when no memory card is installed in the camera. If you set it to Enable Release, you can take a tempo- rary picture, which appears in the monitor with the word *Demo* but isn't recorded anywhere. The feature is provided mainly for

Figure 1-29: Setting the Slot Empty Release Lock option to Release Locked prevents you from taking pictures when no memory card is installed.

use in camera stores, enabling salespeople to demonstrate the camera without having to keep a memory card installed. I can think of no good reason why anyone else would change the setting from the default, Release Locked.

✏ **Date Imprint:** Through this option, you can choose to imprint the shoot- ing date, date and time, or the number of days between the day you took the picture and another date that you specify. This feature works only with pictures that you shoot in the JPEG file format; see Chapter 3 for details about file formats.

The default setting, which disables the imprint, is the best way to go, however; you don't need to permanently mar your photos to find out when you took them. Every picture file includes a hidden vat of text data, called *metadata,* that records the shooting date and time, as well as all the camera settings you used — f-stop, shutter speed, and lots more. You can view this data in the free software provided with your camera as well as in many photo programs. Chapter 5 shows you how.

If you do enable the Date Imprint feature, the word Date appears in the upper left corner of the Shooting Info screen. Also remember that apply- ing some Retouch menu options, such as the Trim function, may crop away the date imprint or leave it illegible.

- ✔ **Storage Folder:** You need to pay attention to this option only if you create custom image folders, an advanced feature you can explore in Chapter 11. If you take that step, you specify which folder you want to use for your next photos through this menu option. You also must specify which folder you want to view during playback. Chapter 5 discusses playback options.

- ✔ **Eye-Fi Upload:** This option (not shown in Figure 1-29) appears on the menu only if you insert an Eye-Fi memory card in your camera. Eye-Fi cards enable you to transmit your files wirelessly to other devices. That's a cool feature, but unfortunately, the cards themselves are more expensive than regular cards. If you do choose to use them and you find yourself in an area that does not allow wireless transmissions (such as hospitals and the like), you can disable the feature through this menu option. You also initiate the wireless transfer through the option.

- ✔ **GPS:** If you attach the optional GPS (Global Positioning System) unit to the camera, head for this menu option and select Position to view the location data the unit reports. Via the second GPS option, Auto Meter Off, you can choose to modify the automatic shutdown of the camera's exposure metering system, which is controlled by the Auto Off Timers option discussed earlier. By default, the Auto Meter Off is set to Enable, and the auto shutdown period is extended by one minute to give the GPS system time to do its thing. Change the setting to Disable, and the meters don't turn off.

- ✔ **Firmware Version:** Select this option and press OK to view what version of the camera *firmware,* or internal software, your camera runs. You see three firmware items, A, B, and L. At the time this book was written, A and B were version 1.00; L was 1.002. Don't worry about what the A, B, and L mean — they simply relate to different aspects of the camera's operation.

Keeping your camera firmware up-to-date *is* important, though, so visit the Nikon Web site (www.nikon.com) regularly to find out whether your camera sports the latest version. You can find detailed instructions on how to download and install any firmware updates on the site.

Restoring Default Settings

You can quickly reset all the options on the Shooting menu by selecting Reset Shooting Options, as shown on the left in Figure 1-30. Likewise, the Setup menu also has a Reset Setup Options item to restore all settings on that menu, as shown on the right.

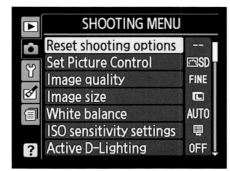
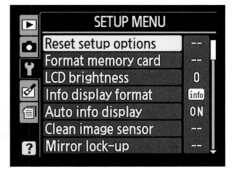

Figure 1-30: Choose the Reset option to return to the default settings for the respective menu.

A couple potential flies in the ointment:

✓ Resetting the Shooting menu defaults wipes out any customizations you made to a Picture Control setting — for example, if you tweaked the Vivid setting to produce even more saturated colors than it does by default. Chapter 8 talks more about this feature.

Additionally, a Shooting menu reset restores the default settings of a couple options not on the menu, including Exposure Compensation, Flash Compensation, Flash mode, and the AF mode. The focus point resets to the center point, and the AE-L/AF-L button returns to its normal operation as well. Visit Chapter 7 for all issues related to flash and exposure; check out Chapter 8 for details about focusing. Chapter 11 explains how to modify the behavior of the AE-L/AF-L button.

✓ More worrisome is that resetting the Setup menu restores the File Number Sequence option to its default, Off, which is most definitely Not a Good Thing. So if you restore the menu defaults, be *sure* that you revisit that option and return it to the On setting. See the preceding section for details.

✓ Resetting the Setup menu does not affect the Video Mode, Flicker Reduction, Time Zone and Date, Language, or Storage Folder options, on the other hand. So you need to adjust those settings individually if needed.

2

Choosing Basic Picture Settings

*E*very camera manufacturer strives to provide a good *out-of-box* experience — that is, to ensure that your initial encounter with the camera is a happy one. To that end, the camera's default settings are carefully selected to make it as easy as possible for you to take a good picture the first time you press the shutter button. On the D3100, the default settings are designed to let you take a picture the same way you do with most automatic, point-and-shoot cameras: You compose the shot, press the shutter button halfway to focus, and then press the button the rest of the way to record the image.

Although you can get a nice picture using the default settings in many cases, they're not designed to produce the optimal results in every shooting situation. Rather, they're established as a one-size-fits-all approach. You may be able to use the defaults to take a decent portrait, for example, but probably need to tweak a few settings to capture action. Adjusting a few options can help turn that decent portrait into a stunning one, too.

So that you can start fine-tuning camera settings to your subject, this chapter explains the most basic picture-taking options, such as the exposure mode, shutter-release mode, and the image size, or resolution. They're not the most exciting options to explore (don't think I didn't notice you stifling a yawn), but they make a big difference in how easily you can capture the photo you have in mind. You also need to understand this core group of camera settings to take best advantage of the advanced color, focus, and exposure controls covered in Part III of the book.

Choosing an Exposure Mode

The first picture-taking setting to consider is the exposure mode, which you select via the Mode dial, as shown in Figure 2-1. Your choice determines how much control you have over two critical exposure settings — aperture and shutter speed — as well as many other options, including those related to color and flash photography. But don't worry if you don't yet know anything about aperture and shutter speed; the camera has many modes designed expressly for those with no photography experience. (When you're ready to explore exposure controls, Chapter 7 spells out everything you need to know.)

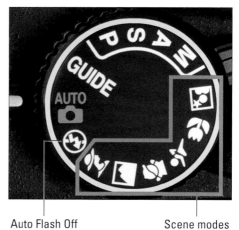

Auto Flash Off   Scene modes

Figure 2-1: The Mode setting determines how much input you have over exposure, color, and other picture options.

Your exposure mode choices break down as follows:

✔ **Fully automatic modes:** For people who haven't yet explored photography concepts such as aperture and shutter speed — or who just aren't interested in "going there" — the D3100 offers the following point-and-shoot modes:

- *Auto:* The camera analyzes the scene in front of the lens and tries to select the most appropriate camera settings to capture the image.

- *Auto Flash Off:* This mode, represented by the icon labeled in Figure 2-1, works just like Auto but disables the flash.

- *Scene modes:* These six modes, labeled in Figure 2-1, automatically select settings geared to capturing specific types of shots: portraits, landscapes, child photos, action, close-ups, and night portraits. You set the Mode dial to the icon that represents the scene type, and the camera does the rest.

Chapter 3 provides details about Auto, Auto Flash Off, and Scene modes. But one critical point to understand now is that these fully automatic modes prevent you from taking advantage of most of the camera's exposure, color, and focus controls. You have access to picture-taking options discussed in this chapter, but that's about it.

✓ **Semi-automatic modes:** To take more creative control but still get some exposure assistance from the camera, choose one of these modes, all detailed in Chapter 7:

• *P (programmed autoexposure):* The camera selects the aperture and shutter speed necessary to ensure a good exposure. But you can choose from different combinations of the two to vary the creative results. For example, shutter speed affects whether moving objects appear blurry or sharp. So you might use a fast shutter speed to freeze action, or you might go the other direction, choosing a shutter speed slow enough to blur the action, creating a heightened sense of motion.

• *S (shutter-priority autoexposure):* You select the shutter speed, and the camera selects the proper aperture to properly expose the image. This mode is ideal for capturing sports or other moving subjects because it gives you direct control over shutter speed.

• *A (aperture-priority autoexposure):* In this mode, you choose the aperture, and the camera automatically chooses a shutter speed to properly expose the image. Because aperture affects *depth of field,* or the distance over which objects in a scene remain in sharp focus, this setting is great for portraits because you can select an aperture that results in a soft, blurry background, putting the emphasis on your subject. For landscape shots, on the other hand, you might choose an aperture that keeps the entire scene sharply focused so that both near and distant objects have equal visual weight.

All three semi-automatic modes give you complete access to all the camera's features. So even if you're not ready to explore aperture and shutter speed yet, go ahead and set the mode dial to P if you need to access a setting that's off limits in the fully automated modes. The camera then operates pretty much as it does in Auto mode but without limiting your ability to control picture settings if you need to do so.

✓ **Manual:** In this mode, you select both the aperture and shutter speed. But the camera still offers an assist by displaying an exposure meter to help you dial in the right settings. You have complete control over all other picture settings, too.

✓ **Guide:** Selecting this setting accesses the guided menu system, which I introduce in Chapter 1 and talk about in a bit more detail in Chapter 3. As a result of choices you make as you step through the guided menu screens, the camera ultimately selects the exposure mode for you.

One very important and often misunderstood aspect about the exposure modes: Although your choice determines your access to exposure and color controls as well as to some other advanced camera features, it has *no* bearing on your *focusing* choices. You can choose from manual focusing or autofocusing in any exposure mode, assuming that your lens offers autofocusing. (Chapter 1 shows you how to set the lens to manual or autofocusing.)

Choosing the (Shutter Button) Release Mode

The *Release mode* determines how you trigger the actual image capture and what happens after you take that step. A switch on top of the camera makes it easy to select a Release mode setting, as shown in Figure 2-2. An icon representing the selected mode appears in the Shooting Info display (refer to the upcoming Figure 2-4).

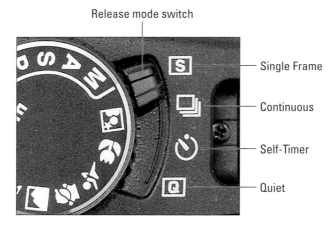

Figure 2-2: Use this switch to shift from Single-Frame mode to Continuous or Self-Timer shooting.

You have the following four options, labeled in Figure 2-2:

 ✔ **Single Frame:** This setting, which is the default, records a single image each time you press the shutter button completely. In other words, this is normal-photography mode.

 ✔ **Continuous:** Sometimes known as *burst mode,* this mode records a continuous series of images as long as you hold down the shutter button. In this mode, designed to make it easier to capture action, you can shoot about three frames per second.

A few critical notes:

- *Flash is disabled.* You can't use flash in Continuous mode because the time that the flash needs to recycle between shots slows down the capture rate too much. So when you set the Release mode switch to Continuous, also set the Mode dial to the Auto Flash Off setting (refer to Figure 2-1) or otherwise disable flash. (In the Scene and Auto modes, set the flash mode to Off; in P, S, A, or M mode, just close the pop-up flash.)

- *Images are stored temporarily in the memory buffer.* The camera has a little bit of internal memory — a *buffer* — where it stores picture data until it has time to record them to the memory card. The number of pictures the buffer can hold depends on certain camera settings, such as resolution and file type (JPEG or Raw). The viewfinder displays an estimate of how many pictures will fit in the buffer; see the sidebar "What does [r 24] in the viewfinder mean?" for details.

  After shooting a burst of images, wait for the memory card access light on the back of the camera to go out before turning off the camera. That's your signal that the camera has successfully moved all data from the buffer to the memory card. Turning off the camera before that happens may corrupt the image file.

  The picture orientation data (horizontal or vertical) of the first image is used for the entire burst of images. So if you rotate the camera during the series of shots, all may not rotate automatically to their proper orientation during playback. See Chapter 5 for more about automatic picture rotation.

- *Your mileage may vary.* Three frames per second is just an approximation. The actual number of frames you can capture in Continuous mode depends on a number of factors, including your shutter speed. At a slow shutter speed, the camera may not be able to reach the maximum frame rate. (See Chapter 7 for an explanation of shutter speed.) Additionally, although you can capture as many as 100 frames in a single burst, the frame rate can drop if the buffer gets full.

✓ **Self-Timer:** Want to put yourself in the picture? Select this mode, press the shutter button, and run into the frame. As soon as you press the shutter button, the AF-assist lamp on the front of the camera starts to blink, and the camera emits a series of beeps (assuming that you didn't disable its voice, a setting I cover in Chapter 1). A few seconds later, the camera captures the image.

At the default settings, the capture-delay time is ten seconds. But you can reduce the delay to just two seconds via the Self Timer Delay option on the Setup menu, as illustrated in Figure 2-3. The current setting is shown with the self-timer symbol and the Release mode icon in the Shooting Info display, as shown in Figure 2-4.

One obscure quirk to note: If you set the shutter speed to Bulb (an option available only in M exposure mode), the shutter closes automatically about 1/10 second after it opens. Chapter 7 explains shutter speed.

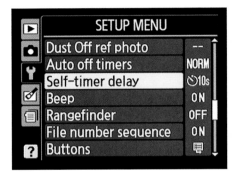
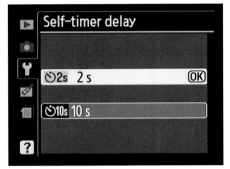

Figure 2-3: You can adjust the self-timer capture delay via the Setup menu.

When you use Self-Timer mode or any time that you don't have your eye to the viewfinder, it's a good idea to remove the little rubber cup that surrounds the viewfinder and then insert the viewfinder cover that shipped with your camera. (Dig around in the accessories box — the cover is a tiny black piece of plastic, about the size of the viewfinder.) Otherwise, light may seep into the camera through the viewfinder and affect exposure. You can also simply use the camera strap or something else to cover the viewfinder in a pinch.

✔ **Quiet:** This setting is designed for situations when you want the camera to be as silent as possible. It disables the autofocus beep and also decreases the internal sounds the camera makes from the time you fully depress the shutter button to the time you lift your finger off the button.

When you use autofocusing, the camera won't release the shutter and capture the picture if it can't achieve focus, no matter what your selected Release mode. Chapter 4 provides details about autofocusing during Live View and movie shooting; Chapter 8 explains autofocusing options for regular (viewfinder) shooting.

Release mode icon

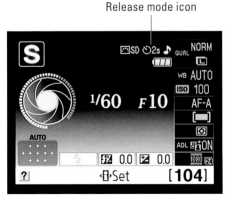

Figure 2-4: The selected Self-Timer Delay setting appears with the Release mode icon in the Shooting Info display.

What does [r 24] in the viewfinder mean?

When you look in your viewfinder to frame a shot, the initial value shown in brackets at the right end of the viewfinder display indicates the number of additional pictures that can fit on your memory card. For example, in the left viewfinder image below, the value shows that the card can hold 856 more images.

As soon as you press the shutter button halfway, which kicks the autofocus and exposure mechanisms into action, that value changes to instead show you how many pictures can fit in the camera's *memory buffer.* In the right image here, for example, the r 24 value tells you that 24 pictures can fit in the buffer.

So what's the *buffer?* It's a temporary storage tank where the camera stores picture data

until it has time to fully record that data onto the camera memory card. This system exists so that you can take a continuous series of pictures without waiting between shots until each image is fully written to the memory card.

When the buffer is full, the camera automatically disables the shutter button until it catches up on its recording work. Chances are, though, that you'll very rarely, if ever, encounter this situation; the camera is usually more than capable of keeping up with your shooting rate.

For more information about rapid-fire photography, see the section on action photography in Chapter 9. And for help translating the other viewfinder information shown in the figures here, check out Chapter 7.

`5OOF5.6` `ISO AUTO [856]`   `5OOF5.6` `ISO AUTO [r 24]`

Adding Flash

The built-in flash on your D3100 offers an easy, convenient way to add light to a scene. For even more lighting power, you can attach an external flash head to the camera via the *hot shoe* on top of the camera, labeled in Figure 2-5. (The hot shoe contacts are covered by a little black insert when you receive the camera; leave the cover in place until you're ready to attach a flash.)

Because the features of external flash heads vary from model to model, this book concentrates on making the best use of the built-in flash. If you need help using an external flash, though, one of the best places to start is www.strobist.com, a Web site loaded with flash photography tips and techniques. (*Strobe* is another word for *flash.*) Nikon also offers many resources on the subject at its Web site, www.nikon.com.

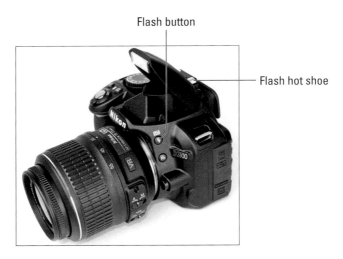

Flash button

Flash hot shoe

Figure 2-5: In P, S, A, and M modes, press the Flash button to use the built-in flash.

The next two sections provide the fundamentals of using the built-in flash; Chapter 7 discusses more advanced aspects of flash photography with the D3100.

Enabling flash

Whether you have any control over the flash depends on your exposure mode, as follows:

✔ **Auto, Portrait, Child, Close-Up, and Night Portrait mode:** The built-in flash pops up and fires automatically if the camera thinks the existing lighting is insufficient. However, you can disable the flash by changing the Flash mode, explained in the next section. What you *can't* do is force the flash to fire if the camera thinks the ambient light is sufficient to expose the image. That limitation can be problematic for outdoor daytime portraits and close-ups, which often can benefit from a little bit of extra light, even on a sunny day. Chapter 7 has some further advice on the subject.

✔ **Landscape, Sports, and No Flash:** Flash is disabled. That setup makes sense for No Flash mode, of course. But why no flash in Sports and Landscape mode, you ask? Well, Sports mode is designed to enable you to capture moving subjects, and the flash can make that more difficult because it needs time to recycle between shots. On top of that, the maximum shutter speed possible with the built-in flash is 1/200 second, which often isn't fast enough to ensure a blur-free subject. Finally, action photos usually aren't taken at a range close enough for the flash to reach the subject, which is also the reason why flash is disabled for Landscape mode.

✔ **Guide mode:** In Guide mode, available flash controls depend on the path you take through the guided menus. For example, if you select the Easy Operations menu item and then select Close-ups as the type of photo you want to take, you can choose from three Flash modes: Auto, Auto with Red-Eye Reduction, and Off. To get to the flash options, select the More Settings menu item after you select the picture type. Chapter 3 provides additional details about Guide mode photography.

 ✔ **P, S, A, and M:** You have complete control over the flash. To raise the flash, press the Flash button, labeled in Figure 2-5. To disable it, just close the flash by pressing it down gently.

If you use flash, check out the next section to find out how to set the Flash mode and see Chapter 7 for details on adjusting the flash power. (Look for the section related to Flash Exposure Compensation.) The latter feature works only in the P, S, A, and M exposure modes.

Setting the Flash mode

For exposure modes that allow flash, you can adjust the flash behavior via the *Flash mode* setting. Table 2-1 offers a quick-reference guide to the six basic modes. In addition to these basic modes, the camera also offers some combo modes, such as Auto with Red-Eye Reduction, Slow-Sync with Red-Eye Reduction, and the like.

Table 2-1		Flash Mode Quick-Reference Guide
Symbol	*Flash Mode*	*What It Does*
⚡ AUTO	Auto	Fires the flash automatically if the camera thinks the ambient light is insufficient or the subject is backlit
⚡	Fill	Fires the flash regardless of the ambient light
⚡(off)	Off	Disables the flash
⚡👁	Red-Eye Reduction	AF-assist lamp lights briefly before the flash goes off to help reduce red-eye reflections
⚡ SLOW	Slow-Sync	Results in a longer-than-normal exposure time so that the background is illuminated by ambient light and the foreground is lit by the flash
⚡ REAR	Rear-Curtain Sync	When combined with a slow shutter speed, causes illuminated, moving objects (such as car headlights) to appear as long, trailing fingers of light behind the subject

You can check the current Flash mode in the Shooting Info display, as shown on the left in Figure 2-6. The viewfinder display doesn't advise you of the specific Flash mode but instead just displays the universal lightning bolt icon when the flash is enabled, as shown on the right in the figure.

If you disable the flash and the camera thinks you're making a mistake, the flash symbol blinks in the viewfinder. You also see a blinking question mark in both the viewfinder and Shooting Info display, indicating that you can press the Zoom Out button to display a help screen with advice on getting a better exposure.

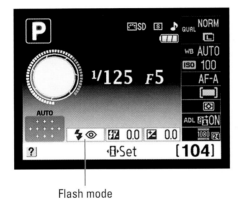
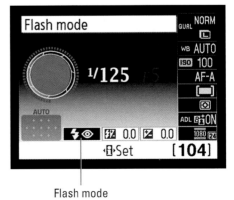

Flash mode

Flash enabled

Figure 2-6: Look here to check flash status.

To change the Flash mode, use either of these two methods:

✔ **Flash button plus Command dial:** Press and hold the Flash button (refer to Figure 2-5) to display the screen shown in Figure 2-7. Keep holding the button as you rotate the Command dial to cycle through the Flash modes available for your selected exposure mode.

✔ **Quick Settings screen:** You can also change the Flash mode by using the Quick Settings screen. Press the Info Edit button twice to shift to the screen and then use the Multi Selector to highlight

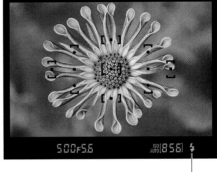

Flash mode

Figure 2-7: The fastest way to change the Flash mode is to hold down the Flash button while rotating the Command dial.

the Flash mode icon, as shown on the left in Figure 2-8. Press OK to display the right screen in the figure, highlight your choice, and press OK. (See Chapter 1 if you need help using the Quick Settings display.)

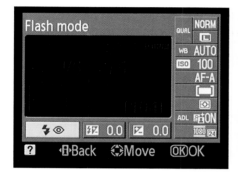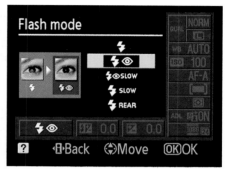

Figure 2-8: You also can change the Flash mode by using the Quick Settings screen.

Now for the bad news: When you try to change the Flash mode, you'll quickly discover that you have access to only a couple Flash modes when you shoot in the fully automatic exposure modes (Auto, Auto Flash Off, and the Scene modes). For the Auto, Portrait, Child, Close-Up, and Night Portrait modes, the flash mode reverts to the default setting if you switch to another exposure mode. Additionally, you don't have access to Flash Compensation, which enables you to diminish or strengthen the burst of light the flash produces, as well as a few other flash features your camera offers. Bummer, as the youngsters say.

You can find details about which Flash modes are available in each of the fully automatic exposure modes in Chapter 3. For details about remaining flash features, see Chapter 7.

Choosing the Right Quality Settings

Almost every review of the D3100 contains glowing reports about the camera's top-notch picture quality. As you've no doubt discovered, those claims are true: This baby can create large, beautiful images.

What you may *not* have discovered is that Nikon's default Image Quality setting isn't the highest that the D3100 offers. Why, you ask, would Nikon do such a thing? Why not set up the camera to produce the best images right out of the box? The answer is that using the top setting has some downsides. Nikon's default choice represents a compromise between avoiding those disadvantages while still producing images that will please most photographers.

Whether that compromise is right for you, however, depends on your photographic needs. To help you decide, the rest of this chapter explains the Image Quality setting, along with the Image Size setting, which is also critical to the quality of images that you print. Just in case you're having quality problems related to other issues, though, the next section provides a handy quality-defect diagnosis guide.

If you already know what settings you want to use and just need some help finding out how to select the options, skip to the very last section of the chapter.

Diagnosing quality problems

When I say *picture quality,* I'm not talking about the composition, exposure, or other traditional characteristics of a photograph. Instead, I'm referring to how finely the image is rendered in the digital sense.

Figure 2-9 illustrates the concept: The first example is a high-quality image, with clear details and smooth color transitions. The other examples show five common digital-image defects.

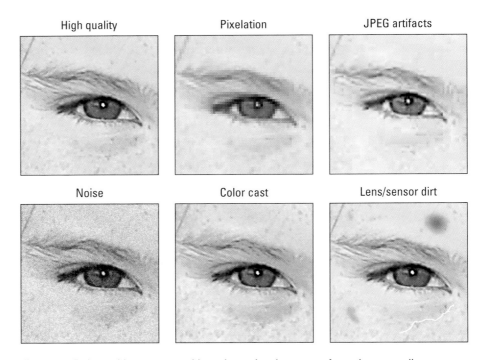

Figure 2-9: Refer to this symptom guide to determine the cause of poor image quality.

Each of these defects is related to a different issue, and only one is affected by the Image Quality setting on your D3100. So if you aren't happy with your image quality, first compare your photos to those in the figure to properly diagnose the problem. Then try these remedies:

- **Pixelation:** When an image doesn't have enough *pixels* (the colored tiles used to create digital images), details aren't clear, and curved and diagonal lines appear jagged. The fix is to increase image resolution, which you do via the Image Size control. See the next section, "Considering image size: How many pixels are enough?" for details.

- **JPEG artifacts:** The "parquet tile" texture and random color defects that mar the third image in Figure 2-9 can occur in photos captured in the JPEG *(jay-peg)* file format, which is why these flaws are referred to as *JPEG artifacts.* This is the defect related to the Image Quality setting; see "Understanding Image Quality options (JPEG or Raw)," later in this chapter, to find out more.

- **Noise:** This defect gives your image a speckled look, as shown in the lower-left example in Figure 2-9. Noise can occur with very long exposure times or when you choose a high ISO Sensitivity setting on your camera. You can explore both issues in Chapter 7.

- **Color cast:** If your colors are seriously out of whack, as shown in the lower-middle example in the figure, try adjusting the camera's White Balance setting. Chapter 8 covers this control and other color issues.

- **Lens/sensor dirt:** A dirty lens is the first possible cause of the kind of defects you see in the last example in the figure. If cleaning your lens doesn't solve the problem, dust or dirt may have made its way onto the camera's image sensor. See the sidebar "Maintaining a pristine view," later in this chapter, for information on safe lens and sensor cleaning.

When diagnosing image problems, you may want to open the photos in ViewNX 2 or some other photo software and zoom in for a close-up inspection. Some defects, especially pixelation and JPEG artifacts, have a similar appearance until you see them at a magnified view. (See Part II for information about using ViewNX 2.)

I should also tell you that I used a little digital enhancement to exaggerate the flaws in my example images to make the symptoms easier to see. With the exception of an unwanted color cast or a big blob of lens or sensor dirt, these defects may not even be noticeable unless you print or view your image at a very large size. And the subject matter of your image may camouflage some flaws; most people probably wouldn't detect a little JPEG artifacting in a photograph of a densely wooded forest, for example.

In other words, don't consider Figure 2-9 as an indication that your D3100 is suspect in the image quality department. First, *any* digital camera can produce these defects under the right circumstances. Second, by following the guidelines in this chapter and the others mentioned in the preceding list, you can resolve any quality issues that you may encounter.

Considering image size: How many pixels are enough?

Pixels are the little square tiles from which all digital images are made. You can see some pixels close up in the right image in Figure 2-10, which shows a greatly magnified view of the eye area in the left image.

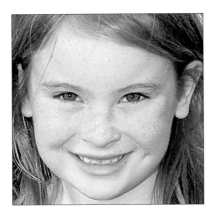 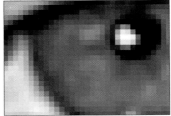

Figure 2-10: Pixels are the building blocks of digital photos.

Pixel is short for *picture element.* The number of pixels in an image is referred to as *resolution.* You can define resolution either in terms of the *pixel dimensions* — the number of horizontal pixels and vertical pixels — or total resolution, which you get by multiplying those two values. This number is usually stated in *megapixels,* or MP for short, with one megapixel equal to one million pixels. For example, the D3100 offers a maximum resolution of 4608 x 3072 pixels, which translates to about 14.2 megapixels.

You control resolution on the D3100 via the Image Size setting. You can choose from three settings: Large, Medium, and Small; Table 2-2 lists the resolution values for each setting. (Megapixel values are rounded off.)

Table 2-2	Image Size (Resolution) Options
Setting	**Resolution**
Large	4608 x 3072 (14.2 MP)
Medium	3456 x 2304 (8.0 MP)
Small	2304 x 1536 (3.5 MP)

However, if you select Raw (NEF) as your file format, all images are captured at the Large setting. You can vary the resolution only when choosing JPEG as the file format. The upcoming section "Understanding Image Quality options (JPEG or Raw)" explains file formats.

To choose the right Image Size setting, you need to understand the three ways that pixel count affects your pictures:

✓ **Print size:** Pixel count determines the size at which you can produce a high-quality print. If you don't have enough pixels, your prints may exhibit the defects you see in the pixelation example in Figure 2-9, or worse, you may be able to see the individual pixels, as in the right example in Figure 2-10. Depending on your photo printer, you typically need anywhere from 200 to 300 pixels per linear inch, or *ppi,* of the print. To produce an 8 x 10 print at 200 ppi, for example, you need a pixel count of 1600 x 2000, or just less than 2 megapixels.

Even though many photo editing programs enable you to add pixels to an existing image, doing so isn't a good idea. For reasons I won't bore you with, adding pixels — known as *upsampling* — doesn't enable you to successfully enlarge your photo. In fact, upsampling typically makes matters worse. The printing discussion in Chapter 6 includes some example images that illustrate this issue.

✓ **Screen display size:** Resolution doesn't affect the quality of images viewed on a monitor, television, or other screen device the way it does for printed photos. Instead, resolution determines the *size* at which the image appears. This issue is one of the most misunderstood aspects of digital photography, so I explain it thoroughly in Chapter 6. For now, just know that you need *way* fewer pixels for onscreen photos than you do for printed photos. In fact, even the Small resolution setting on your camera creates a picture too big to be viewed in its entirety in most e-mail programs.

✓ **File size:** Every additional pixel increases the amount of data required to create a digital picture file. So a higher-resolution image has a larger file size than a low-resolution image.

Large files present several problems:

- You can store fewer images on your memory card, on your computer's hard drive, and on removable storage media such as a CD-ROM.

- The camera needs more time to process and store the image data on the memory card after you press the shutter button. This extra time can hamper fast-action shooting.

- When you share photos online, larger files take longer to upload and download.

- When you edit your photos in your photo software, your computer needs more resources and time to process large files.

As you can see, resolution is a bit of a sticky wicket. What if you aren't sure how large you want to print your images? What if you want to print your photos *and* share them online?

I take the better-safe-than-sorry route, which leads to the following recommendations about which Image Size setting to use:

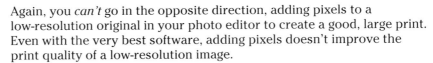

- **Always shoot at a resolution suitable for print.** You then can create a low-resolution copy of the image in your photo editor for use online. In fact, your camera offers a built-in resizing option; Chapter 6 shows you how to use it.

Again, you *can't* go in the opposite direction, adding pixels to a low-resolution original in your photo editor to create a good, large print. Even with the very best software, adding pixels doesn't improve the print quality of a low-resolution image.

- **For everyday images, Medium is a good choice.** I find the Large setting (14.2 MP) to be overkill for most casual shooting, which means that you're creating huge files for no good reason. Keep in mind that even at the Small setting, your pixel count (2304 x 1536) is approximately what you need to produce an 8-x-10-inch print at 200 ppi.

- **Choose Large for an image that you plan to crop, print very large, or both.** The benefit of maxing out resolution is that you have the flexibility to crop your photo and still generate a decent-sized print of the remaining image. Figures 2-11 and 2-12 offer an example. When I was shooting this photo, I couldn't get any closer to the bee — okay, didn't *want* to get closer to the bee — than the first picture shows. But because I had the resolution cranked up to Large, I could later crop the shot to the composition you see in Figure 2-12 and still produce a great print. In fact, I could have printed the cropped image at a much larger size than fits here.

✔ **Reduce resolution if shooting speed is paramount.** If you're shooting action and the shot-to-shot capture time is slower than you want — that is, the camera takes too long after you take one shot before it lets you take another — dialing down the resolution may help. Also see Chapter 9 for other tips on action photography.

After you decide which resolution setting is right for your picture, visit the section "Setting Image Size and Quality," at the end of this chapter.

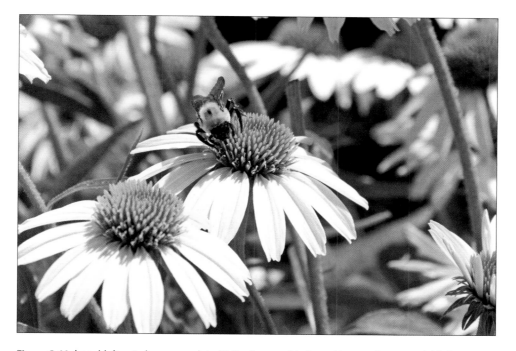

Figure 2-11: I couldn't get close enough to fill the frame with the subject, so I captured this image at the Large resolution setting.

Understanding Image Quality options (JPEG or Raw)

If I had my druthers, the Image Quality option on the D3100 would instead be called File Type because that's what the setting controls.

Here's the deal: The file type, more commonly known as a file *format*, determines how your picture data is recorded and stored. Your choice does impact picture quality, but so do other factors, as outlined at the beginning of this chapter. In addition, your choice of file type has ramifications beyond picture quality.

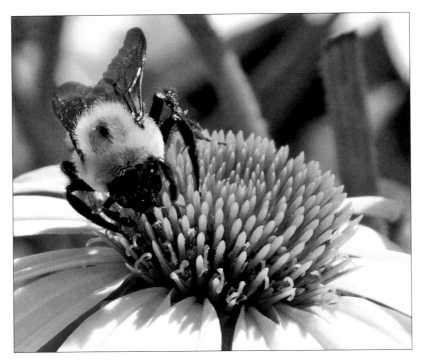

Figure 2-12: A high-resolution original enabled me to crop the photo tightly and still have enough pixels to produce a quality print.

At any rate, your D3100 offers the two file types common on most of today's digital cameras: JPEG and Camera Raw, or just Raw for short, which goes by the specific moniker NEF *(Nikon Electronic Format)* on Nikon cameras. The next sections explain the pros and cons of each format. If your mind is already made up, skip ahead to "Setting Image Size and Quality," near the end of this chapter, to find out how to make your selection.

Don't confuse *file format* with the Format Memory Card option on the Setup menu. That option erases all data on your memory card; see Chapter 1 for details.

JPEG: The imaging (and Web) standard

Pronounced *jay-peg*, this format is the default setting on your D3100, as it is for most digital cameras. JPEG is popular for two main reasons:

- ✓ **Immediate usability:** All Web browsers and e-mail programs can display JPEG files, so you can share them online immediately after you shoot them. The same can't be said for Raw (NEF) files, which must be processed and converted to JPEG files before you can share them online. And although you can view and print your camera's Raw files in Nikon ViewNX 2 without converting them, many third-party photo programs don't enable you to do that. You can read more about the conversion process in the upcoming section "Raw (NEF): The purist's choice."

- ✓ **Small files:** JPEG files are smaller than Raw files. And smaller files consume less room on your camera memory card and in your computer's storage tank.

The downside — you knew there had to be one — is that JPEG creates smaller files by applying *lossy compression.* This process actually throws away some image data. Too much compression leads to the defects you see in the JPEG artifacts example in Figure 2-9.

Fortunately, your camera enables you to specify how much compression you're willing to accept. You can choose from three JPEG settings, which produce the following results:

- ✓ **JPEG Fine:** At this setting, the compression ratio is 1:4 — that is, the file is four times smaller than it'd otherwise be. In plain English, that means that very little compression is applied, so you shouldn't see many compression artifacts, if any.

- ✓ **JPEG Normal:** Switch to Normal, and the compression ratio rises to 1:8. The chance of seeing some artifacting increases as well.

- ✓ **JPEG Basic:** Shift to this setting, and the compression ratio jumps to 1:16. That's a substantial amount of compression and brings with it a lot more risk of artifacting.

Note, though, that even the JPEG Basic setting on your D3100 doesn't result in anywhere near the level of artifacting that you see in my example in Figure 2-9. Again, that example is exaggerated to help you be able to recognize artifacting defects and understand how they differ from other image quality issues. In fact, if you keep your image print or display size small, you aren't likely to notice a great deal of quality difference between the Fine, Normal, and Basic compression levels, although details in the Fine and Normal versions may appear slightly crisper than the Basic one. It's only when you greatly enlarge a photo that the differences become apparent.

Given that the differences between the compression settings aren't that easy to spot until you enlarge the photo, is it okay to stick with the default setting — Normal — or even drop down to Basic to capture smaller files? Well, only you can decide what level of quality your pictures demand. For me, the added file sizes produced by the Fine setting aren't a huge concern, given that the prices of memory cards fall all the time. Long-term storage is more of an issue; the larger your files, the faster you fill your computer's hard drive and the more DVDs or CDs you need for archiving purposes. But in the end, I prefer to take the storage hit in exchange for the lower compression level of the Fine setting. You never know when a casual snapshot is going to be so great that you want to print or display it large enough that even minor quality loss becomes a concern. And of all the defects that you can correct in a photo editor, artifacting is one of the hardest to remove.

To make the best decision, do your own test shots, carefully inspect the results in your photo editor, and make your own judgment about what level of artifacting you can accept. Artifacting is often much easier to spot when you view images onscreen. It's difficult to reproduce artifacting here in print because the printing press obscures some of the tiny defects caused by compression. Your inkjet prints are more likely to reveal these defects.

If you don't want *any* risk of artifacting, bypass JPEG altogether and change the file type to Raw (NEF). Or consider your other option, which is to record two versions of each file, one Raw and one JPEG. The next section offers details.

Preserving the quality of edited photos

If you retouch pictures in your photo software, don't save the altered images in the JPEG format. As explained in the section "JPEG: The imaging (and Web) standard," elsewhere in this chapter, JPEG creates smaller files by eliminating some image data, a process called *lossy compression*.

Every time you alter and save an image in the JPEG format, you apply another round of lossy compression. And with enough editing, saving, and compressing, you can eventually get to the level of image degradation shown in the JPEG example in Figure 2-9. (Simply opening and closing the file does no harm.)

Instead, always save your edited photos in a nondestructive format. TIFF, pronounced *tiff,* is a good choice and is a file-saving option available in most photo-editing programs. Should you want to share the edited image online, create a JPEG copy of the TIFF file when you finish making all your changes. That way, you always retain one copy of the photo at the original quality captured by the camera. You can read more about TIFF in Chapter 6, in the section related to processing Raw images. The same chapter explains how to create a JPEG copy of a photo for online sharing.

Raw (NEF): The purist's choice

The other picture file type you can create on your D3100 is *Camera Raw,* or just *Raw* (as in uncooked) for short.

Each manufacturer has its own flavor of Raw. Nikon's is NEF, for *Nikon Electronic Format,* so you see the three-letter extension NEF at the end of Raw filenames.

Raw is popular with advanced, very demanding photographers, for the following reasons:

- ✔ **Greater creative control:** With JPEG, internal camera software tweaks your images, adjusting color, exposure, and sharpness as needed to produce the results that Nikon believes its customers prefer. With Raw, the camera simply records the original, unprocessed image data. The photographer then copies the image file to the computer and uses special software — a *Raw converter* — to produce the actual image, making decisions about color, exposure, and so on at that point. The upshot is that "shooting Raw" enables you, not the camera, to have the final say on the visual characteristics of your image.

- ✔ **Higher bit depth:** *Bit depth* is a measure of how many distinct color values an image file can contain. JPEG files restrict you to 8 bits each for the red, blue, and green color components, or *channels,* that make up a digital image, for a total of 24 bits. That translates to roughly 16.7 million possible colors. On the D3100, a Raw file delivers a higher bit count, collecting 12 bits per channel. (Chapter 8 provides more information about the red-green-blue makeup of digital images.)

  Although jumping from 8 to 12 bits sounds like a huge difference, you may not really ever notice any difference in your photos — that 8-bit palette of 16.7 million values is more than enough for superb images. Where having the extra bits can come in handy is if you really need to adjust exposure, contrast, or color after the shot in your photo-editing program. In cases where you apply extreme adjustments, having the extra original bits sometimes helps avoid a problem known as *banding* or *posterization,* which creates abrupt color breaks where you should see smooth, seamless transitions. (A higher bit depth doesn't always prevent the problem, however, so don't expect miracles.)

- ✔ **Best picture quality:** Because Raw doesn't apply the destructive compression associated with JPEG, you don't run the risk of the artifacting that can occur with JPEG.

But of course, as with most things in life, Raw isn't without its disadvantages. To wit:

✔ **You can't do much with your pictures until you process them in a Raw converter.** You can't share them online, for example, or put them into a text document or multimedia presentation. You can view and print them immediately if you use the free Nikon ViewNX 2 software, but most other photo programs require you to convert the Raw files to a standard format first. Ditto for retail photo printing. So when you shoot Raw, you add to the time you must spend in front of the computer instead of behind the camera lens. Chapter 6 shows you how to process your Raw files using Nikon ViewNX 2 as well as the converter built into the camera.

✔ **Raw files are larger than JPEGs.** Unlike JPEG, Raw doesn't apply lossy compression to shrink files. In addition, Raw files are always captured at the maximum resolution available on your camera, even if you don't really need all those pixels. For both reasons, Raw files are significantly larger than JPEGs, so they take up more room on your memory card and on your computer's hard drive or other picture-storage device.

✔ **To get the full benefit of Raw, you need software other than Nikon ViewNX 2.** The ViewNX 2 software that ships free with your camera does have a command that enables you to convert Raw files to JPEG or to TIFF, introduced in the nearby sidebar. However, this free tool gives you limited control over how your original data is translated in terms of color, exposure, and other characteristics — which defeats one of the primary purposes of shooting Raw. The same is true for the Raw converter built into the camera.

Nikon Capture NX 2 offers a sophisticated Raw converter, but it costs about $180. (Sadly, if you already own Capture NX, you need to upgrade to version 2 to open the Raw files from your D3100.) Chapter 6 talks more about this software and other programs that provide good Raw conversion tools.

Whether the upside of Raw outweighs the down is a decision that you need to ponder based on your photographic needs, your schedule, and your computer-comfort level. If you decide to try Raw shooting, you can select from the following two Image Quality options:

✔ **RAW:** This setting produces a single Raw file at the maximum resolution (14.2 megapixels).

✔ **RAW+JPEG:** This setting produces two files: the standard Raw file plus a JPEG Fine version. Both files are captured at the maximum resolution, so remember that creating two files for every image eats up substantially more memory card space than sticking with a single file.

I often choose the Raw+JPEG Fine option when I shoot pictures I want to share right away with people who don't have software for viewing Raw files. I upload the JPEGs to a photo-sharing site where everyone can view them and then I process the Raw versions of my favorite images for my own use when I have time. Having the JPEG version also enables you to display your photos on a DVD player or TV that has a slot for an SD memory card — most can't display Raw files but can handle JPEGs. Ditto for portable media players and digital photo frames.

My take: Choose JPEG Fine or Raw (NEF)

At this point, you may be finding all this technical goop a bit much — I recognize that panicked look in your eyes — so allow me to simplify things for you. Until you have time or energy to completely digest all the ramifications of JPEG versus Raw, here's a quick summary of my thoughts on the matter:

- If you require the absolute best image quality and have the time and interest to do the Raw conversion, shoot Raw. See Chapter 6 for more information on the conversion process.

- If great photo quality is good enough for you, you don't have wads of spare time, or you aren't that comfortable with the computer, stick with JPEG Fine.

- If you don't mind the added file-storage space requirement and want the flexibility of both formats, choose Raw+JPEG Fine.

- If you go with JPEG only, stay away from JPEG Normal and Basic. The tradeoff for smaller files isn't, in my opinion, worth the risk of compression artifacts. As with my recommendations on image size, this fits the "better safe than sorry" formula: You never know when you may capture a spectacular, enlargement-worthy subject, and it'd be a shame to have the photo spoiled by compression defects.

Setting Image Size and Quality

To sum up this chapter:

- The Image Size and Image Quality options both affect the quality of your pictures and also play a large role in image file size.

- Choose a high Image Quality setting — Raw (NEF) or JPEG Fine — and the maximum Image Size setting (Large), and you get top-quality pictures and large file sizes.

✔ Combining the lowest Quality setting (JPEG Basic) with the lowest Size setting (Small) greatly shrinks files, enabling you to fit lots more pictures on your memory card, but it also increases the chances that you'll be disappointed with the quality of those pictures, especially if you make large prints.

You can view the current Image Size and Image Quality settings in the Shooting Info screen, in the area labeled in Figure 2-13. (Press the Info button or Info Edit button to access the screen.) To adjust the settings, you have the following choices:

✔ **Quick Settings display:** Press the Info Edit button twice — once to bring up the Shooting Info display and then again to shift to the Quick Settings screen. (Or press the Info button to bring up the Shooting Info screen and press the Info Edit button to toggle to the Quick Settings display.)

Use the Multi Selector to highlight the Image Quality option, located in the top-right corner, as shown on the left in Figure 2-14. Press OK to view the second screen in the figure, where you can select the option you want to use. Highlight your choice and then press OK.

Repeat the process to set the Image Size option, which is right below the Image Quality setting on the Quick Settings screen.

✔ **Shooting menu:** As an alternative, you can adjust the settings via the Shooting menu, as shown in Figure 2-15. *Note:* If you use the guided menus instead of the regular menus, you access the Size and Quality options through the Set Up category, not the Shoot section, and your settings apply only to pictures you take in Guide mode. See Chapter 1 for more information about the guided menus, including the reasons why I suggest you stick with the regular menus.

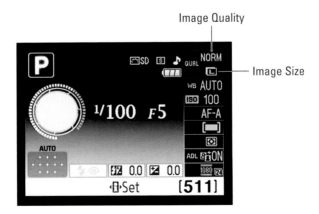

Figure 2-13: The current Image Quality and Image Size settings appear here.

File size   Shots remaining

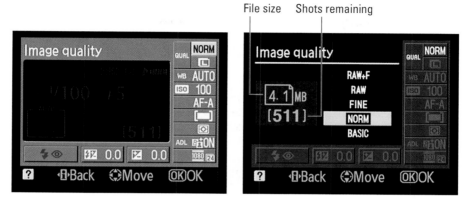

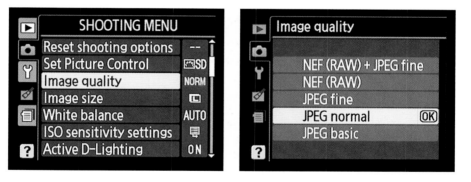

Figure 2-14: You can use the Quick Settings screen to change the Image Size and Quality settings.

Figure 2-15: You also can set Image Size and Image Quality via the Shooting menu.

 ✔ **Use the Fn button with the Command dial:** Through the Buttons option on the Setup menu, you can set the Fn button to access the Image Quality and Image Size options. Then you hold down the button while rotating the Command dial to cycle through the various combinations of Image Size and Image Quality. See Chapter 11 to find out more about this button customization. (Normally, the Fn button is set to provide access to the ISO Sensitivity option.)

However you adjust the Size and Quality options, remember that when you choose the Raw (NEF) or Raw+JPEG Fine format, you don't need to worry about the Image Size setting. For these formats, all pictures are automatically captured at the Large resolution, and you can't choose a lower resolution setting.

Adjusting the Image Size or Image Quality setting changes the picture file size, which changes the number of new shots you can fit on the current memory card. If you adjust the options through the Quick Settings screen, the display reports the resulting file size and shots remaining values in the area highlighted in Figure 2-14. You also can view the shots remaining value in the Shooting Info screen and viewfinder.

Keep in mind that certain other factors also affect file size, such as the level of detail and color in the subject. If you're interested, the camera manual contains a table that shows the approximate file sizes that result from each combination of the Image Size and Image Quality settings, along with information about how many pictures you can expect to fit on a 4GB memory card at those file sizes.

Maintaining a pristine view

Often lost in discussions of digital photo defects — compression artifacts, pixelation, and the like — is the impact of plain-old dust and dirt on picture quality. But no matter what camera settings you use, you aren't going to achieve great picture quality with a dirty lens. So make it a practice to clean your lens on a regular basis, using one of the specialized cloths and cleaning solutions made expressly for that purpose.

If you continue to notice random blobs or hair-like defects in your images (refer to the last example in Figure 2-9), you probably have a dirty *image sensor*. That's the part of your camera that does the actual image capture — the digital equivalent of a film negative, if you will.

Your D3100 offers an automated, internal sensor-cleaning mechanism. By default, this automatic cleaning happens every time you turn the camera on or off. You also can request

a cleaning session at any time via the Clean Image Sensor command on the Setup menu. (Chapter 1 has details on this menu option.)

But if you frequently change lenses in a dirty environment, the internal cleaning mechanism may not be adequate, in which case a manual sensor cleaning is necessary. You can do this job yourself, but . . . I don't recommend it. Image sensors are pretty delicate beings, and you can easily damage them or other parts of your camera if you aren't careful. Instead, find a local camera store that offers this service. In my area (central Indiana), sensor cleaning costs from $30–$50.

One more cleaning tip: Never — and I mean *never* — try to clean any part of your camera using a can of compressed air. Doing so can not only damage the interior of your camera, blowing dust or dirt into areas where it can't be removed, but also crack the external monitor.

3

Taking Great Pictures, Automatically

*A*re you old enough to remember the Certs television commercials from the 1960s and '70s? "It's a candy mint!" declared one actor. "It's a breath mint!" argued another. Then a narrator declared the debate a tie and spoke the famous catchphrase: "It's two, two, two mints in one!"

Well, that's sort of how I see the Nikon D3100. On one hand, it provides a full range of powerful controls, offering just about every feature a serious photographer could want. On the other, it offers automated photography modes that enable people with absolutely no experience to capture beautiful images. "It's a sophisticated photographic tool!" "It's as easy as 'point and shoot!'" "It's two, two, two cameras in one!"

Now, my guess is that you bought this book for help with your camera's advanced side so that's what other chapters cover. This chapter, however, is devoted to your camera's easiest shooting modes, showing you how to get the best results in your camera's fully automatic modes, including Auto, Portrait mode, Sports mode, and the other Scene modes. In addition, a section at the end of the chapter helps you start taking a little more creative control with an assist from Guide mode.

Note: Information in this chapter assumes that you're using the viewfinder to compose your pictures. Things work a little differently in Live View mode, which enables you to use the monitor instead of the viewfinder, so Chapter 4 concentrates on that shooting option.

Setting Up for Automatic Success

Your D3100 offers eight fully automatic exposure modes, which you access via the Mode dial, as shown in Figure 3-1. Your choices include Auto, which is a general purpose, point-and-shoot type of option, Auto Flash Off, which does the same thing as Auto but without flash, plus six Scene modes, which are geared to shooting specific types of pictures.

Fully automatic exposure modes   Release mode switch

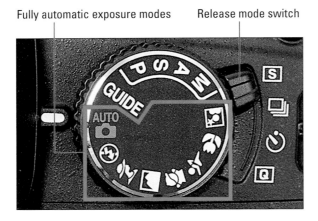

Figure 3-1: You can select from eight fully automatic, point-and-shoot photography modes.

These modes are designed for people without any knowledge of photography. You just frame the shot and press the shutter button. But even in these automatic modes, you have a few ways to control the camera's behavior. You can adjust the following settings:

- **Release mode:** This setting determines the number of images that are recorded with each press of the shutter button and the timing of each shot. Chapter 2 details this option, but here's a quick recap of the available settings:

- *Single Frame:* Records a single picture immediately after you depress the shutter button fully. Use this setting for normal photography.

- *Continuous:* Records up to three frames per second for as long as you hold down the shutter button. Try this setting when shooting action shots; just remember that you can't use the built-in flash during continuous shooting.

- *Self-Timer:* Captures the image a few seconds after you press the shutter button, enabling the photographer to step from behind the camera and into the shot. The default delay is 10 seconds, but you can shorten it to 2 seconds via the Self-Timer Delay option on the Setup menu.

- *Quiet:* Works like Single mode but silences the camera's normal operating sounds as much as possible. Try this mode in situations where camera noise might be disruptive.

Choose the Release mode via the switch labeled in Figure 3-1.

✔ **Focusing:** You can enjoy autofocusing, if your lens supports it, or focus manually. On the D3100 kit lens, select the setting via the switch labeled in Figure 3-2.

The camera's initial autofocusing behavior depends on the exposure mode you select. I detail the default behavior in the upcoming sections that explain the automatic exposure modes; Chapter 8 provides information about advanced focusing features.

✔ **Vibration Reduction:** When enabled, this feature helps produce sharper images by compensating for camera movement that can occur when you handhold the camera. On the kit lens, turn Vibration Reduction on or off via the VR switch, labeled in Figure 3-1. Select On for handheld photography; set the switch to Off when you mount the camera on a tripod. See Chapter 1 for additional details.

✔ **Flash:** Flash is disabled in Sports, Landscape, and Flash Off modes. In the other modes, you can choose from

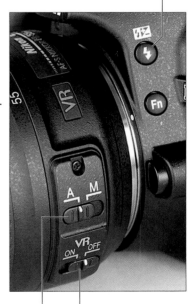

Flash button

Vibration Reduction switch

Auto/Manual focus switch

Figure 3-2: You can choose automatic or manual focusing in any exposure mode (if your lens supports auto-focusing).

a few Flash modes; see Table 3-1 for a summary of which Flash modes work with which exposure modes. The default Flash mode is Auto, which raises and fires the built-in flash if the camera thinks additional light is needed.

The fastest way to change the Flash mode is to press and hold the Flash button, labeled in Figure 3-2, and then rotate the Command dial. You can view the setting in the Shooting Info screen; Chapter 2 provides details.

✔ **Image Quality and Image Size:** By default, pictures are recorded at the Large Image Size setting, producing a 14.2 MP (megapixel) image, and the Normal Image Quality setting, which creates a JPEG picture file with a moderate amount of compression. Chapter 2 explains both options and offers advice on when you may want to stray from the default settings.

✔ **Exposure:** In the Scene modes, you have access to one exposure-adjustment option, ISO Sensitivity, which determines how much light is needed to properly expose the image. At the default setting, Auto, the camera adjusts the ISO Sensitivity as needed. This option is a little complex, so I save it for Chapter 7; stick with Auto for now.

✔ **Advanced Shooting menu options:** You also can control the following more advanced Shooting menu options:

- *Auto Distortion Control:* This feature attempts to correct for the slight distortion that can occur when you shoot with wide-angle or extreme telephoto lenses. Leave this one set to its default, Off, until you explore the details in Chapter 8.

- *Color Space:* Again, stick with the default setting, sRGB, until you delve into the advanced color issues covered in Chapter 8.

- *Noise Reduction:* This feature tries to compensate for image defects that can occur when you use a high ISO setting or a long exposure time. Chapter 7 explains the pros and cons of enabling the feature.

If you're not up to sorting through any of these choices, just leave them all at their default settings and skip to the next section to get step-by-step help with taking your first pictures. After all, the defaults are chosen because they're the best solutions for most shooting scenarios. See the end of Chapter 1 to find out how to restore the default Shooting menu and Setup menu options.

Table 3-1	Flash Modes Available in Automatic Exposure Modes	
Mode Symbol	**Mode Name**	**Available Flash Modes**
AUTO	Auto	Auto, Auto with Red-Eye Reduction, Off
(flash off)	Auto Flash Off	Off
(portrait)	Portrait	Auto, Auto with Red-Eye Reduction, Off
(landscape)	Landscape	Off
(child)	Child	Auto, Auto with Red-Eye Reduction, Off
(sports)	Sports	Off
(close-up)	Close-Up	Auto, Auto with Red-Eye Reduction, Off
(night portrait)	Night Portrait	Auto Slow-Sync, Auto Slow-Sync with Red-Eye Reduction, Off

As Easy As It Gets: Auto and Auto Flash Off

 In Auto mode, the camera analyzes the scene in front of the lens and selects the picture-taking options that it thinks will best capture the image. All you need to do is compose the scene and press the shutter button.

 Auto Flash Off mode does the exact same thing, except flash is disabled. This mode provides an easy way to ensure that you don't break the rules when shooting in locations that don't permit flash: museums, churches, and so on.

The following steps walk you through the process of taking a picture in both modes. Remember that these steps assume that you're using the viewfinder, which is the best option in most cases. Chapter 4 explains why and shows you how to take pictures in Live View mode.

 Before you work through the steps, though, adjust the viewfinder to your eyesight so that you get an accurate idea of whether the scene is in focus. (Chapter 1 shows you how.) Also select your focusing method, Release mode, Vibration Reduction setting, and other options as outlined in the preceding section.

1. **Set the Mode dial to Auto or Auto Flash Off.**

2. **Looking through the viewfinder, frame the image so that your subject appears under one of the 11 focus points, as shown in Figure 3-3.**

   The *focus points* are those tiny rectangles surrounded by brackets to make them a little easier to see. I labeled one of the little guys in the figure.

3. **If focusing manually, twist the focusing ring on the lens until the scene appears in focus.**

   On the kit lens, set the lens switch to M before turning the focusing ring to avoid damaging the lens. If you use another lens, check the lens manual for instructions. Either way, also see Chapter 8 for additional information that may help you achieve better results when focusing manually.

4. **Press and hold the shutter button halfway down.**

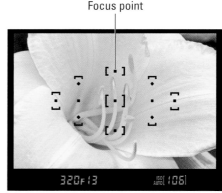

Figure 3-3: The markings in the viewfinder indicate autofocus points.

   At this point, the following occurs:

   - *Exposure metering begins.* The autoexposure meter analyzes the light and selects initial aperture (f-stop) and shutter speed settings, which are two critical exposure controls. These two settings appear in the viewfinder; in Figure 3-3, the shutter speed is 1/320 second, and the f-stop is f/13. (Chapter 7 explains these two options in detail.)

   - *If you set the Mode dial to Auto in Step 1, the built-in flash may pop up if the camera thinks additional light is needed.* By default, the Flash mode is set to Auto, which means that the camera decides when additional light is necessary. You also can select Auto with Red-Eye Reduction, which fires a brief pre-flash to help minimize red-eye. Again, though, the camera fires the flash only if the light is sufficiently dim.

     To go flash free, set the Flash mode to Off or, easier yet, just set the Mode dial to the Auto Flash Off icon. See Chapter 2 to find out how to adjust the Flash mode.

   - *If autofocusing is enabled, the camera's autofocus system begins to do its thing.* In dim light, a little lamp located on the front of the camera, just to the left of the shutter button, may shoot out a beam of light. That lamp, called the *autofocus-assist illuminator,* or *AF-assist lamp* for short, helps the camera measure the distance between your subject and the lens so that it can better establish focus.

When the camera has established focus, one or more of the points turns red, as shown in Figure 3-4, for a split second. The red focus points represent the areas of the frame that are now in focus. In the display at the bottom of the viewfinder, the green focus indicator, labeled in the figure, lights to give you further notice that focus has been achieved.

The autoexposure meter continues monitoring the light up to the time you take the picture, so the f-stop and shutter speed values in the viewfinder may change if the lighting conditions change.

Selected focus points

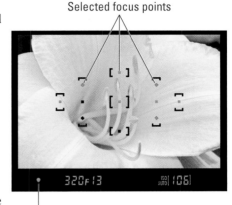

Focus indicator light

Figure 3-4: The green light indicates that the camera has locked focus on the objects under the red focus points.

5. **Press the shutter button the rest of the way down to record the image.**

While the camera sends the image data to the camera memory card, the memory card access lamp lights, as shown in Figure 3-5. Don't turn off the camera or remove the memory card while the lamp is lit, or you may damage both camera and card.

When the recording process is finished, the picture appears briefly on the camera monitor. If the picture doesn't appear or you want to take a longer look at the image, see Chapter 5, which covers picture playback.

I need to add a few important points about working in the Auto and Auto Flash Off modes:

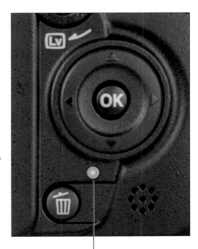

Memory card access lamp

Figure 3-5: The memory card access lamp lights while the camera sends the picture data to the card.

✔ **Exposure:** If an exposure meter blinks in the viewfinder or Shooting Info display, the camera can't select settings that will properly exposure the picture. See Chapter 7 for details about reading the exposure meter and coping with exposure problems. In dim lighting, adding flash may do the trick, however.

✔ **Autofocusing:** Autofocusing behavior is determined by two settings, the AF-area mode and the Focus mode, both explained fully in Chapter 8. By default, the camera uses these settings:

- *AF-area mode:* The Auto Area option is selected, which means that the camera selects which autofocus points to use when establishing focus. Chapter 8 explains how to modify this autofocusing behavior.

- *Focus mode:* The default setting is AF-A, which stands for *auto-servo autofocus.* If the subject isn't moving, focus remains locked as long as you hold the shutter button halfway down. But if the camera detects motion, it continually adjusts focus up to the time you press the button fully to record the picture. To ensure that focus is correct, you must keep your subject within the area of the view-finder covered by the focusing points. You can't alter this aspect of the focusing system as you can in the advanced exposure modes (P, S, A, and M). Your only other option is to switch to manual focusing. See Chapter 8 for details.

In some cases, no amount of fiddling with the autofocus settings will help your camera lock focus where you intend. Some subjects just give autofocusing systems fits: Highly reflective objects, subjects behind fence bars, and scenes in which little contrast exists between the subject and the background are just a few potential problem areas. In such situations, just set the lens to manual focusing and handle the focusing job yourself.

I purposely didn't include an example of a photo taken in Auto or Auto Flash Off modes because, frankly, the results that these settings create vary widely depending on how well the camera detects whether you're trying to shoot a portrait, landscape, action shot, or whatever, as well as on lighting conditions. But the bottom line is that both take a one-size-fits-all approach that may or may not take best advantage of your camera's capabilities. So if you want to more consistently take great pictures instead of merely good ones, I encourage you to explore the exposure, focus, and color information found in Part III so that you can abandon this mode in favor of modes that put more photographic decisions in your hands. At the very least, step up to one of the Scene modes, detailed in the next section.

More focus factors to consider

When you focus the lens, either in autofocus or manual focus mode, you determine only the point of sharpest focus. The distance to which that sharp-focus zone extends from that point — what photographers call the *depth of field* — depends in part on the *aperture setting,* or *f-stop,* which is an exposure control. Some of the D3100's Scene modes are designed to choose aperture settings that deliver a certain depth of field.

The Portrait setting, for example, uses an aperture setting that shortens the depth of field so that background objects are softly focused — an artistic choice that most people prefer for portraits. On the flip side of the coin, the Landscape setting selects an aperture that produces a large depth of field so that both foreground and background objects appear tack sharp.

Another exposure-related control, *shutter speed,* plays a focus role when you photograph moving objects. Moving objects appear blurry at slow shutter speeds; at fast shutter speeds, they appear sharply focused. On your D3100, the camera chooses a fast shutter speed in Sports mode.

A fast shutter speed can also help safeguard against allover blurring that results when the camera moves during the exposure. The faster the shutter speed, the shorter the exposure time, which reduces the time that you need to keep the camera absolutely still. If you're using the Nikon D3100 kit lens, you can also improve your odds of shake-free shots by enabling the Vibration Reduction feature. (Set the VR switch on the lens to the On position.) For a very slow shutter speed, using a tripod is the best way to avoid camera shake; be sure to turn *off* VR when you do so.

Keep in mind, too, that the range of f-stops and shutter speeds the camera can select in any of the automatic exposure modes depends on the lighting conditions. When you're shooting at night, for example, the camera may not be able to select a shutter speed fast enough to stop action even in Sports mode.

If you want to manipulate focus and depth of field to a greater extent than the automated exposure modes allow, start by exploring the advanced Guide mode shooting options covered at the end of this chapter. Then visit Chapters 7 and 8 to find out how to take complete control over these picture characteristics.

Taking Advantage of Scene Modes

In Auto and Auto Flash Off modes, the camera tries to figure out what type of picture you want to take by assessing what it sees through the lens. If you don't want to rely on the camera to make that judgment, your D3100 offers six *Scene modes,* which select settings designed to capture specific scenes in ways that are traditionally considered best from a creative standpoint. For example, most people prefer portraits that have softly focused backgrounds. So in Portrait mode, the camera selects settings that can produce that type of background. In the next sections, you can read about the unique features of each of the Scene modes.

To see whether you approve of how your camera approaches the different scenes, take some test shots. If you aren't happy with the results, you can try adjusting the basic settings explored at the start of this chapter, in the section "Setting Up for Automatic Success." But to really take creative control, switch to one of the advanced exposure modes (P, S, A, or M) and then check out Chapters 7–9 to find out how to manipulate whatever aspect of the picture isn't to your liking.

Portrait and Child modes

The Portrait and Child modes are so closely related that it makes sense to consider them together.

First, Portrait mode. This mode selects an aperture setting designed to produce a short depth of field, which results in a slightly blurry background and thus puts the visual emphasis on your subject. Figure 3-6 offers an example. However, this effect occurs only if your subject is at least a few feet from the background. The extent to which the background blurs also depends on the other depth-of-field factors that I discuss in Chapter 8. Portrait mode also selects settings designed to produce natural skin tones.

Child mode, represented by the toddler icon you see in the margin here, offers a slight variation on the theme. Child mode differs from Portrait mode in the following key ways:

Portrait mode

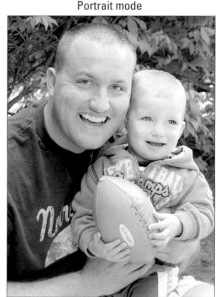

Figure 3-6: Portrait mode produces a softly focused background and natural skin tones.

- ✔ In Child mode, the camera renders hues that are traditionally found in clothing and backgrounds more boldly than in Portrait mode. In Figure 3-7, for example, notice that the football and the little boy's shorts are noticeably more vivid than in the Portrait mode example in Figure 3-6. Skin tones are left natural, although they, too, can appear a little more saturated, depending on the subject and the lighting.

- ✔ Child mode tries to use a slightly faster shutter speed than Portrait mode. The idea is that a faster shutter speed, which "freezes" action, helps you get a sharp picture of children who aren't sitting perfectly still. In order to allow the faster shutter speed, a higher ISO Sensitivity setting is used in Child mode.

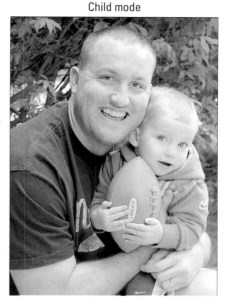

Child mode

Understand that the aperture and shutter speed the camera selects in either mode depend greatly on the available light, the subject, and the range of aperture settings on your lens. Sometimes you may see very little difference between the two modes except for the more-vivid background colors of Child mode. In dim lighting, you also may spot more *noise,* an image defect that gives the picture a speckled look, in Child mode, because of the increased ISO setting. (Chapter 7 explains all this stuff.)

Both modes have these traits in common:

Figure 3-7: Child mode renders non-skin tones more vividly than Portrait mode.

✔ **Autofocusing:** Autofocusing works as it does for Auto mode, described earlier in this chapter. The camera selects which focus points to use, and focus is locked at the time you press the shutter button halfway *unless* the camera senses motion. In that case, focus is adjusted up to the time you take the picture. If you have trouble autofocusing, you can switch to manual focusing.

✔ **Flash:** You can choose from Auto, Auto with Red-Eye Reduction, or Off. You can't enable the flash, though, if the camera doesn't think extra lighting is needed. This restriction can be problematic when shooting outdoor portraits, which often benefit from a small pop of flash light even in bright sunlight. See Chapter 7 for an example as well as some other tips on shooting portraits by flash light.

In my experience, the biggest decision about whether to use Portrait or Child mode depends on your color preferences. I prefer Portrait mode because the strengthened background colors in Child mode can easily distract the eye from the subject's face, which should be the point of emphasis in any portrait.

Landscape mode

 Whereas Portrait mode aims for a very shallow *depth of field* (small zone of sharp focus), Landscape mode — which is designed for capturing scenic vistas, city skylines, and other large-scale subjects — goes the other route, selecting an aperture setting (f-stop) that produces a large depth of field. As a result, objects both close to the camera and at a distance appear sharply focused. Figure 3-8 offers an example.

Note these other factoids about Landscape mode:

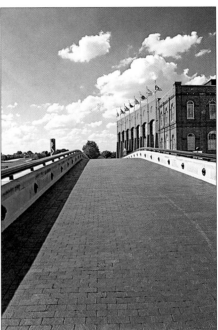

Figure 3-8: Landscape mode produces a large zone of sharp focus and also boosts color intensity slightly.

- ✔ **Depth of field:** As with Portrait mode, the camera manipulates depth of field by adjusting the aperture setting (f-stop). To produce the larger depth of field, the camera tries to use a high f-stop value, which means a very small aperture. But in dim lighting, the camera may be forced to open the aperture to allow enough light into the camera to properly expose the photo, so the depth of field may not be enough to keep the entire landscape in sharp focus. It may also use a slow shutter speed, which means a tripod is necessary to avoid blurry images.

- ✔ **Color and contrast:** This mode boosts color saturation and contrast slightly to produce the kind of bold, rich hues that most people prefer in landscape pictures. In addition, greens and blues are emphasized. If you want more control, switch to an advanced exposure mode (P, S, A, or M) and see Chapter 8 for details.

- ✔ **Autofocusing:** As with Auto mode, the camera selects the focus point for you, locking focus at the time you press the shutter button halfway. The exception occurs when something moves in front of the lens; if the camera sense the motion, it adjusts focus as needed until you take the picture. See Chapter 8 for help with all this autofocus stuff.

- ✔ **Flash:** The built-in flash is disabled, which is typically no big deal: Because of its limited range, a built-in flash is of little use when shooting most landscapes anyway. However, if you attach an external flash unit, you can use it in this mode. (Chapter 7 discusses external flash units.)

Sports mode

Sports mode activates a number of settings that can help you photograph a moving object, whether it's an athlete, a race car, or a romping dog like the one in Figure 3-9. That's my Wheaten Terrier furkid exhibiting his normal reaction to hearing me yell, "Dinner!" (Come to think of it, that's *my* reaction to a dinner bell, too. . . .)

Here's what you need to know about using Sports mode:

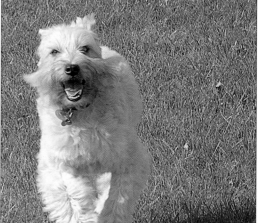

Sports mode

Figure 3-9: To capture moving subjects without blur, try Sports mode.

✔ **Shutter speed:** To catch a moving subject without blur, you need a fast shutter speed. So in Sports mode, the camera automatically chooses that fast shutter speed for you.

In dim lighting, the camera may not be able to select a very fast shutter speed and still deliver a good exposure. And because getting a good exposure trumps all, the shutter speed the camera uses may not be fast enough to "freeze" action, especially if your subject is moving very quickly.

In Figure 3-9, the camera selected a shutter speed that did, in fact, catch my boy in mid-romp, although if you look very closely, you can see some slight blurring of his beard. Because of the very bright light, the camera also selected a small aperture setting, which produces a large depth of field — so the grass in the background is as sharply focused as that in the foreground. To fully understand these issues, explore Chapters 7 and 8.

✔ **Autofocusing:** The camera sets the AF-area mode option to the Dynamic Area mode. Chapter 8 provides full details, but here's the short story: You use the Multi Selector to indicate which focusing point you want the camera to use when calculating the initial focusing distance. But if the object moves out of that point, the camera tries to draw focus information from the other points. With luck, your subject will move within one of the focus points before you record the image.

Additionally, Sports mode sets the Focus mode to AF-A, which means that if the camera detects motion, it continually adjusts focus up to the time you fully depress the shutter button and take the shot. Your other option is MF mode, for manual focusing. (Chapter 8 details the Focus mode options as well.)

If your subject moves after you press the shutter button halfway, be sure that you adjust the framing so that the subject remains under one of the focus points. Otherwise, the camera may not lock focus on the subject correctly.

✔ **Flash:** The built-in flash is disabled. That can be a problem in low-light situations, but it also enables you to shoot successive images more quickly because the flash needs a brief period to recycle between shots. If you own an external flash unit, however, you can use it in Sports mode if you like; just be aware that you may sacrifice in the speed-shooting department because of the necessary flash-recycle time. Additionally, even with an external flash, you're limited to a maximum shutter speed of 1/200 second, which may not be fast enough to freeze a fast-moving subject.

Experiment with setting the Release mode to the Continuous setting when photographing action. In Continuous mode, the camera keeps taking pictures as long as you hold down the shutter button, letting you capture as many as three frames per second. See Chapter 2 for details about the Release mode.

Close Up mode

Switching to Close Up mode doesn't enable you to focus at a closer distance to your subject than normal as it does on some non-SLR cameras. The close-focusing capabilities of your camera depend entirely on the lens you bought, so check your lens manual for details.

Close Up mode does affect your pictures in the following ways, however:

✔ **Depth of field:** Close Up mode, like Portrait mode, selects an aperture setting designed to produce short depth of field, which helps keep background objects from competing for attention with your main subject, as shown in Figure 3-10. As with Portrait mode, though, how much the background blurs varies depending on the available light (which determines the aperture setting the camera can use), the distance between your subject and the background, as well as the lens focal length, all outlined in Chapter 8. The picture in Figure 3-10 features extremely limited depth of field — notice that even part of the caterpillar is far enough from the focus point to be slightly soft.

✔ **Autofocusing:** At the default settings, the camera sets the AF-area mode setting to Single Point AF-area, meaning that it looks to only a single focus point to establish focus. Initially, the center point is selected, but you can press the Multi Selector to choose a different point. Or follow the instructions in Chapter 8 to choose an entirely different AF-area mode option.

As for the Focus mode, also covered in Chapter 8, the camera uses the AF-A setting. Again, that means that focus locks when you press the shutter button halfway. But if the camera detects motion, it adjusts focus as needed, up to the time you take the picture. Your only other alternative is to use manual focusing.

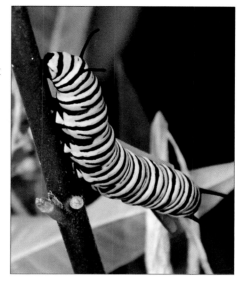

Figure 3-10: Close Up mode helps emphasize the subject by throwing the background out of focus.

✔ **Flash:** You can set the Flash mode to Auto, Auto with Red-Eye Reduction, and Off. (I urge you, though, to be very careful about using the built-in flash when you shoot a person or animal at close range — that strong burst of light isn't healthy for the eyes.)

Chapter 9 offers additional tips on close-up photography.

Night Portrait mode

This goal of this mode is to deliver a better-looking flash portrait at night (or in any dimly lit environment). It does so by constraining you to using Auto Slow-Sync, Auto Slow-Sync with Red-Eye Reduction, or Off Flash modes. In the first two Flash modes, the camera selects a shutter speed that results in a long exposure time. That slow shutter speed enables the camera to rely more on ambient light and less on the flash to expose the picture, which produces softer, more even lighting. If you disable flash, an even slower shutter speed is used.

I cover the issue of long-exposure and slow-sync flash photography in detail in Chapter 7. For now, the critical thing to know is that the slower shutter speed means that you probably need a tripod. If you try to handhold the camera, you run the risk of moving the camera during the long exposure, resulting in a blurry image. Enabling Vibration Reduction, if your lens offers that feature, can help, but for nighttime shooting, even that may not permit successful handheld shooting. Your subjects also must stay perfectly still during the exposure, which can add to the challenge.

Autofocusing in this mode works the same way as in Portrait mode, described earlier in this chapter.

Getting More Creative with Guide Mode

The Scene modes achieve their different effects in part by adjusting *depth of field* (the zone of sharp focus) and the amount of motion blur. Shifts in depth of field are produced by changing the aperture setting (f-stop), and motion blur is controlled via shutter speed.

Part III gives you the foundation you need to really understand these aspects of your pictures. But if you aren't ready to dive into the details, a Guide mode feature makes it easy to play around with depth of field and motion blur to a greater extent than the Scene modes allow. Guide mode enables you to adjust the amount of background blurring, whereas the Scene modes set the depth of field for you. Additionally, whereas Sports mode always tries to use a fast shutter speed to freeze action, Guide mode lets you use a slow shutter speed to intentionally blur a moving object, which can create a heightened sense of motion. I took this approach when shooting the carnival ride featured in Figure 3-11, for example, using a shutter speed of 1/4 second.

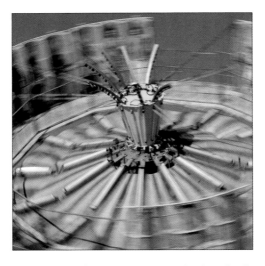

Figure 3-11: In Guide mode, blur motion by selecting the Show Water Flowing option and then choosing a slow shutter speed.

Try it out:

1. **Set the Mode dial to Guide.**

   You see the initial Guide Mode screen on the monitor, as shown on the left in Figure 3-12.

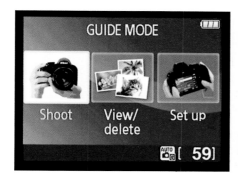 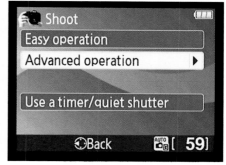

Figure 3-12: Select Advanced Operation to access settings that enable you to adjust depth of field and motion blur.

2. **Highlight Shoot and press OK.**

   You see the screen shown on the right in Figure 3-12.

3. **Highlight Advanced Operation and press OK.**

   The monitor presents the following five creative options, as shown in Figure 3-13:

   - *Soften Backgrounds:* Select this option to create a short depth of field, meaning that your subject will be in sharp focus but objects at a distance will appear blurry. Remember that despite the name of the option, objects at a distance in *front* of the subject will also appear softly focused.

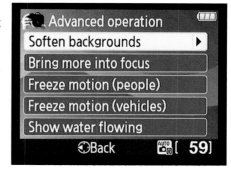

Figure 3-13: The first two options let you manipulate depth of field; the others enable you to freeze or blur motion.

   - *Bring More into Focus:* Select this option for any shot where you want a large depth of field so that both foreground and background objects appear sharp.

- *Freeze Motion (People):* Choose this setting to capture any subject — human or not — that's moving at a moderate pace, such as a trumpet player in a marching band or a duck swimming across a pond.

- *Freeze Motion (Vehicles):* Select this option for any fast-moving subject, whether it's a passing car, a soccer player kicking the ball across the field, or a running dog.

- *Show Water Flowing:* Choose this option to get help setting the camera to blur motion, as I did for my example in Figure 3-11. Why Show Water Flowing as the setting name? Well, when you photograph a waterfall (or any flowing water), a shutter slow speed blurs the water enough to give it a misty, romantic look. (Chapter 9 has an example.)

Using a tripod is a must when you use a slow shutter speed. Otherwise, camera shake can blur the whole picture, not just the moving objects. Remember to turn off Vibration Reduction when you use a tripod (and no, enabling that feature won't be enough to ensure a shake-free shot at shutter speeds slow enough to blur water). For most people, shutter speeds slower than 1/60 second create problems, but it varies depending on your lens and physical limitations. See Chapter 7 for more information.

4. **Highlight the creative effect you want to try and press OK.**

A screen with some basic information appears. For example, if you select Soften Backgrounds in Step 3, you see the screen shown on the left in Figure 3-14.

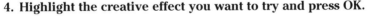

F-stop   Shutter speed

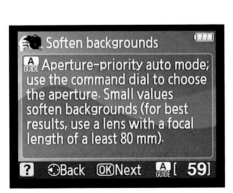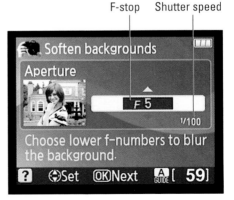

Figure 3-14: These screens guide you through the process of setting the aperture or shutter speed.

For the creative options that affect depth of field (Soften Backgrounds and Bring More into Focus), the camera sets the exposure mode to A, aperture-priority autoexposure, as indicated on the left screen in Figure 3-14. In aperture-priority autoexposure mode, you select the f-stop, or aperture setting, and the camera selects the shutter speed that will produce a good exposure. For the other three options, the camera shifts to the S, shutter-priority autoexposure, mode, which asks you to select the shutter speed. The camera than chooses the f-stop needed to expose the picture. (In either case, the Mode dial remains set to Guide; the shift to A or S mode happens internally.)

5. **After reading the information screen, press OK.**

You see a screen where you can see the current f-stop or shutter speed value, depending on the effect you selected. If you selected Soften Backgrounds, for example, you see the screen shown on the right in Figure 3-14.

6. **Press the Multi Selector up or down to change the f-stop or shutter speed value.**

As you do, the little picture preview updates to illustrate how your picture will be affected. (The change to the preview can be pretty subtle, so don't drive yourself crazy if you can't see much difference when you change the setting.)

The preview screen also shows you the shutter speed the camera has selected to go with your f-stop setting, as shown on the right in Figure 3-14. Or, if you're using one of the freeze/blur motion options, the screen displays the f-stop the camera needs to use to expose the picture at the shutter speed you select. Either way, keep an eye on that shutter speed and remember to use a tripod for slow speeds.

7. **Press OK.**

A screen appears similar to the one on the left in Figure 3-15.

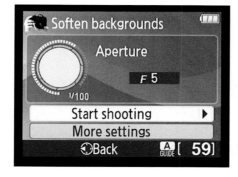
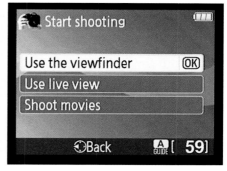

Figure 3-15: Choose these two options when you're ready to actually compose and shoot the picture.

If you're ready to take the picture, choose Start Shooting and press OK. On the next screen, shown on the right in the figure, choose Use the Viewfinder, as shown on the right in the figure, and press OK to exit the guided menus and take the picture. Or, to play with additional options, select More Settings, press OK, and follow the onscreen prompts until you eventually get to the Start Shooting screen.

As you can see from exploring these steps, my earlier statement that Guide mode "makes it easy" to adjust depth of field or motion blur uses "easy" as a relative term. You have to wade through a lot of menu screens, some of which aren't completely user-friendly. For example, the screen on the left in Figure 3-14 tells you to use a lens with a focal length of at least 80mm for best results. The camera offers that recommendation because as you increase the lens focal length, you decrease depth of field, multiplying the effect you get from choosing a low f-stop setting. But if you aren't acquainted with the term focal length, that's not much help. And nowhere in the menu screens related to the Show Water Flowing option are you warned to use a tripod when selecting a slow shutter speed — an oversight that may cause many beginners to wind up with a big, blurry mess.

My overall take is this: You don't need to know a whole lot more than what I spelled out in these steps to use the A (aperture-priority autoexposure) or S (shutter-priority autoexposure) modes. And in those modes, you can dial in the aperture or shutter speed you want much more quickly than going the guided menu route. You also gain control over all the camera's other picture options, which are limited in Guide mode. That said, any time you need a reminder of whether you change aperture or shutter speed to produce your desired creative goal, these Guide mode screens offer a handy assist.

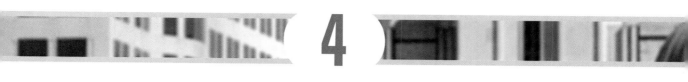

4

Exploring Live View
and Movie Making

*L*ike many newer dSLR cameras, the D3100 offers *Live View,* a feature that enables you to use the monitor instead of the viewfinder to compose photos. Turning on Live View is also the first step in recording a movie; in fact, using the viewfinder isn't possible when you shoot movies.

In many respects, taking a picture in Live View mode is no different from regular, through-the-viewfinder photography. But a few critical steps, including focusing, work very differently when you switch on Live View. So the first part of this chapter explains everything you need to know about Live View focusing as well as other aspects of the Live View system — including precautions to take to keep the camera from overheating. Following that, you can find details on taking still photos in Live View mode and shooting, viewing, and editing movies.

Using Your Monitor as a Viewfinder

The basics of taking advantage of Live View on the D3100 are pretty simple:

- **Switching to Live View mode:** Rotate the little lever on the Live View switch to the right and release it. Figure 4-1 shows you where to find the control. As soon as you take this step, you hear a sort of clicking sound as the internal mirror that normally sends the image from the lens to the viewfinder flips up, permitting the Live View preview to start. Then the scene in front of the lens appears on the monitor, and you no longer can see anything in the viewfinder.

- **Adjusting camera settings:** You can use all the usual tactics:

  - *Quick Settings screen:* Press the Info Edit button to access the Quick Settings screen; press again to return to the Live View display after you adjust settings.

  - *Menus:* When you press the Menu button, the camera exits Live View mode and displays the normal menu screen. You must rotate the Live View switch to return to Live View mode after you select the options you want to use.

- **Shooting photos:** Things work the same as for viewfinder photography, with the exception of focusing. See the upcoming section "Exploring Your Focusing Options," in this chapter, for details.

- **Recording movies:** Press the red movie button to start and stop recording.

- **Exiting Live View mode:** Rotate the Live View switch or press the Menu or Playback button. The camera also automatically disables Live View if you turn the camera off and on again.

As you may have guessed from the fact that I devoted a whole chapter to the topic of Live View and movie recording, these points comprise just the start of the story, however. The next two sections provide some additional general information that

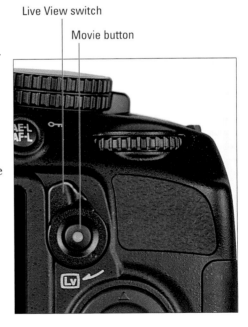

Live View switch

Movie button

Figure 4-1: Use this switch to toggle Live View on and off; press the red button to start and stop movie recording.

applies to both still photography and movie recording; later sections get into the nitty gritty of taking pictures in Live View mode and using the movie functions.

Live View safety tips

Whether your goal is a still image or a movie, be aware of the following tips and warnings any time you enable Live View:

- ✔ **Cover the viewfinder to prevent light from seeping into the camera and affecting exposure.** The camera ships with a little cover designed just for this purpose. To install it, first remove the little rubber eyecup that surrounds the viewfinder; just slide the eyecup up and out of the little groove that holds it in place. Then slide the cover down into the groove and over the viewfinder. (Orient the cover so that the word *Nikon* embossed into the plastic faces the viewfinder.)

- ✔ **By default, the monitor turns off after 30 seconds of inactivity.** A little countdown timer appears in the upper-left corner of the monitor, as shown in Figure 4-2.

  When you're composing still life images such as the one in the figure or other shots that require a bit of arranging, the 30-second monitor-off timing can be maddeningly short. Fortunately, you can delay the automatic shutdown via the Auto Off Timers

Auto Shutoff timer

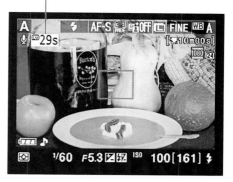

Figure 4-2: This timer tells you how many seconds remain until the camera turns off automatically.

option on the Setup menu. After choosing the menu option, select Custom, as shown on the left in Figure 4-3, and press OK to display the options shown on the right in the figure. Select Live View and press OK to reveal a screen containing the available timer settings (30 seconds, 1 minute, 3 minutes, and 5 minutes). Make your selection and press OK. Then highlight Done and press OK again to lock in your changes.

Choosing the Long menu option (refer to the left screen in Figure 4-3) also changes the delay time to 3 minutes, but going that route also affects the timing of automatic shutdown for the exposure meter, image review, menu display, and playback display. Chapter 1 spells out how the three settings affect shutdown for the various features. Both the Short and Normal options set the Live View shutdown at 30 seconds, by the way.

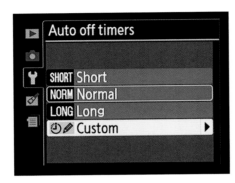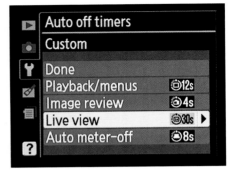

Figure 4-3: Adjust the delay time for automatic monitor shutdown via this menu option.

✔ **Using Live View for an extended period can harm your pictures and the camera.** When you work in Live View mode, the camera's innards heat up more than usual, and that extra heat can create the right electronic conditions for *noise,* a defect that gives your pictures a speckled look. Chapter 7 contains an illustration of this defect, which also is caused by long exposure times and high ISO Sensitivity settings.

Perhaps more critically, the increased temperatures can damage the camera itself. For that reason, Live View is automatically disabled after one hour of shooting — or earlier, if the camera detects a critical heat level. In extremely warm environments, you may not be able to use Live View mode for very long before the system shuts down.

When the camera is 30 seconds or less from shutting down your Live View session to avoid overheating, the countdown timer shown in Figure 4-2 appears to let you know how many seconds you have to wrap things up. The heat-related shutdown occurs regardless of the settings you choose for the Auto Off Timers menu option.

✔ **Aiming the lens at the sun or other bright lights also can damage the camera.** Of course, you can cause problems doing this even during normal shooting, but the possibilities increase when you use Live View. You not only can harm the camera's internal components but also the monitor.

✔ **Some lights may interfere with the Live View display.** The operating frequency of some types of lights, including fluorescent and mercury-vapor lamps, can create electronic interference that causes the monitor display to flicker or exhibit odd color banding. Changing the Flicker Reduction option on the Setup menu may resolve this issue. You're supposed to match the setting to the frequency of the electrical current being used by the lights, but if you're not sure what that frequency is and an electrical engineer isn't handy, just try changing the setting and see which one works best. You can choose from two options, 50 Hz and 60 Hz, as shown in Figure 4-4. (In the U.S., the standard frequency is 60 Hz, and in Europe, it's 50 Hz.)

Either way, the interference affects only the monitor display; the flicker or banding doesn't show up in your pictures or movies.

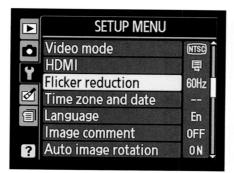
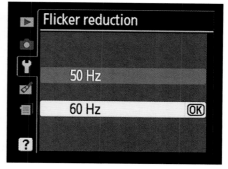

Figure 4-4: To reduce display flickering that can occur when you shoot by fluorescent light, try changing the Flicker Reduction setting.

- **Live View puts additional strain on the camera battery.** The monitor is a big consumer of battery juice. Keep an eye on the battery level icon to avoid running out of power at a critical moment.

- **The risk of camera shake during handheld shots is increased.** When you use the viewfinder, you can help steady the camera by bracing it against your face. But with Live View, you have to hold the camera away from your body to view the monitor, making it harder to keep the camera absolutely still. As Chapter 7 explains, any camera movement during the exposure can blur the shot, so using a tripod is the best course of action for Live View photography. If you do handhold the camera, enabling Vibration Reduction can help compensation for a bit of camera shake; Chapter 1 discusses this feature in more detail.

- **The display can be difficult to see clearly in bright sunlight.** If you've ever used a point-and-shoot camera that doesn't have a viewfinder, you're probably well aware of this problem. Although the D3100 monitor is of high quality, the display still can wash out in bright light, making it hard to see small details in the scene.

Because of these complications, I don't use Live View for still photography very often. Rather, I think of it as a special-purpose tool geared to situations where framing with the viewfinder is cumbersome. I find Live View most helpful for still-life, tabletop photography, especially in cases that require a lot of careful arrangement of the scene.

For example, I have a shooting table that's about waist high. Normally, I put my camera on a tripod, come up with an initial layout of the objects I want to photograph, set up my lights, and then check the scene through the viewfinder. Then there's a period of refining the object placement, the lighting, and so on. If I'm shooting from a high angle, requiring the camera to be positioned above the table and pointing downward, I have to stand on my tiptoes or get a stepladder to check things out through the viewfinder between each compositional or lighting change. At lower angles, where the camera is tabletop height or below, I have to either bend over or kneel to look through the viewfinder, causing no end of later aches and pains to back and knees. With Live View, I can alleviate much of that bothersome routine (and pain) because I can usually see how things look in the monitor no matter what the camera position.

Customizing the Live View display

Whether you're shooting movies or still photos, you can choose from the following display styles in Live View mode. Press the Info button to cycle through the different styles.

- **Show Indicators:** By default, the display uses this mode, which reveals the shooting data shown in Figure 4-5. Later sections of this chapter detail what each of the little symbols indicates.

- **Hide Indicators:** To declutter the screen a little, press the Info button to cycle from the default display to this mode, which presents only the information shown on the left in Figure 4-6.

- **Framing Grid:** Press Info one more time to display a grid over the image, as shown on the right in Figure 4-6. The grid is helpful when you need to precisely align objects in your photo. To return to the default display, give the Info button one more push.

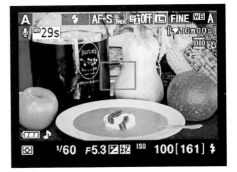

Figure 4-5: In the default Live View mode, you see this shooting data on the monitor.

If you connect your camera to an HDMI (High-Definition Multimedia Interface) device, you no longer see the live scene on your camera monitor. Instead, the view appears on your video display. In that scenario, the arrangement of the shooting information on the screen may appear slightly different than in the examples in this chapter. Also note that if you connect the camera to an HDMI-CEC device, you can't record a movie or take a picture in Live View mode. See the Chapter 5 section related to connecting the camera to a television for more HD details.

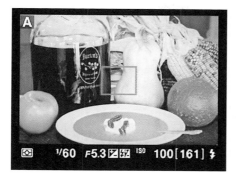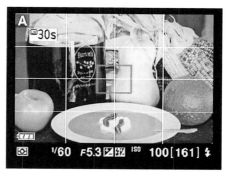

Figure 4-6: Press the Info button to change the display style.

Exploring Your Focusing Options

As with viewfinder photography, you can opt for autofocusing or manual focusing during Live View shooting, assuming that your lens supports both. If you use the kit lens, set the switch shown in Figure 4-7 to the A position for autofocusing and to the M position to focus manually. (With other lenses, check the lens instruction manual for help.)

Auto/Manual focus switch

Focus mode

AF-area mode

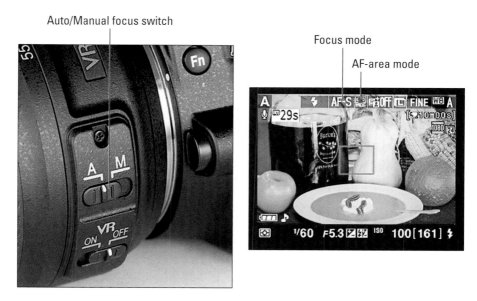

Figure 4-7: These options control the camera's focusing performance in Live View mode.

Both Live View and viewfinder photography also offer two options that tweak the camera's focusing performance:

- ✔ **Focus mode:** This option determines whether autofocusing is disabled, so you can focus manually, or, if you choose autofocusing, when the autofocus system kicks into gear. For movie recording, it also determines whether focus is continually adjusted throughout the recording.

- ✔ **AF-area mode:** With this option, you specify what part of the frame the autofocus system should consider when establishing focus.

At the default Live View display setting, the current Focus mode and AF-area mode settings appear at the top of the monitor, as shown on the right in Figure 4-7.

The settings available for Live View, however, are different from those provided for viewfinder photography. See the next two sections to explore the Live View offerings; visit Chapter 8 for information about the Focus mode and AF-area mode settings available for viewfinder photography.

Choosing a Focus mode: Auto, continuous auto, or manual?

Through the Focus mode setting, you tell the camera whether you want to use autofocus or manual focusing and, if you opt for autofocusing, choose from two types of autofocusing.

Here's how things work at each of the Focus mode settings:

- ✔ **AF-S (single-servo autofocus):** The camera locks focus when you depress the shutter button halfway. (This focus setting is one of the few that works the same during Live View shooting as it does during viewfinder photography.) Generally speaking, AF-S works best for focusing on still subjects. For movie recording, you can release the shutter button after focus is locked.

- ✔ **AF-F (full-time servo autofocus):** At this setting, the autofocus motor goes to work immediately — it doesn't wait for you to press the shutter button halfway. For still photography, you press the shutter button halfway when you're ready to lock focus.

  For movie recording, the camera adjusts focus continuously throughout the recording as long as you don't press the shutter button halfway. You still can lock focus at any time by pressing the shutter button halfway, though. Release the button, and continuous autofocusing begins again.

  This feature has a downside: If you shoot a movie with sound recording enabled, the camera's microphone picks up the sound of the autofocus motor. So if pristine audio is your goal, use AF-S and set focus before you begin recording, or abandon autofocus altogether and focus manually. As another option, you can disable sound recording on the camera and then buy a separate audio recording device to capture sound. You then can combine the soundtrack and the video footage in a video-editing program. (Obviously, this option is for real video buffs only.)

 MF (manual focus): Select this option to focus manually, by twisting the focusing ring on the lens.

 With the kit lens and some other lenses, simply moving the switch on the lens from the A (autofocus) to M (manual focus) position automatically selects the MF Focus mode setting. But if your lens doesn't have such a switch, the camera many not choose the right Focus mode setting, so double-check to be sure.

You can view the current Focus mode setting in the area labeled in the right figure in Figure 4-7. To adjust the setting, press the Info Edit button to bring up the Quick Settings screen. Highlight the Focus mode icon, as shown on the left in Figure 4-8, and press OK to display the second screen in the figure. Select your choice, press OK, and then press the Info Edit button again to return to the Live View display (or just press the shutter button halfway and release it).

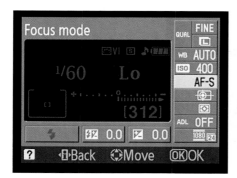 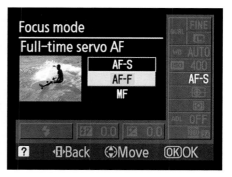

Figure 4-8: Change the Focus mode via the Quick Settings screen.

Selecting a focusing target (AF-area mode)

Through the AF-area mode, you give the camera's autofocusing system instructions on what part of the frame contains your subject so that it can set the focusing distance correctly.

As with the Focus mode, the Live View AF-area mode options are different than the ones available for viewfinder photography, which I detail in Chapter 8. For Live View photography and movie recording, you can choose from the following settings:

✔ **Face Priority:** Designed for portrait shooting, this mode attempts to hunt down and lock focus on faces when you press the shutter button halfway. This setting is the only one available if you use the Auto or Auto Flash Off exposure modes, and is the default setting in Portrait, Child, Landscape, or Night Portrait mode. Keep in mind that Face Detection typically works only when your subjects are facing the camera. If no faces are detected, focus is set initially at the center of the frame, as in Wide Area mode, described next.

✔ **Wide Area:** In this mode, you use the Multi Selector to move a little rectangular focusing frame around the screen to specify your desired focusing spot. (You can see the frame in the right screen in Figure 4-7.) When you press the shutter button halfway, the camera locks focus on objects within the focusing frame. This mode is the default for the Sports exposure mode and for P, S, A, and M nodes.

✔ **Normal Area:** This mode works the same way as Wide Area autofocusing but uses a smaller focusing frame. The idea is to enable you to base focus on a very specific area. It's the default mode for pictures you take in the Close Up exposure mode.

With such a small focusing frame, however, you can easily miss your focus target when handholding the camera. If you move the camera slightly, and the focusing frame shifts off your subject as a result, focus will be incorrect. So for best results, use a tripod in this mode.

✔ **Subject Tracking:** This mode tracks a subject as it moves through the frame and is designed for focusing on a moving subject. But note that subject tracking isn't always as successful as you might hope. For a subject that occupies only a small part of the frame — say, a butterfly flitting through a garden — autofocus may lose its way. Ditto for subjects moving at a face pace, subjects getting larger or smaller in the frame (when moving toward you and then away from you, for example), or scenes in which not much contrast exists between the subject and the background. Oh, and scenes in which there's a great deal of contrast can create problems, too. My take on this feature is that when the conditions are right, it works well, but otherwise, the Wide Area setting gives you a better chance of keeping a moving subject in focus.

Again, Auto and Auto Flash Off modes don't permit you to change the AF-area setting. In other modes, use either of these two techniques:

✓ **Quick Settings display:** Press the Info Edit button to shift to Quick Settings mode. Then highlight the AF-area mode icon, as shown on the left in Figure 4-9. Press OK to access a screen containing the four focusing options, as shown on the right. Highlight your choice, press OK, and then press the Info Edit button again to exit the Quick Settings screen.

✓ **Shooting menu:** As an alternative, you can change the setting via the Shooting menu. Select AF-Area Mode from the menu and then press OK to display the left screen in Figure 4-10. Then choose Live View to display the list of options, as shown on the right. Any time you press the Menu button, the camera exits Live View mode. So after you change the menu setting, you must flip the Live View switch to get back to the Live View display.

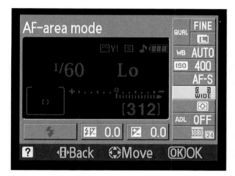
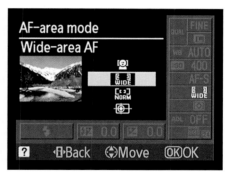

Figure 4-9: The fastest route to adjusting the AF-area mode is through the Quick Settings screen.

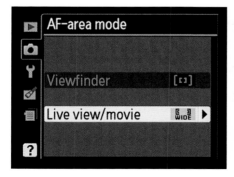
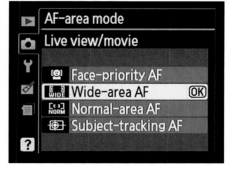

Figure 4-10: You can change the AF-area mode via the Shooting menu, but you must temporarily exit Live View mode to do so.

Choosing the right focusing pairs

To recap, the way the camera sets focus during Live View and movie shooting depends on your Focus mode and AF-area mode settings. If you use the kit lens (or a similar lens), you also need to set the switch on the lens barrel to either A for autofocusing or M for manual focusing.

Until you get fully acquainted with all the various combinations of Focus mode and AF-area mode and can make your own decisions about which pairings you like best, I recommend the following settings:

✏ **For moving subjects:** Set the Focus mode to AF-F and the AF-area mode to Wide Area. You also can try the Subject Tracking AF-area mode, but remember that the camera usually can't track subjects that are moving very rapidly, are small with respect to the rest of the scene, and so on.

✏ **For stationary subjects:** Set the Focus mode to AF-S and the AF-area mode to Wide Area. Or, if you're shooting a portrait, give the Face Priority AF-area option a try. Note that in a group shot, the camera usually locks on the closest face.

✏ **For difficult-to-focus subjects:** If the camera has trouble finding the right focusing point when you use autofocus, don't spend too much time fiddling with the different autofocus settings. Just set the camera to manual focusing and twist the focusing ring to set focus yourself.

✏ **For movies with sound enabled:** To avoid hearing the sound of the autofocus motor during the recording, which can occur with the AF-F Focus mode, use manual focusing or select the AF-S autofocus mode and lock focus before you start recording.

Autofocusing in Live View and movie mode

After setting the lens focus switch to A (if your lens has that feature) and choosing your Focus mode and AF-area mode settings, take these steps to focus:

1. **Locate the focusing frame in the Live View display.**

   The appearance of the frame depends on the AF-area mode, as follows:

   • *Wide Area and Normal Area:* You see a rectangular focusing frame, labeled in Figure 4-11. (The figure shows the frame at the size it appears in Wide Area mode; it's smaller in Normal Area mode.)

• *Face Priority:* If the camera locates faces, you see a yellow focusing frame around each one, as shown on the left in Figure 4-12. Note that one of the frames has double yellow lines — in the figure, it's the rightmost frame. The double yellow line indicates the face that the camera will use to set focusing distance.

Focusing frame

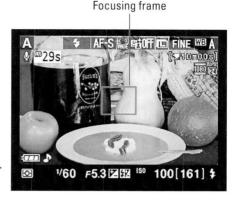

Figure 4-11: The red box represents the focusing frame in Wide Area and Normal Area AF-area mode.

If you don't see the highlight, the camera can't detect your subject's face, and it will set focus on the center of the frame.

• *Subject Tracking:* A focusing frame like the one shown on the right in Figure 4-12 appears.

Selected face   Subject Tracking focus frame

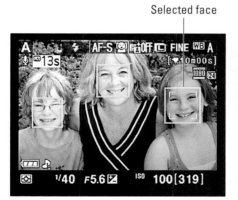 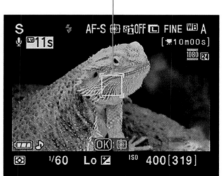

Figure 4-12: The focusing frame appears differently in Face Priority mode (left) and Subject Tracking mode (right).

2. **Use the Multi Selector to position the focusing frame over your subject.**

For example, I moved the focus frame over the garnish on the soup bowl for my example image, as shown on the left in Figure 4-13.

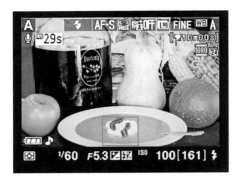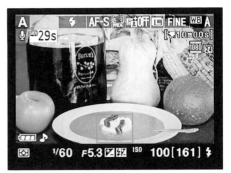

Figure 4-13: The focus frame turns green if the autofocus system was successful.

 In Face Priority mode, you can use the Multi Selector to move the box with the double-yellow border — which indicates the final focusing point — from face to face in a group portrait. In the Wide Area and Normal Area modes, press OK to quickly move the focus point to the center of the frame.

3. In Subject Tracking mode, press OK to initiate focus tracking.

If your subject moves, the focus frame moves with it. To stop tracking, press OK again. (You may need to take this step if your subject leaves the frame — press OK to stop tracking, reframe, and then press OK to start tracking again.)

4. In AF-S Focus mode, press the shutter button halfway to focus.

If the camera can focus successfully, the focus frame turns green, as shown on the right in Figure 4-13. You also hear a little beep (assuming you didn't disable the beep, which you can do via the Setup menu). Focus remains locked as long as you keep the shutter button pressed halfway.

 For movie recording, you can release the shutter button after focus is set.

5. In AF-F mode, check the focus frame.

Again, you don't press the shutter button halfway to focus in this mode — focusing occurs automatically. So just watch for the focus frame to turn green, indicating the camera found the focus target.

6. (Optional) Magnify the display to double-check focus.

After setting focus, you can press the Zoom In button to magnify the scene and check focus. Each press gives you a closer look at the subject.

As when you magnify an image when you're viewing photos in Playback mode, a small thumbnail in the corner of the monitor appears, with the yellow highlight box indicating the area that's currently being magnified, as shown in Figure 4-14. Press the Multi Selector to scroll the display if needed.

To zoom out, press the Zoom Out button until you see the entire scene.

While the display is zoomed, you can press the shutter button halfway again to reset focus if needed — you don't have to zoom out to take that step.

Magnified area

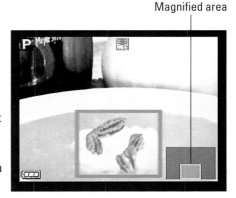

Figure 4-14: Press the Zoom In button to magnify the display and double-check focus.

Manual focusing in Live View and movie mode

For manual focusing, simply set the focus switch on the lens to M (assuming that you're using the kit lens or a similarly featured lens) and then twist the focusing ring to bring the scene into focus. But do note a few quirks about manual focusing in Live View and movie mode:

- The focusing frame doesn't turn green when you set focus as it does with autofocusing.

- Even with manual focusing, you still see the focusing frame; its appearance depends on the current AF-area mode setting. In Face Priority mode, the frame will automatically jump into place over a face, if it detects one. And if you press OK when Subject Tracking mode is enabled, the camera tries to track the subject under the frame until you press OK again. I find these two behaviors irritating, so I always set the AF-area mode to Wide Area or Normal Area for manual focusing.

- You can press the Zoom In button to check focus in manual mode just as you can during autofocusing. See Step 6 in the preceding section for details. Press the Zoom Out button to reduce the magnification level.

Shooting Still Pictures in Live View Mode

After sorting out the focusing options, the rest of the steps involved in taking a picture in Live View mode are essentially the same as for viewfinder photography. The following steps outline the process:

1. **Turn the Mode dial (on top of the camera) to select an exposure mode.**

   Remember, the exposure mode determines what picture settings you can control. Chapter 3 introduces you to the fully automatic modes (Auto, Auto Flash Off, the Scene modes, and Guide mode). Chapter 7 provides help with the advanced modes (P, S, A, and M).

2. **Enable Live View by pressing the Live View switch to the right and releasing it.**

   Figure 4-15 offers a reminder of where to find the switch. The monitor displays your subject onscreen, and the viewfinder stalks away in a huff.

Focusing frame   Live View switch

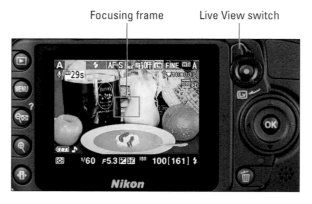

Figure 4-15: Press the Live View switch to the right and release it to enter and exit Live View mode.

In Guide mode, you actually don't have to flip the switch: Instead, when you reach the final guided screens, as shown in Figure 4-16, select Start Shooting (left screen) and then Use Live View (right screen). The camera enters into Live View mode automatically.

3. **Review the current picture settings (exposure, focus mode, and so on).**

   In Live View mode, the Shooting Info screen, which normally displays the critical picture settings, isn't available. But you can view most of the same settings on the Live View display, as shown in Figure 4-17. This display mode is the default; to view other displays, press the Info button. Note that some settings, such as Exposure Compensation and Flash Compensation, appear only when those features are enabled. (See Chapter 7 for information about those two options.)

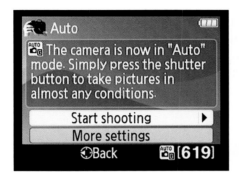 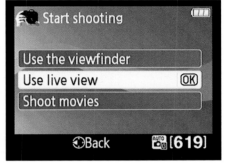

Figure 4-16: In Guide mode, you can shift to Live View by selecting these options on the final guided menu screens.

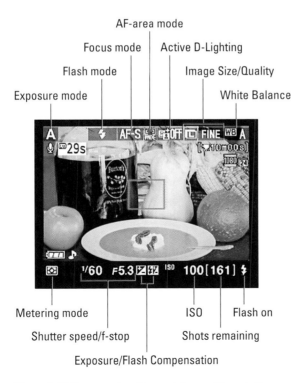

Figure 4-17: You can view these picture settings in the default Live View display mode.

4. **Select the Focus mode and AF-area mode settings.**

   Both can be adjusted via the Quick Settings display. The preceding sections of this chapter help you select the right settings.

5. **Adjust other picture settings as you do for viewfinder photography.**

   The fastest option for most settings is to press the Info Edit button to toggle to the Quick Settings display. Chapter 1 shows you how to navigate that display if you need help.

   If you press the Menu button to adjust a menu option, the monitor turns off briefly as the camera shifts out of Live View mode. Flip the Live View switch to return to Live View mode after you adjust the menu settings.

6. **If focusing manually, twist the focusing ring to set focus.**

7. **If autofocusing, use the Multi Selector to position the focusing frame over your subject.**

   The appearance of the frame varies depending on your selected AF-area mode, as outlined earlier in this chapter. If you're shooting a group portrait and select the Face Priority mode, you may see a frame over more than one face — the frame with the double lines is the one the camera plans to use to set focus.

8. **In AF-F Autofocus mode, wait for the focus frame to turn green and then press the shutter button halfway to lock focus.**

9. **In AF-S Autofocus mode, press the shutter button halfway to focus.**

   Focus is locked when the focus frame turns green.

   Regardless of the autofocus mode, exposure metering is adjusted up to the time you take the picture.

10. **Press the shutter button the rest of the way to take the picture.**

Just two more pertinent points to wrap up the class on Live View photography:

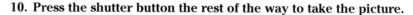

✔ **In Auto or Auto Flash Off mode, the camera may switch automatically to one of the Scene modes.** In the Auto and Auto Flash Off modes, the camera makes a guess about what type of scene you want to capture. Then it automatically chooses one of the four Scene modes — Portrait, Landscape, Close Up, or Night Portrait — and displays the icon for that exposure mode in the upper-left corner of the monitor. (The Mode dial itself doesn't actually rotate to the chosen setting — the camera just uses the properties of the Scene mode to take the picture.) Or, if the camera determines that your subject doesn't fall into one of those four categories, it sticks with the Auto or Auto Flash Off mode.

✔ **Exposure compensation adjustments aren't always reflected by the monitor brightness.** When you increase or decrease exposure using this feature, available only in the P, S, A, and M modes, the image on the monitor becomes brighter or darker only up to shifts of +/– EV 3.0, even though you can select values as high as +5.0 and as low as –5.0. See Chapter 7 to get a primer on Exposure Compensation.

Shooting Digital Movies

Your D3100 offers the ability to record digital movies — and it can even create high-def movies that look stunning on a large TV screen.

Although recording live action with a dSLR involves a few limitations and difficulties that you don't experience with a real video camera, it's a fun option to have onboard nonetheless. The next section explains how to choose recording options, such as resolution; following that, you can find step-by-step instructions for recording, playing, and editing a movie.

Setting recording options

You can modify the way that your movies are recorded in several ways. Here's the preflight checklist to go through before you press the record button:

✔ **Quality:** This critical setting determines the frame size, aspect ratio, and frame rate of the movie.

The *frame rate* determines the smoothness of the playback. At the default setting, movies have a frame rate of 24 *frames per second, or fps,* which is the standard for film motion pictures. You also can choose a frame rate of 30 fps, the same as television quality video in the United States and other countries that follow the NTSC video standard, or 25 fps, the rate used in countries that follow the PAL standard.

You access the option via the Movie Settings option the Shooting menu, as shown on the left in Figure 4-18. Press OK to display the second screen in the figure. Then choose Quality and press OK to reveal the screen shown in Figure 4-19. The Quality settings shake out as follows:

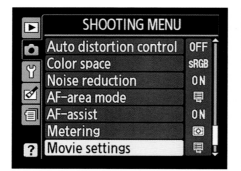

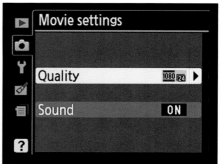

Figure 4-18: Set the movie quality and enable audio recording via the Shooting menu.

- *1920 x 1080 at 24 fps:* This setting is the default and produces a full high-definition (HD) movie that has a 16:9 aspect ratio, the same ratio of HD television sets and many newer computer monitors. Although playback at 24 fps may be a little choppier than your favorite TV show, it should be fine for most uses.

- *1280 x 720 at 30 fps:* This setting also produces a 16:9 frame but at standard HD resolution and higher frame rate. You can use this setting for television sets that use the NTSC video format.

Figure 4-19: The Quality settings determine frame size, aspect ratio, and frames per second.

- *1280 x 720 at 25 fps:* This one works just like the preceding option except uses a frame rate of 25 fps. Choose this option for movies you plan to view on televisions that follow the PAL video standard.

- *1280 x 720 at 24 fps:* Again, the only difference between this and the preceding two options is a lower frame rate. Playback may be a little less smooth than at 30 fps, but should still be acceptable.

- *640 x 424 at 24 fps:* Movies recorded at this setting have an aspect ratio of 3:2 (the same as still photos from your camera), a frame rate of 24 fps, and a significantly lower resolution than the other settings.

On some Nikon cameras that offer movie recording, the maximum length of your movie varies depending on the Quality setting. But on the D3100, you can record up to 10 minutes of action no matter what setting you select, presuming that you have enough space left on your memory card. The largest file size is produced by the 1920 x 1080 setting: A 10-minute movie creates a 1.4GB file. The same length movie at a resolution of 1280 x 720 creates files ranging from 800MB (for 30 and 25 fps) to 640MB (for 24 fps). And the 640 x 424 setting requires 340MB to store a 10-minute movie.

✐ **Sound recording:** You also control whether the camera's built-in microphone records sound via the Movie Settings menu option. But this one's much simpler than the Quality option: To record sound, just set the Sound option to On (refer to the right screen in Figure 4-18). To shoot a silent movie, turn the option to Off.

If you enable sound, note the position of the microphone: It's the little three-holed area above the D3100 logo, on the front of the camera. Make sure that you don't inadvertently cover up the microphone with your finger. And keep in mind that anything *you* say will be picked up by the mike along with any other audio present in the scene.

✐ **Exposure:** The camera automatically sets exposure based on the light throughout the entire scene. But depending on the setting of the Mode dial, you can take advantage of two exposure controls:

- *Exposure compensation:* When the Mode dial is set to P, S, or A, you can apply Exposure Compensation, but only to a limit of EV +3.0 or –3.0 rather than the usual five steps that are possible during normal photography. See Chapter 7 to find out more about this feature. To adjust the setting, press and hold the Exposure Compensation button while rotating the Command dial.

- *Autoexposure lock:* In any exposure mode except Auto or Auto Flash Off, you can lock exposure at the current settings by pressing and holding the AE-L/AF-L button. Chapter 7 also tells you more about autoexposure lock.

✐ **Focusing:** You can choose auto or manual focusing and control focusing behavior via the Focus mode and AF-area mode settings. Earlier parts of this chapter provide a primer in focusing.

✐ **White Balance and Picture Control:** The colors in your movie are rendered according to the current White Balance and Picture Control settings. Chapter 8 explains how to adjust these settings, but you have control over them only when the Mode dial is set to P, S, A, or M.

One more technical point: Movies are created in the MOV format, which means you can play them on your computer using most movie-playback programs. If you want to view your movies on a TV, you can connect the camera to the TV, as explained in Chapter 5. Or if you have the necessary computer software, you can convert the MOV file to a format that a standard DVD player can recognize and then burn the converted file to a DVD disk. You also can edit your movie in a program that can work with MOV files.

Starting and stopping recording

After you establish all the options explained in the preceding section, there's not much left to do to shoot a movie:

1. **Rotate the Live View switch to the right and release it to switch to Live View mode.**

   By default, the shooting information shown in Figure 4-20 appears along with your subject in the monitor. You can view the Quality setting, whether sound is enabled, and the length of the movie that will fit in the remaining space on your memory card.

2. **Set focus as outlined earlier in this chapter.**

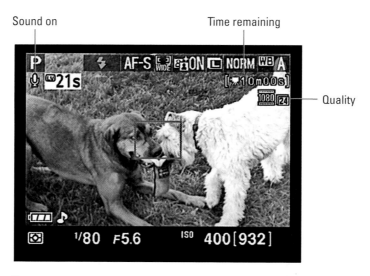

Figure 4-20: These settings relate to options available for movie recording.

3. **To begin recording, press the red movie button in the center of the Live View switch.**

Some of the shooting data disappears from the screen, and a red Rec symbol flashes in the top-left corner, as shown in Figure 4-21. As recording progresses, the area labeled time remaining value shows you how many more seconds of video you can record. (The length is dependent on the movie-quality settings you choose and the amount of space on your memory card.) Also note the number found within the

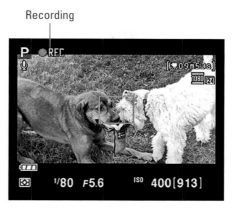

Figure 4-21: The red Rec symbol flashes while recording is in progress.

brackets in the lower-right corner of the screen — 913, in Figure 4-21. That number indicates how many still photos you can fit in the empty card space if you stop recording, and as each second of recording ticks by and card space is depleted, the value that indicates the number of still shots remaining drops.

4. **To stop recording, press the movie button again.**

You can stop your recording and capture a still image in one fell swoop: Just press and hold the shutter button down until you hear the shutter release.

Screening Your Movies

To play your movie, press the Playback button. In single-image playback mode, you can spot a movie file by looking for the little movie-camera icon in the top-left corner of the screen, as shown on the left in Figure 4-22. Press OK to start playback.

In the thumbnail and Calendar playback modes, you see little filmstrip dots along the edges of movie files. This time, press OK twice: once to shift to single-image view and again to start movie playback.

After playback begins, a little playback control icon appears in the lower-right corner of the screen, as shown in Figure 4-23. It represents the Multi Selector and reminds you that you can use these techniques to control the playback:

✔ **Stop playback:** Press the Multi Selector up.

✔ **Pause/resume playback:** Press down to pause playback; press OK to resume playback.

✔ **Fast forward/rewind:** Press the Multi Selector right or left to fast-forward or rewind the movie. Press again to double the fast-forward or rewind speed; keep pressing to increase the speed to 8 times or 16 times normal. Hold the button down to fast-forward or rewind all the way to the end or beginning of the movie.

✔ **Advance frame by frame:** First, press the Multi Selector down to pause playback. Then press the Multi Selector right to advance one frame; press left to go back one frame.

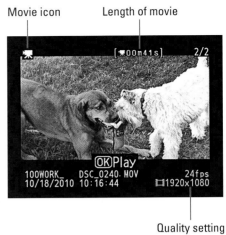

Movie icon   Length of movie

Quality setting

Figure 4-22: The little movie-camera symbol tells you you're looking at a movie file.

✔ **Adjust playback volume:** See the little markings labeled volume control symbols in Figure 4-23? They remind you that you can press the Zoom In button to increase playback volume. For a quieter playback, press the Zoom Out button.

Time remaining

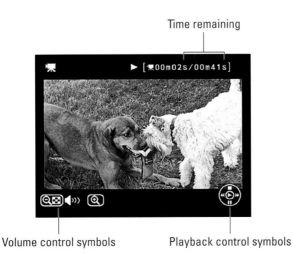

Volume control symbols   Playback control symbols

Figure 4-23: This little icon reminds you to use the Multi Selector to control movie playback.

Chapter 5 explains how to connect your camera to a television so you can play your movies "on the big screen."

Trimming movies

You can do some limited movie editing through the camera's Retouch menu. I emphasize: *limited* editing. You can trim frames from the start of a movie and clip off frames from the end, and that's it.

To eliminate frames from the beginning of the movie, take these steps:

1. **Display your movie in full-frame view.**

2. **Press OK to begin playback.**

3. **When you reach the first frame you want to keep, press the Multi Selector down to pause the movie.**

   The playback screen looks similar to the one on the left in Figure 4-24.

4. **Press the AE-L/AF-L button.**

   Note the symbols centered under the picture frame in the left image in Figure 4-24: They clue you into the fact that you use the AE-L/AF-L button to access the trimming feature. After you press the button, you see the Edit Movie screen, as shown on the right in Figure 4-24.

5. **Highlight Choose Start Point and press OK.**

   The screen appears similar to the one in Figure 4-25. Notice that in the Multi Selector icon, the up arrow point now sports a little scissors icon. That's your cue about how to take the next step . . .

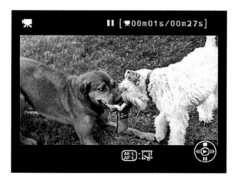
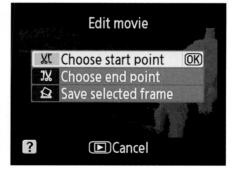

Figure 4-24: After pausing playback, press the AE-L/AF-L button to access the movie-editing tools.

6. **Press the Multi Selector up to lop off all frames that came before the current frame.**

Don't worry that you'll lose your original movie — the trimmed version is saved as a separate file.

After you press the Multi Selector up, you then see a confirmation screen asking for permission to proceed.

7. **Highlight Yes and press OK.**

A message appears telling you that the trimmed movie is being saved. During playback, edited files are indicated by a little scissors icon that appears in the area noted in Figure 4-26.

To instead trim footage from the end of a film, take the same steps, but this time pause playback on the last frame you want to keep in Step 3. Then, in Step 5, select Choose End Point instead of Choose Start Point.

You also can access the Edit Movie option from the Retouch menu, but the process is a little more cumbersome. After you choose the menu option and press OK, you then see the same options as shown on the right in Figure 4-24. Select Choose Start Point or Choose End Point and press OK to display thumbnails of your movie files. Highlight the one you want to edit and press OK. Your movie then appears in full-frame view. Press OK to begin movie playback; from there, everything works as outlined in the steps.

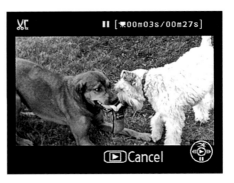

Figure 4-25: Press the Multi Selector up to proceed with the edit.

Trimmed movie icon

Figure 4-26: The scissors tell you that you're looking at an edited movie file.

Saving a movie frame as a still image

In addition to trimming frames from the beginning and end of a movie, you can do a *screen grab* — that is, save a single frame of the movie as a regular image file. Here's how:

1. **Begin playing your movie.**

   Just press the Playback button, locate the movie file, and press OK to begin playback.

2. **When you reach the frame you want to capture, press the Multi Selector down to pause playback.**

3. **Press the AE-L/AF-L button to bring up the Edit Movie screen.**

4. **Choose Save Selected Frame, as shown in Figure 4-27, and press OK.**

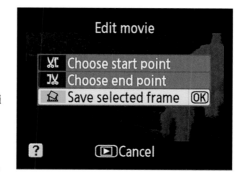

Figure 4-27: Through this option, you can save a single movie frame as a still photo.

5. **Press the Multi Selector up to initiate the screen grab.**

6. **On the confirmation screen that appears, select Yes and press OK.**

   Your frame is saved as a JPEG photo.

Remember a few things about pictures you create this way:

✔ When you view a JPEG image created this way, it's marked with a little movie-snip icon in the upper-left corner, as shown in Figure 4-28.

✔ The resolution of the picture depends on the resolution of the movie. For example, if the movie resolution is 1920 x 1080, the picture has that same number of pixels. The resolution appears in blue, in the lower-right corner of the playback screen, as shown in Figure 4-28.

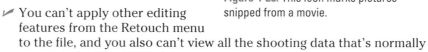

Figure 4-28: This icon marks pictures snipped from a movie.

✔ You can't apply other editing features from the Retouch menu to the file, and you also can't view all the shooting data that's normally associated with a JPEG picture.

For more about JPEG and picture resolution, visit Chapter 2.

Part II

Working with Picture Files

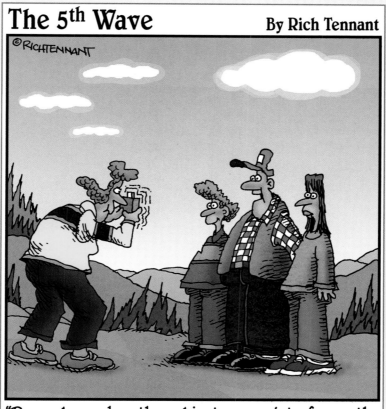

The 5th Wave   By Rich Tennant

"Remember, when the subject comes into focus, the camera makes a beep. But that's annoying, so I set it on vibrate."

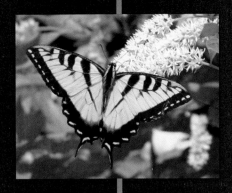

In this part . . .

You have a memory card full of pictures. Now what? Now you turn to the first chapter in this part, Chapter 5, which explains all your camera's picture-playback features, including options that help you evaluate exposure and zoom the display so that you can check small details. The same chapter shows you how to delete lousy pictures and protect great ones from accidental erasure.

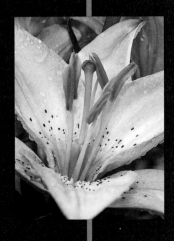

When you're ready to move pictures from the camera to your computer, Chapter 6 shows you the best ways to get the job done. In addition, Chapter 6 offers step-by-step guidance on printing your pictures and preparing them for online sharing.

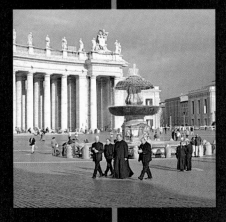

5

Playback Mode: Viewing, Erasing, and Protecting Photos

In This Chapter

▶ Exploring picture playback functions

▶ Deciphering the picture information displays

▶ Understanding histograms

▶ Deleting bad pictures and protecting great ones

▶ Creating an in-camera slide show

▶ Viewing pictures (and movies) on a television set

*W*ithout question, my favorite thing about digital photography is being able to view my pictures on the camera monitor the instant after I shoot them. No more guessing whether I captured the image I wanted or I need to try again; no more wasting money on developing and printing pictures that stink. In fact, this feature alone was reason enough for me to turn my back forever on my closetful of film photography hardware and all the unexposed film remaining from my predigital days.

But seeing your pictures is just the start of the things you can do when you switch your D3100 to playback mode. You also can review all the camera settings you used to take the picture, display graphics that alert you to serious exposure problems, and add file markers that protect the picture from accidental erasure. This chapter tells you how to use all these playback features and also explains how to connect your camera to a television so that you can view your photos and movies on a bigger screen. (For details on movie playback, be sure to visit Chapter 4 as well.)

Setting Playback Timing Preferences

You can control many aspects of how your pictures appear on the camera monitor. Later sections of this chapter explain how to adjust the display after you shift to playback mode. But first, the next few sections talk about a few basic options that determine when your pictures appear and the length of time they remain onscreen.

Adjusting playback timing

By default, the camera monitor turns off after 12 seconds of inactivity during picture playback to save battery power. So if you're looking at a picture or passing around your camera so other people can see the image, the monitor goes dark if you don't either advance to the next picture or use one of the other playback functions discussed in this chapter within 12 seconds.

If you want a longer or shorter interval before the playback cutoff, take these steps:

1. **Select Auto Off Timers on the Setup menu, as shown on the left in Figure 5-1.**

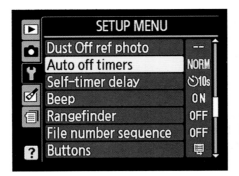
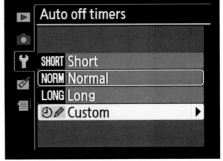

Figure 5-1: Start here to control how long pictures are displayed before automatic monitor shutdown occurs.

2. **Press OK.**

   You see the second screen in Figure 5-1.

3. **Select Custom and press OK to display the screen shown on the left in Figure 5-2.**

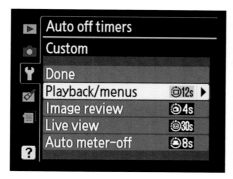
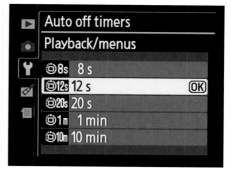

Figure 5-2: Select this option to adjust playback and menu shutoff timing only.

4. **Select Playback/Menus and press OK to display the timing options, shown on the right in Figure 5-2.**

   You can select from intervals ranging from 8 seconds to 10 minutes.

5. **Select your choice and press OK.**

   The screen shown in Figure 5-3 appears.

6. **Highlight Done, as shown in Figure 5-3, and press OK to wrap up things.**

   Any time you see a menu screen that has a Done option, it's important to take the step of highlighting that option and pressing OK. Otherwise, your settings aren't preserved. I add this reminder because I forget to take this step on a regular basis!

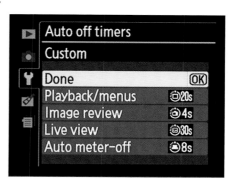

Figure 5-3: To save your changes, highlight Done and then press OK.

As another option, you can choose Long, Normal (the default setting), or Short instead of Custom in Step 3. However, going that route also affects how long the camera displays a picture immediately after you capture the image — known as the *image review period* — as well as the automatic shut-off timing of the exposure meters and Live View display. I prefer to set these options separately, as described in the steps, but in case you're interested, Chapter 1 spells out the various shutdown intervals produced by the Short, Normal, and Long settings.

Adjusting and disabling instant review

After you take a picture, it automatically appears briefly on the camera monitor. By default, this instant-review period lasts 4 seconds. But you can customize this behavior in two ways:

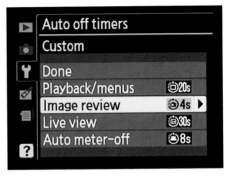

Figure 5-4: You also can adjust the length of the instant-review period through the Auto Off Timers option.

 ✓ **Adjust the length of the instant-review period.** Take the same steps as outlined in the preceding section, but choose Image Review instead of Playback/Menus in Step 4, as shown in Figure 5-4. Press OK to display the timing intervals; you can choose from shutdown timing intervals ranging from 4 seconds to 10 minutes.

 ✓ **Disable instant review.** Because any monitor use is a strain on battery power, consider turning off instant review altogether if your battery is running low. Just call up the Playback menu and set the Image Review option to Off, as shown in Figure 5-5. You can still view your pictures by pressing the Playback button at any time.

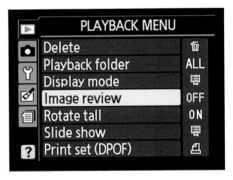

Figure 5-5: Head for the Playback menu to disable instant review altogether.

Enabling Automatic Picture Rotation

When you take a picture, the camera can record the image *orientation* — whether you held the camera normally, creating a horizontally oriented image, or turned the camera on its side to shoot a vertically oriented photo. This bit of data is simply added into the picture file.

During playback, the camera can read the data and automatically rotate the image so that it appears in the upright position, as shown on the left in Figure 5-6. Otherwise, the image isn't rotated and appears as shown on the right side of the figure. The image is also automatically rotated when you view it in Nikon ViewNX 2, Capture NX 2, and some other photo programs that can interpret the data.

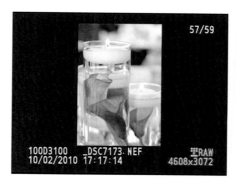 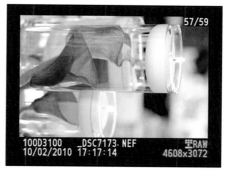

Figure 5-6: You can display vertically oriented pictures in their upright position (left) or sideways (right).

Official photo lingo uses the term *portrait orientation* to refer to vertically oriented pictures and *landscape orientation* to refer to horizontally oriented pictures.

The feature that embeds the rotation data in the file is turned on by default, but the one that rotates the picture during playback is turned off.

To adjust the status of automatic rotation, you need to visit two menus:

1. **On the Setup menu, select Auto Image Rotation, as shown in the left image in Figure 5-7.**

   You need to scroll to the second screen of the menu to get to the Auto Image Rotation option. If you select On, the rotation data is added to the picture file. Select Off to leave out the data.

Figure 5-7: Visit the Setup and Playback menus to enable image rotation.

2. **Display the Playback menu and select the Rotate Tall option, as shown on the right in Figure 5-7.**

   Select On if you want the camera to read the orientation data and rotate vertical pictures. Select Off if you prefer not to rotate the photos during playback. The images are still rotated automatically in photo programs that can read the orientation data in the file. Note that even if you select On, images aren't rotated for the instant-review display, explained in the preceding section.

Shooting with the lens pointing directly up or down sometimes confuses the camera, causing it to record the wrong data in the file. If that issue bothers you, turn off Auto Image Rotation on the Setup menu before you shoot the pictures. The camera then won't record the orientation information as part of the picture file.

Viewing Images in Playback Mode

To take a look at the pictures on your camera memory card, take these steps:

1. **If you created custom image folders, specify which ones you want to view. Otherwise, skip to Step 2.**

   Your D3100 normally organizes pictures automatically into folders that are assigned generic names: 100D3100, 101D3100, and so on. You can see the name of the current folder by looking at the Storage Folder option, found on the last screen of the Setup menu. (The default folder name appears as just D3100 on the menu.)

   You also can create custom folders through that same menu option. (See Chapter 11 for specifics.) If you do, you need to tell the camera whether you want to view only pictures in the current folder or in all folders. Display the Playback menu and highlight Playback Folder, as shown on the left in Figure 5-8. Press OK to display the screen shown on the right in the figure. Select All to view all folders; select Current to view only the active folder. Press OK to exit the screen.

   Again, this step applies only if you create custom folders. If you let the camera handle all folder-creation duties, you can view all pictures on the card regardless of the Playback Folder setting.

 2. **Press the Playback button, labeled in Figure 5-9.**

   The monitor displays the last picture you took, along with some picture data, such as the frame number of the photo. To find out how to interpret the picture information and specify what data you want to see, see the upcoming section "Viewing Picture Data," in this chapter.

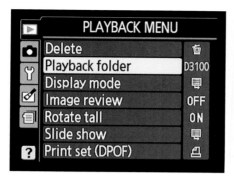
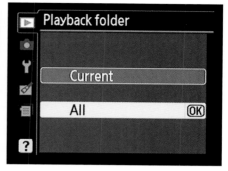

Figure 5-8: If you create custom folders, specify which folder you want to view.

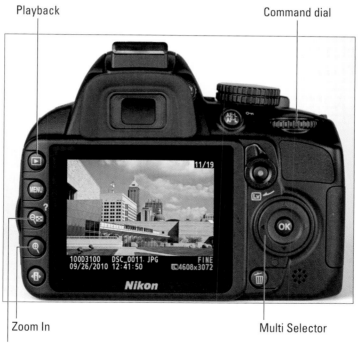

Figure 5-9: Navigate and inspect your photos using these controls.

The figure assumes that the camera is currently set to display a single photo at a time. You can also display multiple images at a time, as explained in the next section.

3. **To scroll through your pictures, rotate the Command dial or press the Multi Selector right or left.**

I highlighted the dial and Multi Selector in Figure 5-9.

Note that in Calendar display view, covered a little later in this chapter, pressing the Multi Selector or rotating the Command dial selects a date on the calendar. See the upcoming section about this display mode for details.

4. **To return to picture-taking mode, press the shutter button halfway and then release it.**

Or just press the Playback button again.

By default, one picture appears to shove the other off the screen as you scroll through your pictures. If you don't like this transition effect, which is named Slide In, you can disable it. Or, for fancier playback, you can opt for the Zoom/Fade transition effect, which works just like its name implies — one frame fades into the next with a zoom effect. To adjust the setting, open the Playback menu and select Display Mode, as shown on the left in Figure 5-10. Press OK to bring up the screen shown on the right in the figure. Choose Transition Effects and press right to bring up the screen offering the three transition settings, as shown in Figure 5-11. Make your selection and press OK one more time.

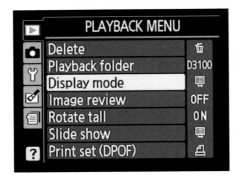 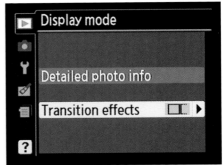

Figure 5-10: Follow this menu path to adjust the transition effect used during playback.

Viewing multiple images at a time

Along with viewing images one at a time, you can choose to display 4 or 9 thumbnails, as shown in Figure 5-12, or fill the screen with a whopping 72 thumbnails. Just press the button shown in the margin here and labeled

Zoom Out/Thumbnail display in Figure 5-9. Press once to cycle from single-picture view to 4-thumbnail view, press again to shift to 9-picture view, and press once more to bring up 72-image view. Press yet again, and you shift to Calendar view, a nifty feature explained in the next section.

 To reduce the number of thumbnails, press the Zoom In button, shown clinging to the margin here and labeled in Figure 5-9. Or to jump immediately to single-frame view without cycling back through all the display modes, just press OK.

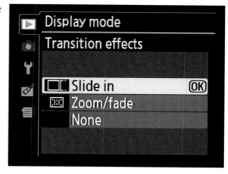

Figure 5-11: The default transition setting is Slide In.

Selected photo

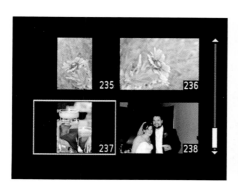 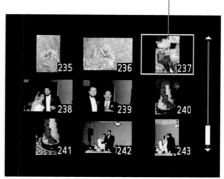

Figure 5-12: You can view multiple image thumbnails at a time.

In any of the thumbnail display modes, use these techniques to navigate your photo collection:

- **Scroll through your pictures.** Rotate the Command dial or press the Multi Selector right or left.

- **Select an image.** As you scroll through your pictures, a yellow box surrounds the currently selected image. For example, in Figure 5-12, Image 237 is selected. To select a different image, use the Command dial or Multi Selector to scroll the display until the highlight box surrounds the image.

✔ **View the selected image at the full-frame size.** Press OK.

After you return to full-frame view, pressing OK displays the Retouch menu. Now you can select a retouch option and apply it to the image. See Chapters 10 and 11 for a look at the tools found on the Retouch menu. But note that the image-viewing information in this chapter deals with still pictures; see Chapter 4 for help with movie playback and applying the one movie-related feature on the Retouch menu, the Edit Movie option.

Displaying photos in Calendar view

In Calendar display mode, you see a little calendar on the monitor, as shown in Figure 5-13. By selecting a date on the calendar, you can quickly navigate to all pictures you shot on that day. On the calendar, a thumbnail-free date indicates that your memory card doesn't contain any photos from that day.

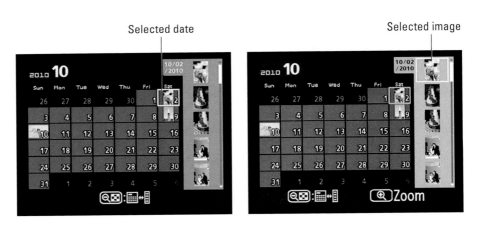

Figure 5-13: Calendar view makes it easy to view all photos shot on a particular day.

The key to navigating Calendar view is the Zoom Out button:

1. **Press the Zoom Out button as needed to cycle through the thumbnail display modes until you reach Calendar view.**

   If you're currently viewing images in full-frame view, for example, you need to press the button four times to get to Calendar view.

2. **Using the Multi Selector or Command dial, move the yellow highlight box over a date that contains an image.**

In the left example in Figure 5-13, for example, the 2nd day of October is selected. (The number of the month appears in the top-left corner of the screen.) After you select a date, the right side of the monitor displays a vertical strip of thumbnails of pictures taken on that date.

3. **To view all thumbnails from the selected date, press the Zoom Out button again.**

   The vertical thumbnail strip becomes active, as shown on the right in Figure 5-13, and you can scroll through the thumbnails by pressing the Multi Selector up and down, or by rotating the Command dial. A second highlight box appears in the thumbnail strip to indicate the currently selected image.

4. **To temporarily display a larger view of the selected thumbnail, hold down the Zoom In button.**

   The image filename appears under the larger preview, as shown in Figure 5-14. When you release the button, the large preview disappears, and the calendar comes back into view.

5. **To jump back to the calendar and select a different date, press the Zoom Out button again.**

   You can just keep pressing the button to jump between the calendar and the thumbnail strip as much as you want.

6. **To exit Calendar view and return to single-image view, press OK.**

   If you want to return to Calendar view, you have to press the Zoom Out button four times to cycle from full-frame view through the different thumbnail display modes.

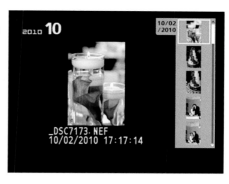

Figure 5-14: Highlight a photo in the thumbnail strip and press the Zoom In button to temporarily display it at a larger size.

Zooming in for a closer view

After displaying a photo in single-frame view, you can magnify it so that you can get a close-up look at important details, such as whether someone's eyes are closed in a portrait. For example, Figure 5-15 shows a magnified view of the candle image featured in Figure 5-14.

Here's the scoop on playback zoom:

Magnified area

> ✔ **Zoom in.** Press the Zoom In button, shown in the margin here. You can magnify the image to a maximum of 14 to 27 times its original display size, depending on the *resolution* (pixel count) of the photo. Just keep pressing the button until you reach the magnification you want.
>
> Note the magnifying glass icon on the button face. The plus sign in the middle is your reminder that this button enlarges the image.

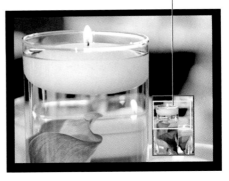

Figure 5-15: Use the Multi Selector to move the yellow outline over the area you want to inspect.

> ✔ **View another part of the magnified picture.** When an image is magnified, a little navigation thumbnail showing the entire image appears briefly in the lower-right corner of the monitor, as shown in Figure 5-15. The yellow outline in this picture-in-picture image indicates the area that's currently consuming the rest of the monitor space. Use the Multi Selector to scroll the yellow box and display a different portion of the image. After a few seconds, the navigation thumbnail disappears; just press the Multi Selector in any direction to redisplay it.

> ✔ **Inspect faces.** If the camera detects faces in the photo, the picture-in-picture thumbnail displays a white border around each detected face, as shown in Figure 5-16. Hold down the Info Edit button and press the Multi Selector right or left to toggle the display from face to face so that you can examine each person at a magnified view, as shown on the right in the figure. (Typically, subjects must be facing forward for the camera to detect a face.)

> ✔ **View more images at the same magnification.** Here's another neat trick: While the display is zoomed, you can rotate the Command dial to display the same area of the next photo at the same magnification. So if you shot the same subject several times, you can easily check how the same details appear in each one.

> ✔ **Zoom out.** To zoom out to a reduced magnification, press the Zoom Out button. This button also sports the magnifying glass symbol, but this time with a minus sign to indicate that it reduces the display size. That little grid-like thingy next to the magnifying glass reminds you that the button also comes into play when you want to go from full-frame view to one of the thumbnail views or Calendar view.

✔ **Return to full-frame view.** When you're ready to return to the normal magnification level, you don't need to keep pressing the Zoom Out button until you're all the way zoomed out. Instead, just press OK, which quickly returns you to the standard, full-frame view.

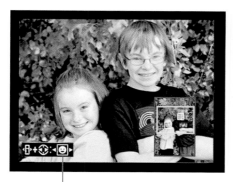 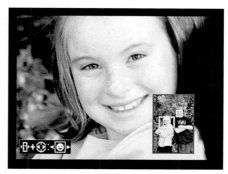

Face Detection symbol

Figure 5-16: The Face Detection feature enables you to quickly inspect faces.

Viewing Picture Data

In single-image picture view, you can choose from five Photo Information modes, each of which presents a different set of shooting data along with the image. To cycle between the different modes, press the Multi Selector up or down.

Note, though, that three of the five modes don't appear unless they are enabled through a menu option. To access them, take these steps:

1. **Open the Playback menu and highlight Display Mode, as shown on the left in Figure 5-17.**

2. **Press OK.**

   The screen shown on the right in Figure 5-17 appears.

3. **Select Detailed Photo Info and press OK.**

   You're presented with the screen shown on the left in Figure 5-18, offering the three hidden display modes: Highlights, RGB Histogram, and Data. (The last item enables the Shooting Data display mode.) A check mark in the box next to a mode means that the mode is enabled. By default, all three modes are off, as shown in the figure.

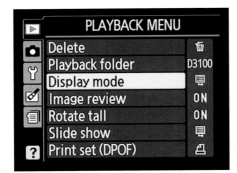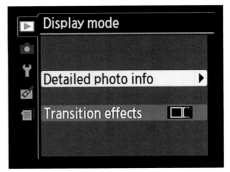

Figure 5-17: You must enable some of the information display modes via the Playback menu.

4. **To toggle a display mode on, highlight it and then press the Multi Selector right.**

A check mark appears in the box for that mode, as shown on the right in Figure 5-18.

5. **After turning on the options you want to use, highlight Done, as shown on the right in Figure 5-18, and press OK.**

The next sections explain exactly what details you can glean from each display mode. I present them here in the order they appear if you cycle through the modes by pressing the Multi Selector down. You can spin through the modes in the other direction by pressing the Multi Selector up.

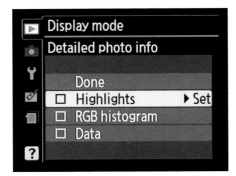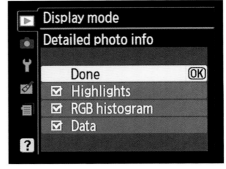

Figure 5-18: Press the Multi Selector right to toggle the highlighted display option on and off.

File Information mode

In this display mode, the monitor displays the data shown in Figure 5-19.

Frame Number/Total Pictures

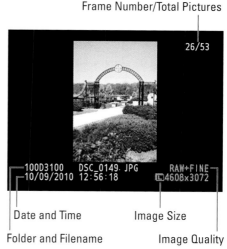

- ✏ **Frame Number/Total Pictures:**
  The first value here indicates the frame number of the currently displayed photo; the second tells you the total number of pictures on the memory card. In Figure 5-19, for example, the image is number 26 out of 53.

Date and Time   Image Size
Folder and Filename   Image Quality

Figure 5-19: In File Information mode, you can view these bits of data.

- ✏ **Folder Name:** Folders are named automatically by the camera unless you create custom folders, an advanced trick you can explore in Chapter 11. The first camera-created folder is 100D3100. Each folder can contain up to 9999 images; when you exceed that limit, the camera creates a new folder and assigns the next folder number: 101D3100, 102D3100, and so on.

- ✏ **Filename:** The camera also automatically names your files.

  Filenames end with a three-letter code that represents the file format, which is either JPG (for JPEG) or NEF (for Raw) for still photos. Chapter 2 discusses these two formats. If you create a dust-off reference image file, an advanced feature designed for use with Nikon Capture NX 2, the camera instead uses the extension NDF. (Because this software must be purchased separately, I don't cover it or the dust-off function in this book.)

  The first three letters of filenames also vary. Here's what the possible three-letter codes indicate:

  - *DSC:* This code means normal, plain-old picture file.

  - *SSC:* This trio appears at the beginning of files that you create with the Small Picture option on the Retouch menu. Chapter 6 discusses this feature.

  - *CSC:* This code is used for images that you alter using other Retouch menu features.

- **_ (underscore):** If you change the Color Space setting on the Shooting menu to the Adobe RGB color profile, a topic you can investigate in Chapter 8, an underscore character precedes the filename. (The exception is for dust-off reference photos, which don't use the underscore.) For photos taken in the default color profiles (sRGB), the underscore appears after the three-letter code, as in DSC_.

Each image is also assigned a four-digit file number, starting with 0001. When you reach image 9999, the file numbering restarts at 0001, and the new images go into a new folder to prevent any possibility of overwriting the existing image files. For more information about file numbering, see the Chapter 1 section that discusses the File Number Sequence option.

- **Date and Time:** Just below the folder and filename info, you see the date and time that you took the picture. Of course, the accuracy of this data depends on whether you set the camera's date and time values correctly, which you do via the Setup menu. Chapter 1 has details.

- **Image Quality:** Here you can see which Image Quality setting you used when taking the picture. Again, Chapter 2 has details, but the short story is this: Fine, Normal, and Basic are the three JPEG recording options, with Fine representing the highest JPEG quality. Raw refers to the Nikon Camera Raw format, NEF.

- **Image Size:** This value tells you the image resolution, or pixel count. See Chapter 2 to find out about resolution.

In the top-left corner of the screen, you may see the following two symbols, labeled in Figure 5-20:

- **Protect Status:** A little key icon indicates that you used the camera's file-protection feature to prevent the image from being erased when you use the camera's Delete function. See "Protecting Photos," later in this chapter, to find out more. (**Note:** Formatting your memory card, a topic discussed in Chapter 1, *does* erase even protected pictures.) This area appears empty if you didn't apply protection.

- **Retouch Indicator:** This icon appears if you used any of the Retouch menu options to alter the image. Remember that the

Protect Status

Retouch Indicator

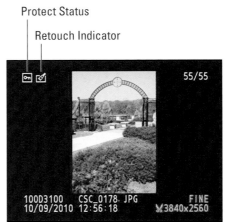

Figure 5-20: These symbols indicate a protected photo and a retouched photo.

image filename also indicates a retouched photo. For example, I used the camera's Trim function to create a cropped version of the scene shown in Figure 5-19, so the filename of the picture in Figure 5-20 begins with CSC. Additionally, the little scissors symbol next to the file size (lower-right corner) indicates that I cropped the original to the current size. Chapter 10 explains the Trim feature.

RGB Histogram mode

Press the Multi Selector down to shift from File Information mode to this mode, which displays your image in the manner shown in Figure 5-21. (*Remember:* You can view your picture in this mode only if you enable it via the Display Mode option on the Playback menu. See "Viewing Picture Data," earlier in this chapter, for help.)

Brightness histogram

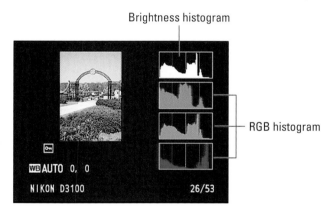

RGB histogram

Figure 5-21: RGB Histogram mode presents exposure and color information in chart-like fashion.

Underneath the image thumbnail, you see just a few pieces of data. As with File Information mode, you see the Protect Status and Retouch Indicator icons if you used those features. The Protect Status icon appears in Figure 5-21, for example. Beneath that, you see the White Balance settings used for the shot. (White Balance is a color feature you can explore in Chapter 8.) Along the bottom row of the display, you see the camera name along with the Frame Number/Total Pictures data, also part of the standard File Information display data.

The core of this display mode, though, are those chart-like thingies called *histograms.* You get two types of histograms: The top one is a Brightness histogram; the three others are collectively called an RGB (red, green, blue) histogram.

The next two sections explain what you can discern from the histograms. But first, here's a cool trick to remember: If you press the Zoom In button while in this display mode, you can zoom the thumbnail to a magnified view. The histograms then update to reflect only the magnified area of the photo. Use the Multi Selector to scroll the display to see other areas of the picture. To return to the regular view and once again see the whole-image histogram, press OK.

Reading a Brightness histogram

You can get an idea of image exposure by viewing your photo on the camera monitor. But if you adjust the brightness of the monitor or the ambient light affects the display brightness, you may not get the real story. The Brightness histogram provides a way to gauge exposure that's a little more reliable.

A Brightness histogram indicates the distribution of shadows, highlights, and *midtones* (areas of medium brightness) in your image. Figure 5-22 shows you the Brightness histogram for the landscape scene shown in Figure 5-21.

The horizontal axis of the histogram represents the possible picture brightness values — the maximum *tonal range,* in photography-speak — from the darkest shadows on the left to the brightest highlights on the right. And the vertical axis shows you how many pixels fall at a particular brightness value. A spike indicates a heavy concentration of pixels. For example, in Figure 5-22, the histogram shows that most pixels fall within the range from black to just a tad lighter than medium brightness range, with few pixels reaching maximum brightness.

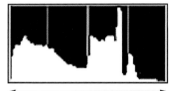

Shadows　　　　　Highlights

Figure 5-22: The Brightness histogram indicates tonal range, from shadows on the left to highlights on the right.

Keep in mind that there is no one "perfect" histogram that you should try to achieve. Instead, interpret the histogram with respect to the distribution of shadows, highlights, and midtones that comprise your subject. You wouldn't expect to see lots of shadows, for example, in a photo of a polar bear walking on a snowy landscape.

Pay attention, however, if you see a very high concentration of pixels at the far right end of the histogram, which can indicate a problem known as *blown highlights* in some circles and *clipped highlights* in others. In plain English, both terms mean that *highlights* — the brightest areas of the image — are so overexposed that areas that should include a variety of light shades are instead totally white. For example, in a cloud image, pixels that should be light to very light gray become white because of overexposure, resulting in a loss of detail in those clouds. On the flip side, a large mass of pixels at the left end of the histogram may indicate clipped shadows and a loss of detail in the darkest areas of the scene.

Understanding RGB histograms

When you view your images in RGB Histogram display mode, you see two histograms: the Brightness histogram, covered in the preceding section, and an RGB histogram. Figure 5-23 offers a sample RGB histogram for your consideration; it reflects the landscape photo in Figure 5-21.

To make sense of an RGB histogram, you first need to know that digital images are called *RGB images* because they're created out of three primary colors of light: red, green, and blue. Whereas the Brightness histogram reflects the brightness of all three color components, or *channels,* RGB histograms enable you to view the values for each channel.

When you look at the brightness data for a channel, though, you're really evaluating

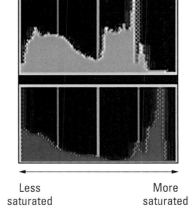

Less saturated   More saturated

Figure 5-23: The RGB histogram can indicate problems with color saturation.

color *saturation.* I don't have space in this book to provide a full lesson in RGB color theory, but the short story is that when you mix together red, green, and blue light and each component is at maximum brightness, you get white. Zero brightness in all three channels gives you black. But if you have maximum red and no blue or green, you have fully saturated red. If you mix together two channels at maximum brightness, you also get full saturation. For example, maximum red and blue produce fully saturated magenta. And wherever colors are fully saturated, you can lose picture detail. For example, a rose petal that should have a range of tones from partially saturated red to fully saturated red may instead be one flat blob of full-on red.

The upshot is that if all the pixels for one or two channels are slammed to the right end of the histogram, you may be losing picture detail due to overly saturated colors. If all three channels show a heavy pixel population at the right end of the histograms, you may have blown highlights — again, because when you have maximum red, green, and blue, you get white. Either way, you may want to adjust your exposure settings and try again.

A savvy RGB histogram reader can also spot color balance issues by looking at the pixel values. But frankly, color balance problems are fairly easy to notice just by looking at the image itself. And understanding how to translate the histogram data for this purpose requires more knowledge about RGB color theory than I have room to present in this book.

For information about manipulating color, see Chapter 8.

Highlights display mode

When the pixels in a photograph are just a little overexposed, it's sometimes possible to bring them back into line by using exposure correction tools in a photo-editing program. But when the highlights are completely *blown* — that is, they're so overexposed that they're full-on white — you're stuck. You can make them darker in your photo editor, but because a darker shade of white is gray, you don't gain any headway. There simply isn't any color information that lets the program know that a pixel is supposed to be very light blue, for example. If you want that blown pixel to be any color other than gray, you simply have to paint the color yourself.

To help you avoid this issue, the D3100 offers Highlights display mode. In this mode, blown highlights are represented by pixels that blink on and off in the camera monitor. For example, the "blinkies" in Figure 5-24 show that the candle flame and a few areas in the glass vase contain blown pixels.

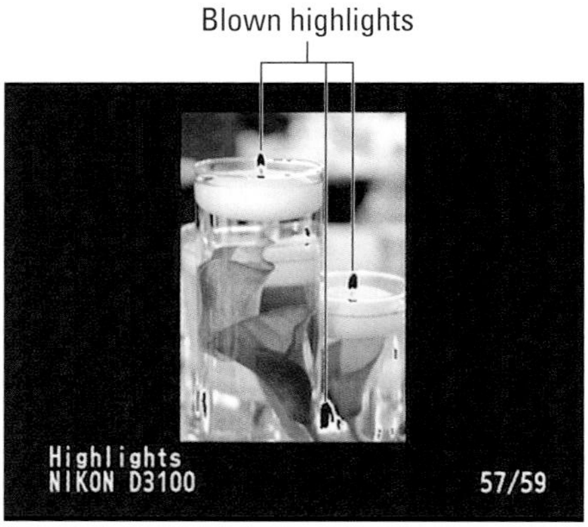

Blown highlights

Like RGB Histogram mode, Highlights mode is provided because simply viewing the image isn't always a reliable way to gauge exposure. To use it, however, you must follow the instructions laid out in the earlier section "Viewing Picture Data," in this chapter, to enable the mode.

Highlights
NIKON D3100   57/59

Figure 5-24: In Highlights mode, blinking areas indicate blown highlights.

Along with the blinking highlight warning, Highlights display mode presents the camera name and the File Number/Total Pictures values, all explained in the earlier section "File Information mode." The label *Highlights* also appears to let you know the current display mode, as shown in Figure 5-24. You also see the Protect Status (key) icon and the Retouch icon if you used those features.

I suggest that you check both the Brightness histogram offered in RGB Histogram display mode and the Highlights display, though, when you're concerned about overexposure. If an image contains only a small area of blown highlights, the histogram may indicate a very small pixel population at the brightest end of the spectrum, leading you to assume that you're okay in the exposure department. But if those blown highlights happen to fall in an important part of your image — someone's face, for example — they can wreck your picture.

On the flip side, just because you see the flashing alerts doesn't mean that you should adjust exposure — the decision depends on where the alerts occur and how the rest of the image is exposed. Consider my candle photo, for example. Yes, small white areas are in the flames and the glass vase. Yet exposure in the majority of the photo is fine. If you reduced exposure to darken those spots, some areas of the flowers would be underexposed. In other words, sometimes you simply can't avoid a few clipped highlights when the scene includes a broad range of brightness values.

Shooting Data display mode

Before you can access this mode, you must enable it via the Display Mode option on the Playback menu. See the earlier section, "Viewing Picture Data," for details. After turning on the option, press the Multi Selector down to shift from Highlights mode to Shooting Data mode.

In this mode, you can view the three screens of information shown in Figure 5-25. Nikon refers to these screens as Shooting Data Page 1, 2, and 3. If you attach the optional GPS unit to the camera, a fourth screen becomes available, listing the GPS data.

Most of the data here won't make any sense to you until you explore Chapters 7 and 8, which explain the exposure, color, and other advanced settings available on your camera. But I do want to call your attention to a couple of factoids now:

- ✔ Press the Multi Selector up or down to move from one Shooting Data screen to the next.

- ✔ The top-left corner of the monitor shows the Protect Status and Retouch Indicator icons, if you used these features. Otherwise, the area is empty. (See the earlier section "File Information mode" for details about these particular features.)

- ✔ The current frame number, followed by the total number of images on the memory card, appears in the lower-right corner of the display.

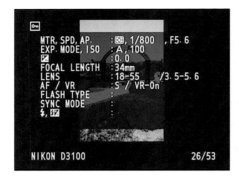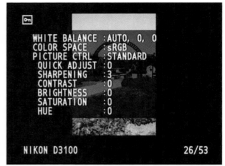

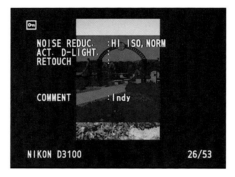

Figure 5-25: You can view the camera settings used to capture the image in Shooting Data display mode.

- ✔ The Comment item, which is the final item on the third screen, contains a value if you use the Image Comment feature on the Setup menu. I cover this option in Chapter 11.

- ✔ If the ISO value on Shooting Data Page 1 (the first screen in Figure 5-25) appears in red, the camera is letting you know that it overrode the ISO Sensitivity setting that you selected in order to produce a good exposure. This shift occurs only if you enable automatic ISO adjustment for the P, S, A, and M exposure modes. See Chapter 7 for details.

Overview Data mode

This mode is the second of the two default photo-information modes. (Meaning, you don't have to enable it via the Display Mode option on the Playback menu to use it.) In this mode, the playback screen contains a small image thumbnail along with scads of shooting data — although not quite as much as Shooting Data mode — plus a Brightness histogram. Figure 5-26 offers a look.

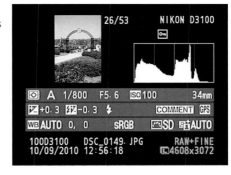

The earlier section "Reading a Brightness histogram" tells you what to make of that part of the screen. Just above the histogram, you see the Protect Status and Retouch Indicator, if you took advantage of those features. The Frame Number/Total Pictures data appears near the upper-right corner of the image thumbnail. For details on that data, see the earlier section "File Information mode." As always, the Protect Status and Retouch Indicator icons appear only if you used those two features; otherwise, the area is empty. (The Protect Status symbol appears in Figure 5-26.)

Figure 5-26: In Overview Data mode, you can view your picture along with the major camera settings you used to take the picture.

To sort out the maze of other information, the following list breaks things down into the five rows that appear under the image thumbnail and histogram. In the accompanying figures as well as in Figure 5-26, I include all possible data simply for the purposes of illustration. (I didn't actually use flash, Flash Compensation, or Exposure Compensation to capture the photo.) If any of the items in the figures don't appear on your screen, it simply means that the relevant feature wasn't enabled when you took the shot.

✔ **Row 1:** This row shows the exposure-related settings labeled in Figure 5-27, along with the focal length of the lens you used to take the shot. Chapter 7 details the exposure settings; Chapter 8 introduces you to focal length.

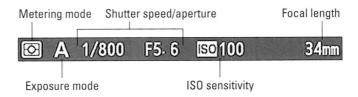

Figure 5-27: Here you can inspect major exposure settings along with the lens focal length.

✔ **Row 2:** This row contains a few additional exposure settings, labeled in Figure 5-28. On the right end of the row, the Comment label appears if you took advantage of the Image Comment feature, covered in Chapter 11, before snapping the picture. Likewise, the GPS item appears only when the option GPS unit was used for the shot. In both cases, switch to the Shooting Data display mode to view the actual comment or GPS data.

Exposure compensation   Flash mode

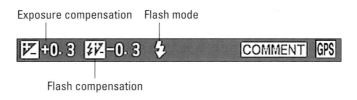

Flash compensation

Figure 5-28: This row contains additional exposure information.

✔ **Row 3:** Shown in Figure 5-29, this row is a mixed bag. Chapter 8 details the first three items, which relate to settings that affect image colors. See Chapter 7 for information about the final item on the row, which shows the Active D-Lighting setting.

White Balance   Picture control

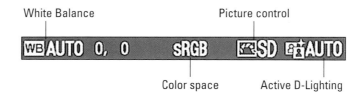

Color space   Active D-Lighting

Figure 5-29: Look at this row for details about advanced color settings and Active D-Lighting.

✔ **Rows 4 and 5:** The final two rows of data (visible in Figure 5-26) show the same information you get in File Information mode, explained earlier in this chapter. Figure 5-19 labels the various bits and pieces, if you forget what's what.

Deleting Photos

You have three options for erasing pictures from a memory card when it's in your camera. The next sections give you the lowdown. (Or is it the down low? I can't seem to keep up.)

Deleting images one at a time

The Delete button is key to erasing single images. But the process varies a little depending on which Playback display mode you use, as follows:

- In single-image view, you can erase the current image by pressing the Delete button.
- In thumbnail view (displaying 4, 9, or 72 thumbnails), use the Multi Selector to highlight the picture you want to erase and then press the Delete button.
- In Calendar view, first highlight the date that contains the image. Then press the Zoom Out button to jump to the scrolling list of thumbnails, highlight a specific image, and press the Delete button.

After you press Delete, you see a message asking whether you really want to erase the picture. If you do, press the Delete button again. Or, to cancel out of the process, press the Playback button.

See the earlier section, "Viewing Images in Playback Mode," for more details about the display modes.

You can also press the Delete button during the instant-review period if you know right away that the picture's a bust. But you have to be quick or the camera returns to shooting mode.

Deleting all photos

To erase all pictures, take these steps:

1. **Display the Playback menu and highlight Delete, as shown in the left image in Figure 5-30.**

2. **Press OK to display the second screen in the figure.**

3. **Highlight All and press the Multi Selector right.**

   You then see a screen that asks you to verify that you want to delete all of your images.

4. **Select Yes and press OK.**

If you create custom image folders, a feature I cover in Chapter 11, be aware that this step deletes only pictures in the folder that is currently selected via the Playback Folder option on the Playback menu. See the section "Viewing Images in Playback Mode," earlier in this chapter, for information.

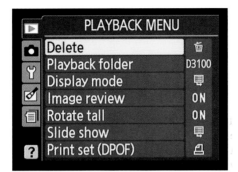
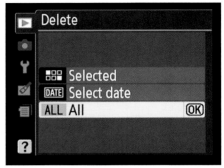

Figure 5-30: To delete all photos, use the Delete option on the Playback menu.

Deleting a batch of selected photos

To erase multiple photos — but not them all — display the Playback menu and highlight Delete, as shown on the left in Figure 5-31. Press OK to display the second screen in the figure.

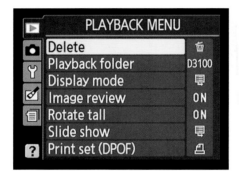
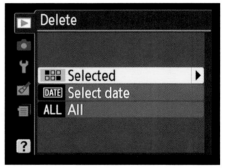

Figure 5-31: The Delete menu option also provides two ways to delete only some pictures from your memory card.

You then have two options for specifying which photos to erase:

✔ **Select photos one-by-one.** To go this route, highlight Selected, as shown on the right in Figure 5-31, and press the Multi Selector right to display a screen of thumbnails, as shown in Figure 5-32. Use the Multi Selector to place the yellow highlight box over the first photo you want to delete and then press the Zoom Out button, shown in the margin here. A little trash can icon, the universal symbol for delete, appears in the upper-right corner of the thumbnail, as shown in the figure.

If you change your mind, press the Zoom Out button again to remove the Delete tag from the image. To undo deletion for all selected photos, press the Playback button.

For a closer look at the selected image, press and hold the Zoom In button. When you release the button, the display returns to normal thumbnail view.

Delete symbol

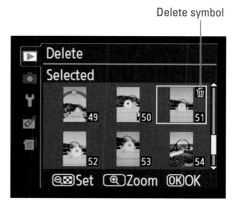

Figure 5-32: Use the Zoom Out button to tag pictures you want to delete.

✔ **Erase all photos taken on a specific date.** This time, choose Select Date from the main Delete screen, as shown on the left in Figure 5-33. Press the Multi Selector right to display a list of dates on which you took the pictures on the memory card, as shown on the right in the figure.

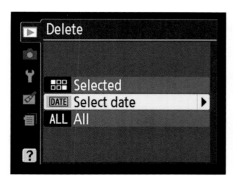
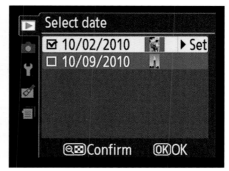

Figure 5-33: With the Select Date option, you can quickly erase all photos taken on a specific date.

Next, highlight a date and press the Multi Selector right. A little check mark appears in the box next to the date, as shown in Figure 5-33, tagging all images taken on that day for deletion. To remove the check mark and save the photos from the digital dumpster, press the Multi Selector right again.

Can't remember what photos are associated with the selected date? Try this:

- To display thumbnails of all images taken on the selected date, as shown on the left in Figure 5-34, press the Zoom Out button.
- To temporarily view the selected thumbnail at full-size view, as shown on the right in the figure, press the Zoom In button.
- To return to the date list, press the Zoom Out button again.

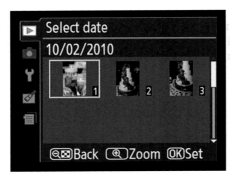 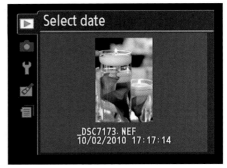

Figure 5-34: Press the Zoom Out button to display thumbnails of all photos taken on the selected date; then press Zoom In to magnify the selected image.

Deleting versus formatting: What's the diff?

In Chapter 1, I introduce you to the Format Memory Card command, which lives on the Setup menu and erases everything on your memory card. What's the difference between erasing photos by formatting and by choosing Delete from the Playback menu and then selecting the All option?

Well, if you happen to have stored other data on the card, such as, say, a music file or a picture taken on another type of camera, you need to format the card to erase everything on it. You can't use Delete to get rid of them.

Also keep in mind that the Delete function affects only the currently selected folder of

camera images. As long as you use the default folder system that the camera creates for you, however, "currently selected folder" is the same as "all images." The section "Viewing Images in Playback Mode," earlier in this chapter, talks more about this issue; Chapter 11 explains how to create custom folders.

One final — and important — note: Although using the Protect feature (explained elsewhere in this chapter) prevents the Delete function from erasing a picture, formatting erases all pictures, protected or not.

After tagging individual photos for deletion or specifying a shooting date to delete, press OK to start deleting. You see a confirmation screen asking permission to destroy the images; select Yes and press OK. The camera trashes the photos and returns you to the Playback menu.

You have one alternative way to quickly erase all images taken on a specific date: In the Calendar display mode, you can highlight the date in question and then press the Delete button instead of going through the Playback menu. You get the standard confirmation screen asking you whether you want to go forward. Press the Delete button again to dump the files. Visit the section "Displaying photos in Calendar view," earlier in this chapter, for the scoop on that display option.

Protecting Photos

You can safeguard pictures from accidental erasure by giving them *protected status.* After you take this step, the camera doesn't allow you to erase a picture by using either the Delete button or the Delete option on the Playback menu.

Formatting your memory card, however, *does* erase even protected pictures. See the nearby sidebar for more about formatting.

The picture protection feature comes in especially handy if you share a camera with other people. You can protect pictures so that those other people know that they shouldn't delete your super-great images to make room on the memory card for their stupid, badly photographed ones. (This step isn't foolproof, though, because anyone can remove the protected status from an image.)

Perhaps more importantly, when you protect a picture, it shows up as a read-only file when you transfer it to your computer. Files that have that read-only status can't be altered. Again, anyone with some computer savvy can remove the status, but this feature can keep casual users from messing around with your images after you download them to your system. Of course, *you* have to know how to remove the read-only status if you plan on editing your photo in your photo software. (***Hint:*** In Nikon ViewNX 2, you can do this by clicking the image thumbnail and then choosing File⇨Protect Files⇨Unprotect.)

Anyway, protecting a picture is easy:

1. Display or select the picture you want to protect.

- In single-image view, just display the photo.

- In 4/9/72 thumbnail mode, use the Multi Selector as needed to place the yellow highlight box over the photo.

- In Calendar view, highlight the date that contains the image and then press the Zoom Out button to jump to the scrolling list of thumbnails. Then move the highlight box over the image.

2. **Press the AE-L/AF-L button.**

   It's just to the left of the Command dial, on the back of the camera. (See the tiny key symbol that appears next to the button? That's your reminder that you use the button to lock a picture.) After you press the button, the same symbol appears on the image display, as shown in Figure 5-35.

3. **To remove protection, display or select the image and press the AE-L/AF-L button again.**

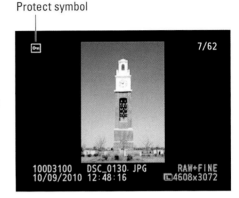

Protect symbol

Figure 5-35: Press the AE-L/AF-L button to prevent accidental deletion of the selected image.

Creating a Digital Slide Show

Many photo-editing and cataloging programs offer a tool for creating digital slide shows that can be viewed on a computer or, if copied to a DVD, on a DVD player. You can even add music, captions, graphics, special effects, and the like to jazz up your presentations.

But if you want to create a simple slide show — that is, one that simply displays the photos on the camera memory card one by one — you don't need a computer or any photo software. You can create and run the show right on your camera. And by connecting your camera to a television, as outlined in the next section, you can present your show to a whole roomful of people.

Two things to note before I walk you through the steps of running a slide show: First, which photos appear depends on the setting of the Playback Folder option. Read more about this setting in the earlier section "Viewing Images in Playback Mode." Second, movies aren't included in the show; for details on how to play movies, see Chapter 4.

Follow these steps to create a simple slide show on your camera:

1. **Display the Playback menu and highlight Slide Show, as shown on the left in Figure 5-36.**

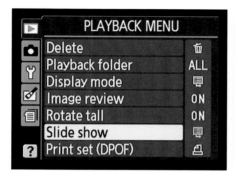 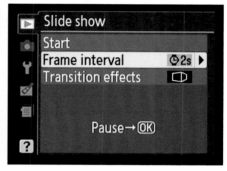

Figure 5-36: Choose Slide Show to set up automatic playback of all pictures on your memory card.

2. **Press OK to display the Slide Show screen shown on the right in Figure 5-36.**

3. **Highlight Frame Interval and press the Multi Selector right.**

   On the next screen, you can specify how long you want each image to display. You can set the interval to 2, 3, 5, or 10 seconds.

4. **Highlight the frame interval you want to use and press OK.**

   You return to the Slide Show screen.

5. **Select Transition Effects, as shown on the left in Figure 5-37, and press OK.**

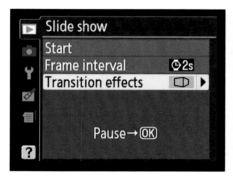 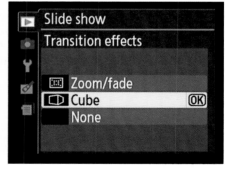

Figure 5-37: Choose the transition effect for your show by using this option.

You see the second screen in the figure. These options control the effect the camera uses when moving from one photo to the next. The Zoom/Fade option works just like the one available for regular, in-camera playback. With the Cube option, pictures sort of rotate into view, as if you're spinning a cube that has a different photo on each side. (Just give both effects a try — they're sort of hard to describe in words.) Select None if you like things plain and simple; the first picture disappears completely before the next one comes into view.

6. **Select a transition option and press OK.**

7. **Highlight Start and press OK.**

   The camera displays your pictures on the camera monitor.

When the show ends, you see a screen offering four options: You can choose to restart the show, adjust the frame interval, change the transition effect, or exit to the Playback menu. Highlight your choice and press OK.

During the show, you can control playback as follows:

✔ **Pause the show.** Press OK. Select Restart and press OK to display pictures again. When you pause the slide show, you also can change the interval — a handy option if the pace is too quick or slow — adjust the transition effect, or exit the show. Just highlight your choice and press OK. If you adjust the timing or transition, resume playback by choosing Restart and pressing OK.

✔ **Exit the show.** You have three options:

   • *To return to full-frame, regular playback,* press the Playback button.

   • *To return to the Playback menu,* press the Menu button.

   • *To return to picture-taking mode,* press the shutter button halfway.

✔ **Skip to the next/previous image manually.** Press the Multi Selector right or left or rotate the Command dial.

✔ **Change the information displayed with the image.** Press the Multi Selector up or down to cycle through the info-display modes. (See the earlier section "Viewing Picture Data" for details on what information is provided in each mode.)

Viewing Your Photos on a Television

Your camera is equipped with a feature that allows you to play your pictures and movies on a television screen. In fact, you have three playback options:

- **Regular (standard definition) video playback:** Haven't made the leap yet to HDTV? No worries: You can set the camera to send a regular standard-definition audio and video signal to the TV. For this option, you need to purchase the Nikon EG-D2 Audio Video Cable, available for around $13. A third-party cable is also fine, but be sure to look in the camera manual for details about what type to buy. You also need to attach the little ferrite cores that shipped in your camera box to the cable. (The cores help improve the video signal.)

- **HDTV playback:** If you have a high-definition television, you can set the camera to high-def playback. However, you need to purchase an HDMI cable to connect the camera and television. You need something called a Type C mini-pin HD cable; prices start at about $20. Nikon doesn't make its own cable, so just look for a quality third-party version.

  By default, the camera decides the proper video resolution to send to the TV after you connect the two devices. But you can set a specific resolution as well. To do so, select HDMI from the Setup menu, press OK, and then choose Output Resolution, as shown in Figure 5-38.

- **For HDMI CEC TV sets:** If your television is compatible with HDMI CEC, your D3100 enables you to use the buttons on the TV's remote control to perform the functions of the OK button and Multi Selector during full-frame picture playback and slide shows. To make this feature work, you must enable it via the Setup menu. Again, start with the HDMI option, but this time select Device Control, as shown in Figure 5-39, and set the option to On.

You need to make one final pre-flight check before connecting the camera and television: Verify the status of the Video Mode setting, located just above the HDMI option on the Setup menu. (Refer to the left screen in Figure 5-38.) You have just two options: NTSC and PAL. Select the video mode used by your part of the world. (In the United States, Canada, and Mexico, NTSC is the standard.) The mode should have been set at the factory to the right option for the country in which you bought your camera, but it never hurts to check.

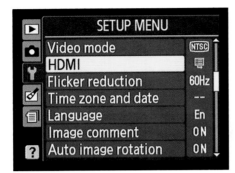

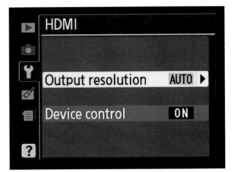

Figure 5-38: Choose the Auto setting if you want the camera to determine the proper resolution of the HD video signal it sends to the television.

After you select the necessary Setup menu options, grab your video cable, turn off the camera, and open the little rubber door on the left side of the camera. There you find two *ports* (connection slots): one for a standard audio/video (A/V) signal and one for the HDMI signal. Figure 5-40 labels the two ports.

The smaller plug on the A/V cable attaches to the camera. If you buy the Nikon cable, the yellow plug goes into your TV's video jack, and the white one goes into your TV's stereo audio jacks. For HDMI playback, a single plug goes to the TV.

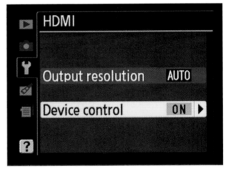

Figure 5-39: To use your HD TV remote control for playback, set the Device Control option to On.

At this point, I need to point you to your specific TV manual to find out exactly which jacks to use to connect your camera. You also need to consult your manual to find out which channel to select for playback of signals from auxiliary input devices. Then just turn on your camera to send the signal to the TV set. If you don't have the latest and greatest HDMI CEC capability (or lost your remote), control playback using the same techniques as you normally do to view pictures on your camera monitor. You can also run a slide show by following the steps outlined in the preceding section.

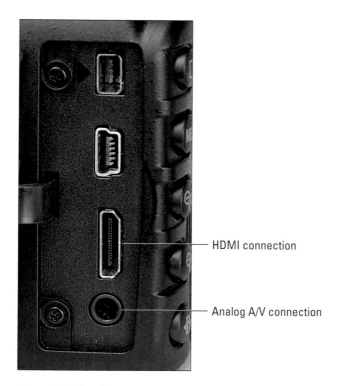

Figure 5-40: The video-out ports are under the little rubber door on the side of the camera.

6

Downloading, Printing, and Sharing Your Photos

_F_or many novice digital photographers, the task of moving pictures to the computer is one of the more confusing aspects of the art form. Unfortunately, providing you with detailed downloading instructions is impossible because the steps vary widely depending on which computer software you use to do the job.

To give you as much help as I can, however, this chapter starts with a quick review of photo software, in case you aren't happy with your current solution. Following that, you can find information about downloading images, converting pictures that you shoot in the Raw format to a standard format, and preparing your pictures for print and online sharing.

Choosing the Right Photo Software

Programs for downloading, archiving, and editing digital photos abound, ranging from entry-level software designed for beginners to high-end options geared to professionals. The good news is that if you don't need serious photo-editing capabilities, you may find a free program that serves your needs — in fact, your camera ships with one free program, Nikon ViewNX 2. The next section offers a look at Nikon ViewNX 2 along with two other freebies; following that, I offer some advice on a few popular programs to consider when the free options don't meet your needs.

Three free photo programs

If you don't plan on doing a lot of retouching or other manipulation of your photos but simply want a tool for downloading and organizing your pictures, one of the following free programs may be a good solution:

✔ **Nikon ViewNX 2:** This program is on the CD that shipped in your camera box. As the name implies, the program provides a simple photo organizer and viewer, plus a few basic photo-editing features, including red-eye removal and exposure and color adjustment filters. You also can use the program to download pictures and to convert Raw files to a standard format. (See Chapter 2 for a primer on file formats.) I show you how to accomplish both tasks later in this chapter.

Figure 6-1 offers a look at the ViewNX 2 window as it appears when you use the Thumbnail Grid view mode, one of three display options available from the View menu.

Selected focus point

Click to hide/display focus point

Click to hide/display Metadata panel

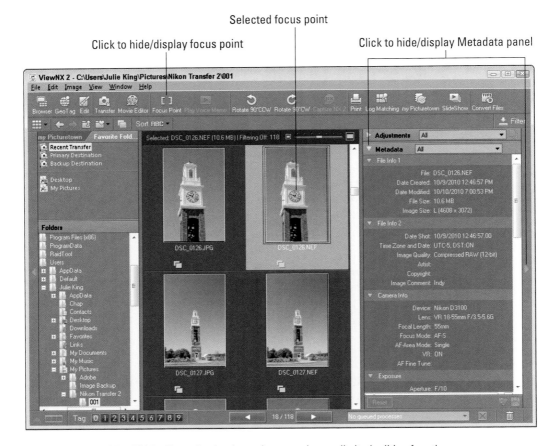

Figure 6-1: Nikon ViewNX 2 offers a basic photo viewer and some limited editing functions.

After you download your photos, you can view camera *metadata* — the data that records the camera settings you used to take the picture — in ViewNX 2. Just display the Metadata panel, located on the right side of the program window, as shown in Figure 6-1. (If the panel is hidden, click the little triangle on the far right side of the window and then click the triangle to the left of Metadata. I labeled both controls in the figure.) Many other photo programs also display metadata, but sometimes can't reveal data that's very camera-specific, such as the Picture Control setting on the D3100. Every camera manufacturer records metadata differently and sometimes vary the data format slightly when introducing new models, so it's a little difficult for software companies to keep up with each new camera.

ViewNX 2 offers another cool feature that most other browsers don't: By clicking the Focus Point button, labeled in Figure 6-1, you can display a little red rectangle that indicates which of the 11 focus points the camera used to establish focus for the shot, which can be helpful when you're trying to troubleshoot focus problems. You see the point only if you used autofocusing when taking the shot, however.

✏ **Apple iPhoto:** Most Mac users are very familiar with this photo browser, built into the Mac operating system. Apple provides some great tutorials on using iPhoto at its Web site (www.apple.com) to help you get started if you're new to the program.

✏ **Windows Photo Gallery:** Some versions of Microsoft Windows also offer a free photo downloader and browser — Windows Photo Gallery or Windows Live Photo Gallery, depending on your version of the Windows operating system.

Of these three programs, only Nikon ViewNX 2 displays all photo files on your computer right away. With the other programs, you must ask the software to search for and catalog your photos. However, if you use the program to handle the picture downloads, it catalogs pictures as part of the process. Check the program's Help system for details on taking the cataloging step and setting up the program as the default download tool.

Advanced photo programs

Any of the programs mentioned in the preceding section can handle simple photo downloading and organizing tasks. But if you're interested in serious photo retouching or digital-imaging artistry, you need to step up to a full-fledged photo-editing program.

As with software in the free category, you have many choices; the following list describes just five widely known programs.

✏ **Adobe Photoshop Elements:** Elements has been the best-selling consumer-level photo-editing program for some time, and for good reason. With a full complement of retouching tools, onscreen guidance for beginners, and an assortment of templates for creating photo projects like scrapbooks, Elements offers all the features that most consumers need. Figure 6-2 shows the Elements editing window with some of the photo-creativity tools displayed to the right of the photo. The program includes a photo organizer as well, along with built-in tools to help you print your photos and upload them to photo-sharing sites. (www.adobe.com, about $100)

✔ **Nikon Capture NX 2:** Shown in Figure 6-3, this Nikon program offers an image browser/organizer plus a wealth of photo-editing tools, including a sophisticated tool for processing Raw images. But as you can see from the figure, it's not exactly geared to casual photographers or novice photo editors, so expect a bit of a learning curve. Nor does this program offer the sort of photo-creativity tools you find in a program like Photoshop Elements (the same is true for the other advanced tools described in this list). (www.nikon.com, about $180)

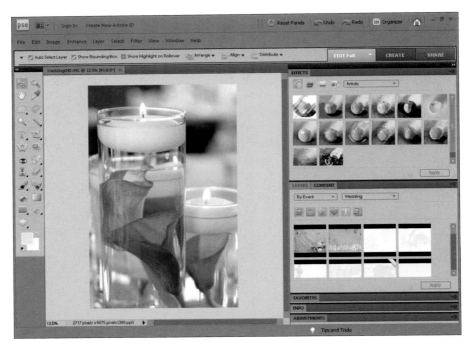

Figure 6-2: Adobe Photoshop Elements offers good retouching tools plus templates for creating scrapbooks, greeting cards, and other photo gifts.

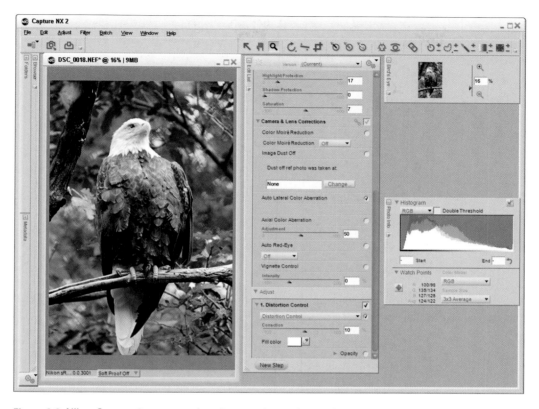

Figure 6-3: Nikon Capture 2 may appeal to photographers who need more robust image editing tools than are found in ViewNX 2.

✒ **Apple Aperture:** Aperture is geared more to shooters that need to organize and process lots of images but typically do only light retouching work — wedding photographers and school-portrait photographers, for example. (www.apple.com, about $200)

✒ **Adobe Photoshop Lightroom:** Lightroom is the Adobe counterpart to Aperture, although in its latest version, it offers some fairly powerful retouching tools as well. Many pro photographers rely on this program or Aperture for all their work, in fact. (www.adobe.com, about $300)

✒ **Adobe Photoshop:** The granddaddy of photo editors, Photoshop offers the industry's most powerful, sophisticated retouching tools, including tools for producing HDR (high dynamic range) and 3D images. In fact, you probably won't use even a quarter of the tools in the Photoshop shed unless you're a digital imaging professional who uses the program on a daily basis — even then, some tools may never see the light of day. (www.adobe.com, about $700)

Not sure which tool you need, if any? Good news: You can download 30-day free trials of all these programs from the manufacturers' Web sites.

Sending Pictures to the Computer

Whatever photo software you choose, you can take the following approaches to downloading images to your computer:

✔ **Connect the camera to the computer via a USB cable.** After connecting the two, the computer sees your camera as just another storage drive, and you then can transfer your images.

To go this route, you must buy the cable, however, because Nikon no longer supplies it with the camera. The official Nikon cable is the UC-E4 USB; you can buy it for about $35. However, if you happen to have another Nikon digital camera lying around, and that camera uses the same cable — it was standard for many Nikon cameras — you can safely use it with your D3100. You can use a third-party cable if you prefer, too. Check the camera manual for details on what cable specifications are required, and be sure to attach the smaller of the two ferrite cores included in your camera box to the cable. (The larger core is used with third-party A/V cables, as outlined in Chapter 5.)

✔ **Use a memory card reader.** With a card reader, you simply pop the memory card out of your camera and into the card reader instead of hooking the camera to the computer. Many computers and printers now have card readers, and you also can buy standalone readers for under $30. *Note:* If you use the new SDHC (Secure Digital High Capacity) or SDXC (Secure Digital eXtended Capacity) cards, the reader must specifically support that type.

✔ **Invest in Eye-Fi memory cards and transfer images via a wireless network.** You can find out more about these special memory cards at the manufacturer's Web site, www.eye.fi. Your computer must be connected to a wireless network for the transfer technology to work.

For most people, I recommend using a card reader. Sending pictures directly from the camera, whether via cable or wirelessly, requires that the camera be turned on during the entire download process, wasting battery power. Additionally, the USB cable works only with specific Nikon cameras, and not all devices can use Eye-Fi memory cards. Card readers, on the other hand, can accept cards from any device that uses SD cards, which are fast becoming the standard storage medium for portable devices.

That said, I include information about cable transfer in the next section in case you happen to have one of those Nikon USB cables around and you don't have a card reader. To use a card reader, skip ahead to "Starting the transfer process," in this chapter.

Because Eye-Fi cards aren't yet in widespread use, I don't cover that transfer technology. If you're an Eye-Fi user, check the instructions that ship with the cards and visit the company's Web site for information on how to set up your card and transfer images from it to your computer. Also check the Eye-Fi compatibility and use details provided in the D3100 manual; look for the section related to the Eye-Fi Upload option on the Setup menu. (The menu item appears only when an Eye-Fi card is installed in the camera.)

Connecting the camera and computer for picture download

If you own a USB cable that's compatible with your camera (see the preceding section), you can connect the camera to the computer and then transfer images to your hard drive via the cable.

The next section explains the actual transfer process; the steps here just walk you through the process of connecting the two devices. You need to follow a specific set of steps when connecting the camera to your computer. Otherwise, you can damage the camera or the memory card.

Also note that for your camera to communicate with the computer, Nikon suggests that your computer runs one of the following operating systems:

  ✔ Windows 7, Vista with Service Pack 2, or XP with Service Pack 3 (Home or Professional edition).

  ✔ Mac OS X 10.4.11, 10.5.8, or 10.6.4

If you use another OS (operating system, for the non-geeks in the crowd), check the support pages on the Nikon Web site (www.nikon.com) for the latest news about any updates to system compatibility. You can always simply transfer images with a card reader, too.

With that preamble out of the way, here are the steps to link your computer and camera:

1. **Check the level of the camera battery.**

   If the battery is low, charge it before continuing. Running out of battery power during the transfer process can cause problems, including lost picture data. Alternatively, if you purchased the optional AC adapter, use that to power the camera during picture transfers.

2. **Turn on the computer and give it time to finish its normal startup routine.**

3. **Turn off the camera.**

4. **Insert the smaller of the two plugs on the USB cable into the USB port on the side of the camera.**

Look under the little rubber door on the left side of the camera for this port, labeled in Figure 6-4.

5. **Plug the other end of the cable into the computer's USB port.**

If possible, plug the cable into a port that's built in to the computer, as opposed to one that's on your keyboard or part of an external USB hub. Those accessory-type connections can sometimes foul up the transfer process.

6. **Turn on the camera.**

What happens now depends on your computer operating system and what photo software you have installed on that system. The next section explains the possibilities and how to proceed with the image transfer process.

7. **When the download is complete, turn off the camera and then disconnect it from the computer.**

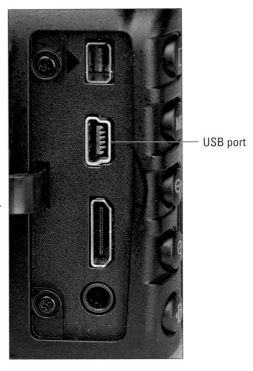

USB port

Figure 6-4: The USB slot is hidden under the rubber door on the left side of the camera.

I repeat: Turn off the camera before severing its ties with the computer. Otherwise, you can damage the camera.

Starting the transfer process

After you connect the camera to the computer or insert a memory card into your card reader, your next step depends, again, on the software installed on your computer and the computer operating system.

Here are the most common possibilities and how to move forward:

✓ **On a Windows-based computer, a Windows message box similar to the one in Figure 6-5 appears.** Again, the figure shows the dialog box as it appears on a computer running Windows 7. Whatever its design, the dialog box suggests different programs that you can use to download your picture files. Which programs appear depend on what you have installed on your system. If you installed Nikon ViewNX 2, for example, the list should contain a Nikon Transfer 2 entry, as shown in the figure. Nikon Transfer 2 is the downloading utility built into ViewNX 2.

In Windows 7 and Vista, just click the transfer program that you want to use. In other versions of Windows, the dialog box may sport an OK button; if so, click that button to proceed.

If you want to use the same program for all your transfers, select the Always Do This for Pictures check box, as shown in the figure. (In other versions of Windows, the check box may have a slightly different name.) The next time you connect your camera or insert a memory card, Windows will automatically launch your program of choice instead of displaying the message box.

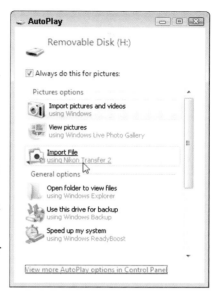

Figure 6-5: Windows may display this initial boxful of transfer options.

- ✔ **An installed photo program automatically displays a photo-download wizard.** For example, the Nikon Transfer 2 downloader or a downloader associated with Adobe Photoshop Elements, iPhoto, or some other photo software may leap to the forefront. Usually, the downloader that appears is associated with the software that you most recently installed. Each new program that you add to your system tries to wrestle control over your image downloads away from the previous program.

If you don't want a program's auto downloader to launch whenever you insert a memory card or connect your camera, you can turn off that feature. Check the software manual to find out how to disable the auto launch.

- ✔ **Nothing happens.** Don't panic; assuming that your card reader or camera is properly connected, all is probably well. Someone simply may have disabled all the automatic downloaders on your system. Just launch your photo software and then transfer your pictures using whatever command starts that process.

As another option, you can use Windows Explorer or the Mac Finder to drag and drop files from your memory card to your computer's hard drive. Whether you connect the card through a card reader or attach the camera directly, the computer sees the card or camera as just another drive on the system. So the process of transferring files is exactly the same as when you move any other file from a CD, DVD, or other storage device onto your hard drive.

Safeguarding your digital photo files

To make sure that your digital photos enjoy a long, healthy life, follow these storage guidelines:

✔ Don't rely on your computer's hard drive for long-term, archival storage. Hard drives occasionally fail, wiping out all files in the process. This warning applies to both internal and external hard drives. At the very least, having a dual-drive backup is in order — you might keep one copy of your photos on your computer's internal drive and another on an external drive. If one breaks, you still have all your goodies on the other one.

✔ Camera memory cards, flash memory keys, and other portable storage devices, such as one of those wallet-sized media players, are similarly risky. All are easily damaged if dropped or otherwise mishandled. And being of diminutive stature, these portable storage options also are easily lost.

✔ The best way to store important files is to copy them to nonrewritable CDs. (The label should say CD-R, not CD-RW.) Look for quality, brand-name CDs that have a gold coating, which offer a higher level of security than other coatings and boast a longer life than your garden-variety CDs.

✔ Recordable DVDs offer the advantage of holding lots more data than a CD. However, be aware that the DVDs you create on one computer may not be playable on another because multiple recording formats and disc types exist: DVD minus, DVD plus, dual-layer DVD, and so on. If you do opt for DVD, look for the archival, gold-coated variety, just as for CDs.

✔ For a double backup, you may want to check into online storage services, such as Mozy (www.mozy.com) and IDrive (www.idrive.com). You pay a monthly subscription fee to back up your important files to the site's servers.

Note, though, the critical phrase here: *double backup.* Online storage sites have a troubling history of closing down suddenly, taking all their customers' data with them. (One extremely alarming case was the closure of a photography-oriented storage site called Digital Railroad, which gave clients a mere 24-hours' notice before destroying their files.) So anything you store online should be also stored on DVD or CD and kept in your home or office. Also note that photo-sharing sites such as Shutterfly, Kodak Gallery, and the like *aren't* designed to be long-term storage tanks for your images. Usually, you get access to only a small amount of file storage space, and the site may require you to purchase prints or other photo products periodically to maintain your account.

In the next section, I provide details on using Nikon Transfer 2 to download your files. Remember, if you use some other software, the concepts are the same, but check your program manual to get the small details. In most programs, you also can find lots of information by simply clicking open the Help menu.

Downloading photos with Nikon ViewNX 2

If you want to use the free Nikon software, Nikon ViewNX 2, to download, view, and organize your photos, dig out the program CD from your camera box and install the software on your system.

Also note that this book features Nikon ViewNX 2 version 2.0.1. If you own an earlier version of the program, visit the Nikon Web site to install the updates. (To find out what version you have installed, open the program. Then, in Windows, choose Help⇨About. On a Mac, choose the About command from the Nikon Transfer or Nikon ViewNX menu.) You also may be able to use the built-in software updater, depending on the age of your software. Open the program and choose Help⇨Check for Updates to give it a go.

One final software-related point: You can use Nikon ViewNX 2 to download your photos and still use any photo-editing or image-management software you prefer. And to do your editing, you don't need to re-download photos — after you transfer photos to your computer, you can access them from any program, just as you can any file that you put on your system. With some programs, you must first take the step of *importing* the photo files, which enables the program to build thumbnails and, in some cases, working copies of your pictures, however.

With that lengthy preamble out of the way, the following steps walk you through the process of downloading via Nikon ViewNX 2:

1. **Attach your camera or insert a memory card into your card reader, as outlined in the first part of this chapter.**

   Depending on what software you have installed on your system, you may see a dialog box asking you how to download your photos. If the window that appears is the Nikon Transfer 2 window, shown in Figure 6-6, skip to Step 3. *Nikon Transfer 2* is the picture-downloading utility built into ViewNX 2.

   Similarly, if you see a Windows dialog box that contains the Nikon Transfer 2 option, as shown in Figure 6-5, click that option and skip to Step 3.

   If nothing happens, don't worry — just travel to Step 2, which shows you how to launch the Nikon Transfer 2 software if it didn't appear automatically.

2. **Launch Nikon Transfer 2, if it isn't already open.**

   To access the transfer tool, open Nikon ViewNX 2 and then choose File⇨Launch Transfer or click the Transfer button at the top of the window. The window shown in Figure 6-6 appears.

Click to display/hide options   Select All   Select Protected

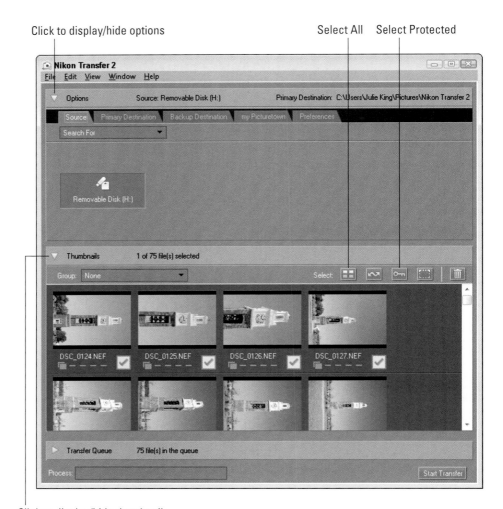

Click to display/hide thumbnails

Figure 6-6: Select the check boxes of the images that you want to download.

3. Display the Source tab to view thumbnails of your pictures, as shown in the figure.

Don't see any tabs? Click the little Options triangle, located near the top-left corner of the window and labeled in Figure 6-6, to display them. Then click the Source tab. The icon representing your camera or memory card should be selected, as shown in the figure. If not, click the icon.

Thumbnails of your images appear in the bottom half of the dialog box. If you don't see the thumbnails, click the arrow labeled in Figure 6-6 to open the thumbnails area.

4. Select the images that you want to download.

A check mark in the little box under a thumbnail tells the program that you want to download the image. Click the box to toggle the check mark on and off.

If you used the in-camera function to protect pictures (see Chapter 5), you can select just those images by clicking the Select Protected icon, labeled in Figure 6-6. To select all images on the card, click the Select All icon instead.

5. Click the Primary Destination tab at the top of the window.

When you click the tab, the top of the transfer window offers options that enable you to specify where and how you want the images to be stored on your computer. Figure 6-7 offers a look.

Choose a storage folder

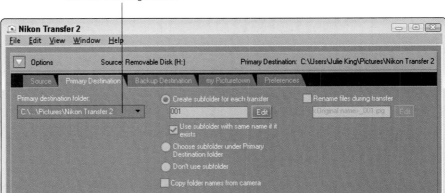

Figure 6-7: Specify the folder where you want to put the downloaded images.

6. Choose the folder where you want to store the images from the Primary Destination Folder drop-down list.

The list is labeled in Figure 6-7. If the folder you want to use isn't in the list, open the drop-down list, choose Browse from the bottom of the list, and then track down the folder and select it.

By default, the program puts images in a Nikon Transfer folder, which is housed inside the My Pictures folder in Windows XP and Pictures in Windows 7, Windows Vista, and on a Mac. That My Pictures or Pictures folder is housed inside a folder that your system creates automatically for each registered user of the computer.

You don't have to stick with this default location — you can put your pictures anywhere you please. But because most photo programs automatically look for pictures in these standard folders, putting your pictures there simplifies things a little down the road. *Note:* You can always move your pictures into other folders after you download them if needed, too.

7. **Specify whether you want the pictures to be placed inside a new subfolder.**

   If you select the Create Subfolder for Each Transfer option, the program creates a new folder inside the storage folder you selected in Step 6. Then it puts all the pictures from the current download session into that new subfolder. You can either use the numerical subfolder name the program suggests or click the Edit button to set up your own naming system. You might find it helpful to go with a folder name that includes the date that the batch of photos was taken, for example. (You can reorganize your pictures into this type of setup after download, however.) If you created custom folders on the camera memory card, an option you can explore in Chapter 11, select the Copy Folder Names from Camera check box to use those folder names instead.

8. **Tell the program whether you want to rename the picture files during the download process.**

   If you do, select the Rename Files during Transfer check box. Then click the Edit button to display a dialog box where you can set up your new filenaming scheme. Click OK after you do so to close the dialog box.

9. **Click the Preferences tab to set the rest of the transfer options.**

   The tab shown in Figure 6-8 takes over the top of the program window. Here you find a number of options that enable you to control how the program operates, as follows:

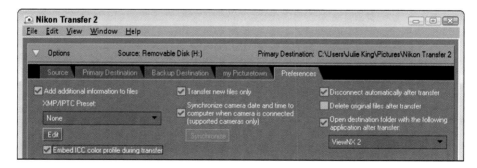

Figure 6-8: Control other aspects of the program's behavior via the Preferences tab.

- *Add Additional Information to Files:* Through this option, you can embed *XMP/IPTC* data in the file. *IPTC* refers to text data that press photographers are often required to tag onto their picture files, such as captions and copyright information. *XMP* refers to a data format developed by Adobe to enable that kind of data to be added to the file. IPTC stands for International Press Telecommunications Council; XMP stands for Extensible Metadata Platform.

  Click the Edit button beneath the option to create and store a preset that contains the data you want to add. On your next visit to the dialog box, you can choose the preset from the drop-down list above the Edit button.

  You also can tag a file with text comments in the camera, using the Comment feature that I cover in Chapter 11.

- *Embed ICC Color Profile during Transfer:* This option relates to the Color Space option on the Shooting menu. Nikon recommends that you enable this option if you capture images using the Adobe RGB color space instead of the default, sRGB space. Otherwise, some photo programs may simply assume that the files are in the sRGB space.

- *Transfer New Files Only:* This option, when selected, ensures that you don't waste time downloading images that you've already transferred but are still on the memory card.

- *Synchronize Camera Date and Time . . . :* If you connect your camera to the computer via USB cable — and again, the cable is an optional purchase — selecting this option tells the camera to reset its internal clock to match the date and time of the computer.

- *Disconnect Automatically after Transfer:* Choose this option to tell the transfer tool to shut itself down automatically when the download is complete.

- *Delete Original Files after Transfer:* Turn off this option, as shown in Figure 6-8. Otherwise, your pictures are automatically erased from your memory card when the transfer is complete. Always make sure the pictures really made it to the computer before you delete them from your memory card. (See Chapter 5 to find out how to use the Delete function on your camera.)

- *Open Destination Folder with the Following Application after Transfer:* By default, Nikon ViewNX 2 starts automatically at the end of the download process if it isn't already open. If you want to use a program other than ViewNX 2 to view and edit your photos, open the drop-down list, choose Browse, and select the program from the dialog box that appears. Click OK after doing so.

Your choices remain in force for any subsequent download sessions, so you don't have to revisit this tab unless you want the program to behave differently.

10. **When you're ready to start the download, click the Start Transfer button.**

It's located in the lower-right corner of the program window. (Refer to Figure 6-6.) After you click the button, the Process bar in the lower-left corner indicates how the transfer is progressing. Again, what happens when the transfer completely depends on the choices you made in Step 9; by default, Nikon Transfer closes, and ViewNX 2 opens, automatically displaying the folder that contains your just-downloaded images.

Processing Raw (NEF) Files

Chapter 2 introduces you to the Raw file format. The advantage of capturing Raw files, or NEF files on Nikon cameras, is that you make the decisions about how to translate the original picture data into an actual photograph. You can specify attributes such as color intensity, image sharpening, contrast, and so on — which are all handled automatically by the camera if you use its other file format, JPEG. You take these steps by using a software tool known as a *Raw converter*.

The bad news: Until you convert your NEF files into a standard file format, you can't share them online or print them from most programs other than Nikon ViewNX 2. You also can't get prints from most retail outlets or open them in many photo-editing programs.

To process your D3100 NEF files, you have the following options:

- **Use the in-camera processing feature.** Through the Retouch menu, you can process your Raw images right in the camera. You can specify only limited image attributes (color, sharpness, and so on), and you can save the processed files only in the JPEG format, but still, having this option is a nice feature.

- **Process and convert in ViewNX 2.** ViewNX 2 also offers a Raw processing feature. Again, the controls for setting picture characteristics are a little limited, but you can save the adjusted files in either the JPEG or TIFF format.

- **Use Nikon Capture NX 2 or a third-party Raw conversion tool.** For the most control over your Raw images, you need to open up your wallet and invest in a program that offers a truly capable converter. See the first part of this chapter for a review of Capture NX 2 as well as some other programs with good Raw converters.

The next two sections show you how to convert Raw files using your camera and ViewNX 2. If you opt for a third-party conversion tool, check the program's Help system for details on how to use the various controls, which vary from program to program.

Processing Raw images in the camera

Through the NEF (RAW) Processing option on the Retouch menu, you can convert Raw files right in the camera — no computer or other software required. I want to share two reservations about this option, however:

✔ First, you can save your processed files only in the JPEG format. As discussed in Chapter 2, that format results in some quality loss because of the file compression that JPEG applies. You can choose the level of JPEG compression you want to apply during Raw processing; you can create a JPEG Fine, Normal, or Basic file. Each of those settings produces the same quality that you get when you shoot new photos in the JPEG format and select Fine, Normal, or Basic from the Image Quality menu.

Chapter 2 details the JPEG options, but, long story short, choose Fine for the best JPEG quality. And if you want to produce the absolute best quality from your Raw images, use a software solution and save your processed file in the TIFF format instead. TIFF is a *lossless* format, which means that all original image quality is retained. TIFF is the publishing industry standard format, so almost every photo program can open TIFF files.

✔ You can make adjustments to exposure, color, and a few other options as part of the in-camera Raw conversion process. Evaluating the effects of your adjustments on the camera monitor can be difficult because of the size of the display compared to your computer monitor. So for really tricky images, you may want to forgo in-camera conversion and do the job on your computer, where you can get a better — and bigger — view of things. If you do go the in-camera route, make sure that the monitor brightness is set to its default position so that you aren't misled by the display. (Chapter 1 shows you how to adjust monitor brightness.)

That said, in-camera Raw processing offers a quick and convenient solution when you need JPEG copies of your Raw images for immediate online sharing — JPEG is the standard format for online use — or to share with someone who doesn't have photo software that can handle Raw images. Follow these steps to get the job done:

1. Press the Playback button to switch to playback mode.

2. **Display the picture you want to process in the single-image (full-frame) view.**

   If necessary, you can shift from thumbnails view to single-image view by just pressing OK. Chapter 5 has more playback details.

3. **Press the OK button.**

   The Retouch menu then appears atop your photo, as shown in Figure 6-9.

4. **Use the Multi Selector to scroll to the NEF (RAW) Processing option, as shown in Figure 6-9.**

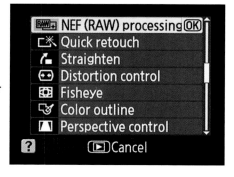

Figure 6-9: In single-image playback mode, press OK to display the Retouch menu over your photo.

5. **Press OK to display your processing options, as shown in Figure 6-10.**

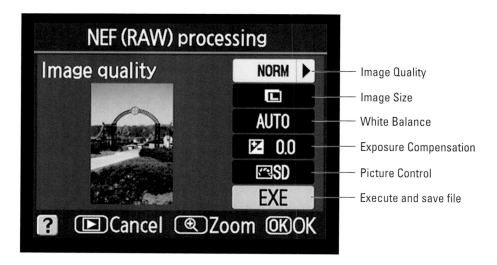

Figure 6-10: Specify Raw conversion settings here.

This screen is command central for specifying what settings you want the camera to use when creating the JPEG version of your Raw image.

6. **Set the conversion options.**

   Along the right side of the screen, you see a vertical column offering five conversion options, which I labeled in Figure 6-10. To establish the setting for an option, highlight it and then press the Multi Selector right. You then see the available settings for the option. For example, if you choose the Exposure Compensation option, you see the screen shown in

Figure 6-11. Use the Multi Selector to highlight the setting you want to use and press OK to return to the main Raw conversion screen.

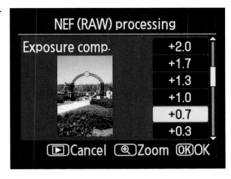

Rather than detailing all the options here, the following list points you to the chapter where you can explore the settings available for each:

Figure 6-11: Select the setting you want to use and press OK.

- *Image Quality:* See the Chapter 2 section related to the JPEG quality settings for details on this option. Choose Fine to retain maximum picture quality.

- *Image Size:* Chapter 2 explains this one, too. Choose Large to retain all the original image pixels.

- *White Balance:* Check out Chapter 8 for details about White Balance options, which affect picture colors.

- *Exposure Compensation:* With this option, you can adjust image brightness by applying Exposure Compensation, a feature that I cover in Chapter 7. For example, I brightened the sample image in Figure 6-11 by setting the value to +0.7.

- *Picture Control:* This option enables you to adjust color, contrast, and image sharpness. For a review of the available settings, see the last part of Chapter 8.

7. **When you finish setting all the conversion options, highlight EXE on the main conversion screen. (Refer to Figure 6-10.) Then press OK.**

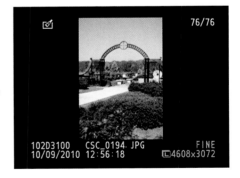

The camera records a JPEG copy of your Raw file and displays the copy in the monitor. To remind you that the image was created with the help of the Retouch menu, the top-left corner of the display sports the little Retouch icon, and the filename of the image begins with CSC rather than the usual DSC, as shown in

Figure 6-12: Filenames of photos you process using the Retouch menu start with CSC.

Figure 6-12. See Chapter 5 for details about filenaming conventions used by the D3100.

Processing Raw files in ViewNX 2

In ViewNX 2, you can convert your Raw files to the JPEG format or, for top picture quality, to the TIFF format. Although the ViewNX 2 converter isn't as full-featured as the ones in Nikon Capture NX 2 and some other photo-editing programs, it does enable you to make some adjustments to your Raw images. Follow these steps to try it out.

1. **Open ViewNX 2 and click the thumbnail of the image that you want to process.**

   You may want to set the program to Image Viewer mode, as shown in Figure 6-13, so that you can see a larger preview of your image. Just choose View⏎Image Viewer to switch to this display mode. To give the photo even more room, also choose Window⏎Filmstrip to turn off the row of thumbnails that normally appears at the bottom of the window.

2. **Display the Adjustments panel on the right side of the program window.**

   I labeled the panel in Figure 6-13. You show and hide this panel and the Metadata panel by clicking the triangle on the far right side of the window. You can then display and collapse the individual panels by clicking the triangles to the left of their names. (I labeled the triangle in the figure.) To allow the maximum space for the Raw conversion adjustments, collapse the Metadata panel, as shown in the figure. If necessary, drag the vertical bar between the image window and the Adjustments panel to adjust the width of the panel.

3. **To display all available image settings, choose All from the Adjustments drop-down list at the top of the panel, as shown in the figure.**

   Unless you use a large monitor, you may need to use the scroll bar on the right side of the panel to scroll the display to see all the options.

4. **Use the panel controls to adjust your image.**

   The preview you see in the image window reflects the default conversion settings chosen by Nikon. But you can play with any of the settings as you see fit. If you need help understanding any of the options, open the built-in help system (via the Help menu), where you can find descriptions of how each adjustment affects your image.

   To return to the original image settings, click the Reset button at the bottom of the panel, labeled in Figure 6-13.

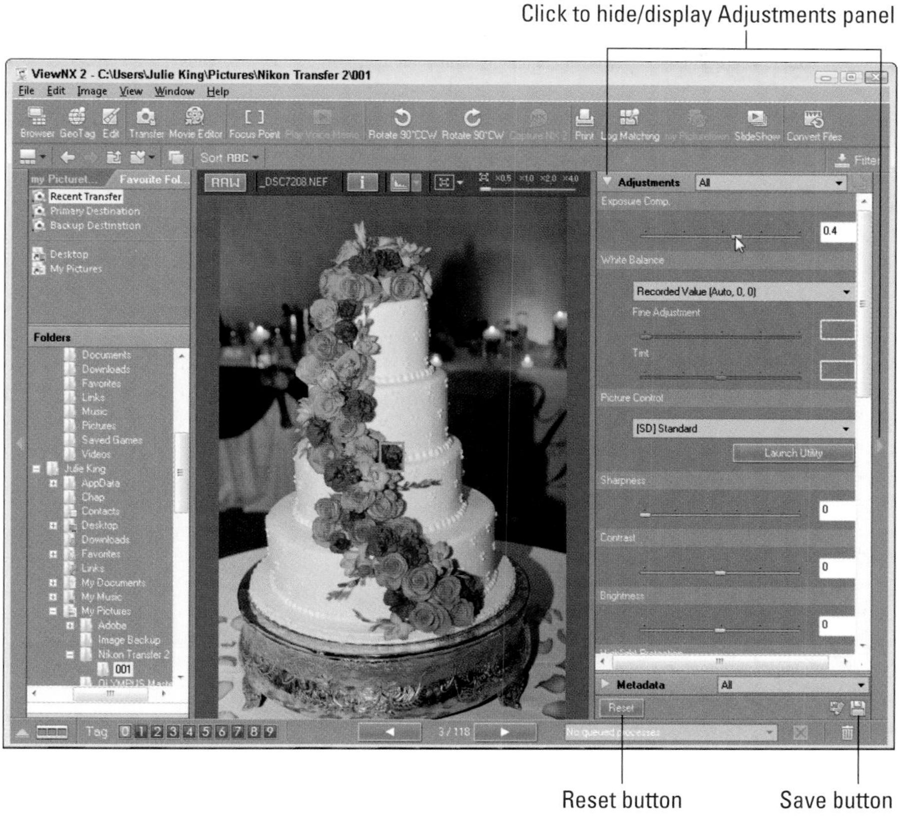

Click to hide/display Adjustments panel

Reset button   Save button

Figure 6-13: Display the Adjustments panel to tweak Raw images before conversion.

5. Click the Save button at the bottom of the panel (refer to Figure 6-13).

This step stores your conversion settings as part of the image file but doesn't actually create your JPEG or TIFF copy of the photo.

6. To save the processed file, choose File⇨Convert Files.

Or just click the Convert Files button on the toolbar at the top of the program window. Either way, you see the Convert Files dialog box, as shown in Figure 6-14.

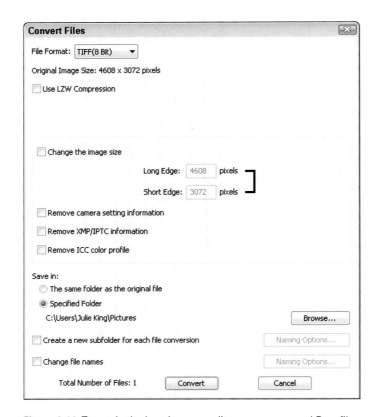

Figure 6-14: To retain the best image quality, save processed Raw files in the TIFF format.

7. Select TIFF (8 Bit) from the File Format drop-down list.

A *bit* is a unit of computer data; the more bits you have, the more colors your image can contain. Although you can create 16-bit TIFF files in the converter, many photo-editing programs either can't open them or limit you to a few editing tools, so I suggest you stick with the standard, 8-bit image option. Your image will contain more than enough colors, and you'll avoid potential conflicts caused by so-called *high-bit* images.

Don't select JPEG; the JPEG format applies *lossy compression,* thereby sacrificing some image quality. If you need a JPEG copy of your processed Raw image for online sharing, you can easily create one from your TIFF version by following the steps laid out near the end of this chapter.

8. Deselect the Use LZW Compression option, as shown in the figure.

Although LZW Compression reduces the file size somewhat and does not cause any quality loss, some programs can't open files that were saved with this option enabled. So turn it off.

9. **Deselect the Change the Image Size check box.**

   This step ensures that you retain all the original pixels in your image, which gives you the most flexibility in terms of generating quality prints at large sizes. For details on this issue, check out Chapter 2.

10. **Deselect each of the three Remove check boxes.**

    If you select the check boxes, you strip image *metadata* — the extra text data that's stored by the camera — from the file. Unless you have some specific reason to do so, clear all three check boxes so that you can continue to access the metadata when you view your processed image in programs that know how to display metadata.

    The first check box relates to data that you can view on the Metadata tab in ViewNX; the first section of the chapter gives you the lowdown. The second box refers to the XMP/IPTC data that you can embed during file transfer; see the section "Downloading photos with Nikon ViewNX 2" for a discussion of that issue. The ICC profile item refers to the image *color space,* which is either sRGB or Adobe RGB on your D3100. Chapter 8 explains the difference.

11. **Select a storage location for the processed TIFF file.**

    You do this in the Save In area of the dialog box. Select the top option to save your processed file in the same folder as the original Raw file. Or, to put the file in a different folder, click the Specified Folder button. The name of the currently selected alternative folder appears below the button, as shown in Figure 6-14. You can change the storage destination by clicking the Browse button and then selecting the drive and folder where you want to put the file.

    By selecting the Create a New Subfolder for Each File Conversion check box, you can put your TIFF file into a separate folder within the destination folder. If you select the box, click the Naming Options button and then specify how you want to name the subfolder.

12. **Specify whether you want to give the processed TIFF a different file-name from the original Raw image.**

    To do so, select the Change File Names check box and then click the Naming Options button and enter the name you want to use.

    If you don't change the filename, the program gives the file the same name as the original Raw file. But you don't overwrite that Raw file because you're storing the copy in a different file format (TIFF). In Windows, the filename of the processed TIFF image has the three-letter extension TIF.

13. **Click the Convert button.**

    A window appears to show you the progress of the conversion process. When the window disappears, your TIFF image appears in the storage location you selected in Step 11.

One neat thing about working with Raw images is that you can easily create as many variations of your photo as you want. For example, you might choose one set of options when processing your Raw file the first time and then use an entirely different set to create another version of the photo. You could create one image in full color, perhaps, and then open the Raw file again and this time launch the Picture Control Utility and create a sepia version of the image.

Planning for Perfect Prints

Images from your D3100 can produce dynamic prints, and getting those prints made is easy and economical, thanks to an abundance of digital printing services in stores and online. For home printing, today's printers are better and less expensive than ever, too. That said, getting the best prints from your picture files requires a little bit of knowledge and prep work on your part, whether you decide to do the job yourself or use a retail lab. To that end, the next three sections offer tips to help you avoid the most common causes of printing problems.

Check the pixel count before you print

Resolution — the number of pixels in your digital image — plays a huge role in how large you can print your photos and still maintain good picture quality. You can get the complete story on resolution in Chapter 2, but here's a quick recap as it relates to printing:

- **Choose the right resolution before you shoot:** Set resolution via the Image Size option, found on the Shooting menu, or via the Quick Settings display.

  You must select the Quality option *before* you capture an image, which means that you need some idea of the ultimate print size before you shoot. When you do the resolution math, remember to take any cropping you plan to do into account.

- **Aim for a minimum of 200 pixels per inch (ppi):** You'll get a wide range of recommendations on this issue, even among professionals. But in general, if you aim for a resolution in the neighborhood of 200 ppi, you should be pleased with your results. If you want a 4-x-6-inch print, for example, you need at least 800 x 1200 pixels.

  Depending on your printer, you may get even better results at a slightly lower resolution. On the other hand, some printers do their best work when fed 300 ppi, and a few request 360 ppi as the optimum resolution. However, using a resolution higher than that typically doesn't produce any better prints.

Unfortunately, because most printer manuals don't bother to tell you what image resolution produces the best results, finding the right pixel level is a matter of experimentation. (Don't confuse *ppi* with the manual's statements related to the printer's dpi. *Dots per inch (dpi)* refers to the number of dots of color the printer can lay down per inch; many printers use multiple dots to reproduce one image pixel.)

If you're printing photos at a retail kiosk or at an online site, the software you use to order prints should determine the resolution of your files and then suggest appropriate print sizes. If you're printing on a home printer, though, you need to be the resolution cop.

What do you do if you don't have enough pixels for the print size you have in mind? You have the following two choices, neither of which provides a good outcome:

- **Keep the existing pixel count and accept lowered photo quality.** In this case, the pixels simply get bigger to fill the requested print size. When pixels grow too large, they produce a defect known as *pixelation:* The picture starts to appear jagged, or stairstepped, along curved or oblique lines. Or, at worst, your eye can make out the individual pixels and your photo begins to look more like a mosaic than, well, like a photograph.

- **Add more pixels and accept lowered photo quality.** In some photo programs, you can add pixels to an image (the technical term for this process is *resampling*). Some other photo programs even resample the photo automatically for you, depending on the print settings you choose.

   Although adding pixels might sound like a good option, it actually doesn't help in the long run. You're asking the software to make up photo information out of thin air, and the resulting image usually looks worse than the original. You don't see pixelation, but details turn muddy, giving the image a blurry, poorly rendered appearance.

Just to hammer home the point and remind you again of the impact of resolution picture quality, Figures 6-15 through 6-17 show you the same image as it appears at 300 ppi (the resolution required by the publisher of this book), at 50 ppi and then resampled from 50 ppi to 300 ppi. As you can see, there's just no way around the rule: If you want the best-quality prints, you need the right pixel count from the get-go.

300 ppi

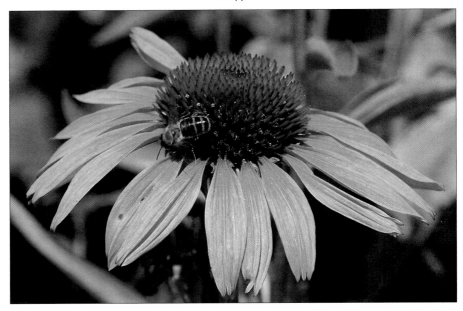

Figure 6-15: A high-quality print depends on a high-resolution original.

50 ppi

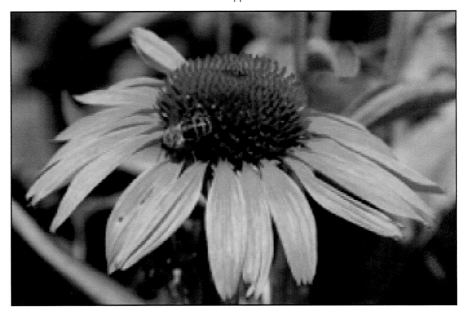

Figure 6-16: At 50 ppi, the image has a jagged, pixelated look.

50 ppi resampled to 300 ppi

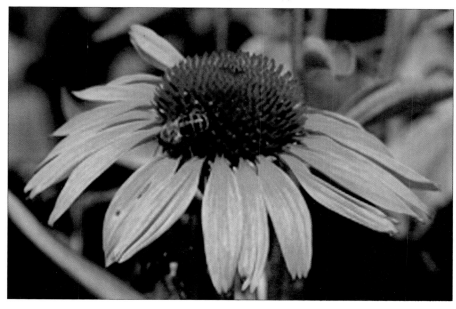

Figure 6-17: Adding pixels in a photo editor doesn't rescue a low-resolution original.

Allow for different print proportions

By default, the D3100 produces images that have a 3:2 aspect ratio, which matches the proportions of a 4-x-6-inch print. To print your photo at other traditional sizes — 5 x 7, 8 x 10, and so on — you need to crop the photo to match those proportions. Alternatively, you can reduce the photo size slightly and leave an empty margin along the edges of the print as needed.

As a point of reference, both images in Figure 6-18 are original, 3:2 images. The red outlines indicate how much of the original can fit within a 5-x-7-inch frame and an 8-x-10-inch frame, respectively.

Chapter 10 shows you how to crop your image using the Trim option on the Retouch menu. You also can usually crop your photo using the software provided at online printing sites and at retail print kiosks. If you plan to simply drop off your memory card for printing at a lab, be sure to find out whether the printer automatically crops the image without your input. If so, use your photo software to crop the photo, save the cropped image to your memory card, and deliver that version of the file to the printer.

5 x 7   8 x 10

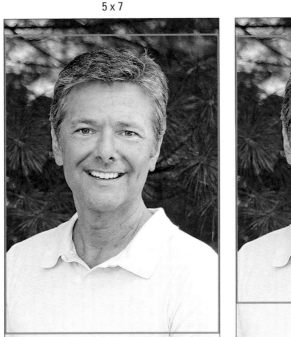
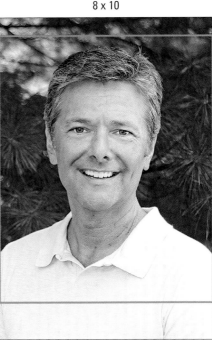

Figure 6-18: Composing your shots with a little head room enables you to crop to different frame sizes.

To allow yourself some printing flexibility, leave at least a little margin of background around your subject when you shoot (refer to Figure 6-18). That way, you don't clip off the edges of the subject, no matter what print size you choose. (Some people refer to this margin padding as *head room,* especially when describing portrait composition.)

Get print and monitor colors in sync

Ah, your photo colors look perfect on your computer monitor. But when you print the picture, the image is too red or too green or has another nasty color tint. This problem, which is probably the most prevalent printing issue, can occur because of any or all the following factors:

- ✔ **Your monitor needs to be calibrated.** When print colors don't match the ones you see on your monitor, the most likely culprit is the monitor, not the printer. If the monitor isn't accurately calibrated, the colors it displays aren't a true reflection of your image colors. The same caveat applies to monitor brightness: You can't accurately gauge the exposure of a photo if the brightness of the monitor is cranked way up or down. It's worth noting that many of today's new monitors are very bright, providing ideal conditions for Web browsing and watching movies but not necessarily for photo editing. So you may need to turn the brightness way, way down to get to a true indication of image exposure.

To ensure that your monitor displays photos on a neutral canvas, you can start with a software-based *calibration utility,* which is just a small program that guides you through the process of adjusting your monitor. The program displays various color swatches and other graphics and then asks you to provide feedback about the colors you see onscreen.

If you use a Mac, its operating system (OS) offers a built-in calibration utility, the Display Calibrator Assistant; Windows 7 offers a similar tool: Display Color Calibration. You also can find free calibration software for both Mac and Windows systems online; just enter the term *free monitor calibration software* into your favorite search engine.

Software-based tools, though, depend on your eyes to make decisions during the calibration process. For a more reliable calibration, you may want to invest in a hardware solution, such as the Huey Pro (about $100, www.pantone.com) or the Spyder3Express (about $90, www.datacolor.com). These products use a device known as a *colorimeter* to accurately measure display colors.

Whichever route you take, the calibration process produces a monitor *profile,* which is simply a data file that tells your computer how to adjust the display to compensate for any monitor color casts or brightness and contrast issues. Your Windows or Mac operating system loads this file automatically when you start your computer. Your only responsibility is to perform the calibration every month or so because monitor colors drift over time.

✔ **One of your printer cartridges is empty or clogged.** If your prints look great one day but are way off the next, the number-one suspect is an empty ink cartridge or a clogged print nozzle or head. Check your manual to find out how to perform the necessary maintenance to keep the nozzles or print heads in good shape.

If black-and-white prints have a color tint, a logical assumption is that your black ink cartridge is to blame, if your printer has one. But the truth is that images from a printer that doesn't use multiple black or gray cartridges always have a slight color tint. Why? Because to create gray, the printer instead has to mix yellow, magenta, and cyan in perfectly equal amounts, and that's a difficult feat for the typical inkjet printer to pull off. If your black-and-white prints have a strong color tint, however, a color cartridge might be empty, and replacing it may help somewhat. Long story short: Unless your printer is marketed for producing good black-and-white prints, you'll probably save yourself some grief by simply having your black-and-whites printed at a retail lab.

When you buy replacement ink, by the way, keep in mind that third-party brands (though perhaps cheaper) may not deliver the same performance as cartridges from your printer manufacturer. A lot of science goes into getting ink formulas to mesh with the printer's ink-delivery system, and the printer manufacturer obviously knows most about that delivery system.

✓ **You chose the wrong paper setting in your printer software.** When you set up a print job, be sure to select the right setting from the paper type option — glossy or matte, for example. This setting affects the way the printer lays down ink on the paper.

✓ **Your photo paper is low quality.** Sad but true: Cheap, store-brand photo papers usually don't render colors as well as the higher-priced, name-brand papers. For best results, try papers from your printer manufacturer; again, those papers are engineered to provide top performance with the printer's specific inks and ink-delivery system.

Some paper manufacturers, especially those that sell fine-art papers, offer downloadable *printer profiles,* which are simply little bits of software that tell your printer how to manage color for the paper. Refer to the manufacturer's Web site for information on how to install and use the profiles. And note that a profile mismatch can also cause incorrect colors in your prints, including the color tint in black-and-white prints alluded to earlier.

✓ **Your printer and photo software fight over color management duties.** Some photo programs offer *color management* tools, which enable you to control how colors are handled as an image passes from camera to monitor to printer. Most printer software also offers color management features. The problem is, if you enable color management controls in both your photo software and printer software, you can create conflicts that lead to wacky colors. Check your photo software and printer manuals for color management options and ways to turn them on and off.

Even if all the aforementioned issues are resolved, however, don't expect perfect color matching between printer and monitor. Printers simply can't reproduce the entire spectrum of colors that a monitor can display. In addition, monitor colors always appear brighter because they are, after all, generated with light.

Finally, be sure to evaluate print colors and monitor colors in the same ambient light — daylight, office light, whatever — because that light source has its own influence on the colors you see. Also allow your prints to dry for 15 minutes or so before you make any final judgments.

DPOF, PictBridge, and computerless printing

The D3100 offers two features that enable you to print directly from your camera or a memory card assuming that your printer offers the required options.

One of the direct-printing features is *Digital Print Order Format,* or *DPOF.* With this option, accessed via the Print Set (DPOF) option on the Playback menu, you select pictures from your memory card to print and then specify how many copies you want of each image. Then, if your photo printer has a Secure Digital (SD) memory card slot (or SDHC/SDXC slots, if you use these new, high-capacity cards) and supports DPOF, you just pop the memory card into that slot. The printer reads your "print order" and outputs just the requested copies of your selected images. (You use the printer's own controls to set paper size, print orientation, and other print settings.)

A second direct-printing feature, *PictBridge,* works a little differently. If you have a PictBridge-enabled photo printer, you can connect the camera to the printer by using an optional USB cable. (You use the same cable as for picture downloads.) A PictBridge interface appears on the camera monitor, and you use the camera controls to select the pictures you want to print. With PictBridge, you specify additional print options from the camera, such as page size and whether to print a border around the photo.

Both DPOF and PictBridge are especially useful when you need fast printing. For example, if you shoot pictures at a party and want to deliver prints to guests before they go home, DPOF offers a quicker option than firing up your computer, downloading pictures, and so on. And, if you invest in one of the tiny portable photo printers on the market today, you can easily make prints away from your home or office. You can take both your portable printer and camera along to your regional sales meeting, for example.

If you're interested in exploring either printing feature, your camera manual provides complete details.

Preparing Pictures for E-Mail and Online Sharing

How many times have you received an e-mail message that looks like the one in Figure 6-19? Some well-meaning friend or relative sent you a digital photo that's so large you can't to view the whole thing on your monitor.

The problem is that computer monitors can display only a limited number of pixels. The exact number depends on the monitor's resolution setting and the capabilities of the computer's video card, but suffice it to say that the average photo from one of today's digital cameras has a pixel count in excess of what the monitor can handle.

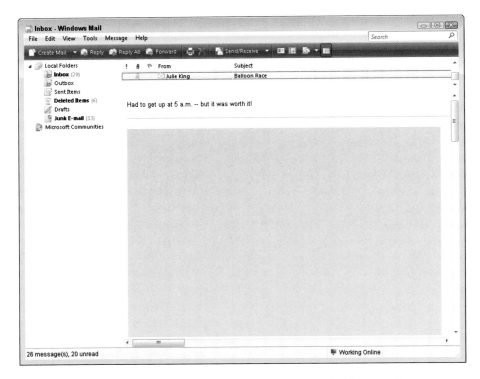

Figure 6-19: The attached image has too many pixels to be viewed without scrolling.

In general, a good rule is to limit a photo to no more than 640 pixels at its longest dimension. That ensures that people can view your entire picture without scrolling, as in Figure 6-20. This image measures 640 x 428 pixels.

This size recommendation means that even if you shoot at your D3100's lowest Image Size setting (2304 x 1536), you wind up with lots more pixels than you need for onscreen viewing. Some new e-mail programs have a photo-upload feature that creates a temporary low-res version for you, but if not, creating your own copy is easy. (Details later.) If you're posting to an online photo-sharing site, you may be able to upload all your original pixels, but many sites have resolution limits.

In addition to resizing high-resolution images, check their file types; if the photos are in the Raw (NEF) or TIFF format, you need to create a JPEG copy for online use. Web browsers and e-mail programs can't display Raw or TIFF files.

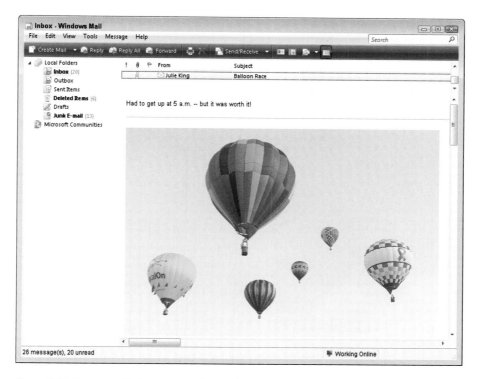

Figure 6-20: Keep e-mail pictures to no larger than 640 pixels wide or tall.

You can tackle both bits of photo prep in the following ways:

- **Use ViewNX 2:** Just choose the Convert Files command, found on the File menu. When the Convert Files dialog box appears, set things up as follows:

  - *Select JPEG as the file format.* Make your choice from the File Format drop-down list, as shown in Figure 6-21.

  - *Set the picture quality level.* Use the Quality slider, labeled in the figure, to set the picture quality, which is controlled by how much JPEG compression is applied when the file is saved. For best quality, drag the slider all the way to the right, but remember the tradeoff: As you raise the quality, less compression occurs, which results in a larger file size. (See Chapter 2 for more information about JPEG compression.)

  - *Set the image size (number of pixels):* To resize the photo, select the Change the Image Size check box and then enter a value (in pixels) for the longest dimension of the photo. The program automatically fills in the other value.

For pictures that you want to share online, also select all three of the Remove check boxes, as shown in the figure, to eliminate adding to file sizes unnecessarily.

The rest of the options work just as they do during Raw conversion; refer to "Processing Raw files in ViewNX 2," earlier in this chapter, for details.

✓ **Use the in-camera tools:** Use the Small Picture option on the Retouch menu to create a small JPEG copy of either a JPEG or Raw original, as outlined in the next two sections.

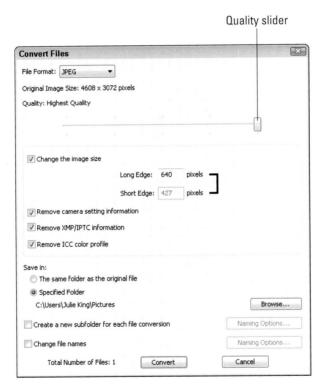

Figure 6-21: In ViewNX 2, select the Convert Files option to create a JPEG version of a Raw or TIFF photo.

One last point about onscreen images: Remember that pixel count has *absolutely no effect* on the quality of pictures displayed onscreen. Pixel count determines only the size at which your images are displayed.

Resizing a single photo

The in-camera resizing tool works on both JPEG and Raw images. If you apply it directly to a Raw image, though, you lose the chance to adjust the image through the camera's Raw conversion tool. So you may prefer to do the conversion first, which creates a JPEG copy at the original size, and then create a small copy of that JPEG image.

Either way, to create a small copy of just one image, take these steps:

1. **Press the Playback button to set your camera to playback mode.**

2. **Display the picture in single-image view.**

   If the monitor currently displays multiple thumbnails, just press OK to switch to single-image view.

3. **Press OK to display the Retouch menu over your image, as shown on the left in Figure 6-22.**

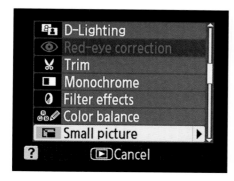
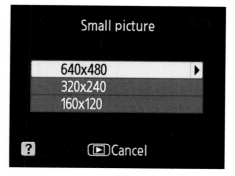

Figure 6-22: The Small Picture feature creates a low-resolution, e-mail–friendly copy of a photo.

4. **Highlight Small Picture and press OK or press the Multi Selector right.**

   You see the screen shown on the right in the figure. You can choose from three size options (stated in pixels) for your small copy.

5. **Highlight the size you want to use for your copy.**

   For pictures that you plan to send via e-mail, choose either 640 x 480 or 320 x 240 pixels unless the recipient is connected to the Internet via a very slow, dial-up modem connection. In that case, you may want to go one step down, to 160 x 120 pixels. (The display size of the picture may be quite small at that setting however, depending on the resolution of the monitor on which the picture is viewed.)

REMEMBER

If you're a math lover, you may have noticed that all the size options create pictures that have an aspect ratio of 4:3, while your original images have an aspect ratio of 3:2. The camera trims the small-copy image as needed to fit the 4:3 proportions. Unfortunately, you don't have any input over what portion of the image is cropped away.

6. **Press OK or press the Multi Selector right.**

A screen appears, asking you to confirm that you want to create a small copy.

7. **Highlight Yes and press OK.**

The camera duplicates the selected image and *downsamples* (eliminates pixels from) the copy to achieve the size you specified in Step 5. Your original picture file remains untouched.

When you view your small-size copies on the camera monitor, they appear surrounded by a gray border, as shown in Figure 6-23. A tiny Retouch icon appears on the display as well. Note that you can't zoom in to magnify the view of small-size copies as you can your original images.

Pictures that you create using the Small Picture feature are given filenames that start with the letters SSC. The camera automatically assigns a file number. (The number is different from that of your original file, unfortunately.)

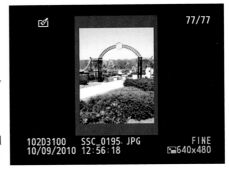

Figure 6-23: The gray border indicates a small-size copy.

Resizing a batch of images

TIP

If you want to create small copies of several photos on your memory card, you can save time by using the following alternative in-camera resizing process. (As with the steps outlined in the preceding section, these steps work with both JPEG and Raw files.)

1. **Press the Menu button and then display the Retouch menu.**

2. **Select the Small Picture option, as shown in Figure 6-24, and press OK.**

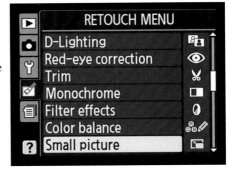

Figure 6-24: Start directly from the Retouch menu to resize a bunch of pictures at the same time.

You see the screen shown on the left in Figure 6-25.

3. **Select Choose Size to display the screen shown on the left in Figure 6-25.**

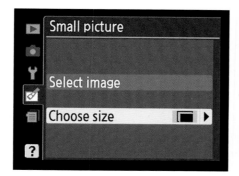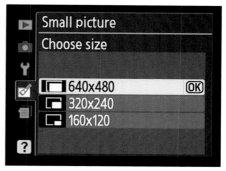

Figure 6-25: You can choose from these three sizes for your small copy.

4. **Highlight the size you want to use and press OK.**

   You return to the Small Picture screen (left screen in Figure 6-25).

5. **Choose Select Image and press OK to display thumbnails of all your pictures, as shown in Figure 6-26.**

Resize icon

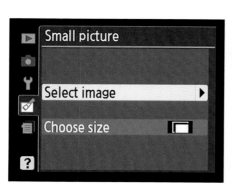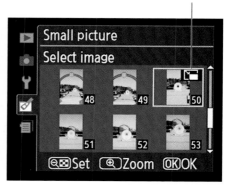

Figure 6-26: Press the Zoom Out button to tag a picture for resizing.

6. **Move the yellow highlight box over a thumbnail and press the Zoom Out button to "tag" the photo for copying.**

   You see a little icon in the top-right corner of the thumbnail; press the button again to remove the tag if you change your mind.

7. After selecting all your pictures, press OK to display the copy-confirmation screen.

8. Highlight Yes and press OK once more to wrap things up.

Part III
Taking Creative Control

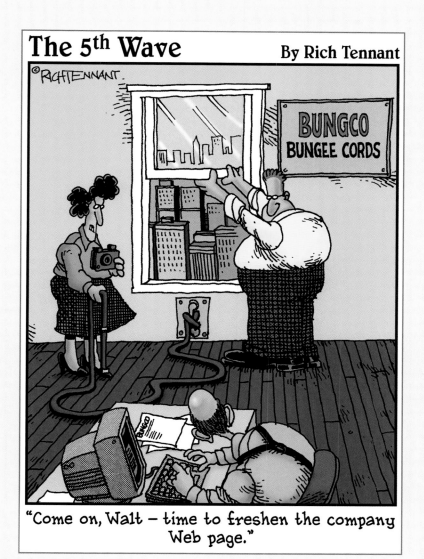

The 5th Wave   By Rich Tennant

BUNGCO
BUNGEE CORDS

"Come on, Walt – time to freshen the company Web page."

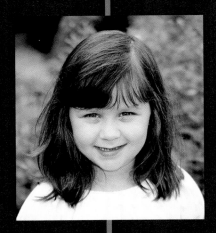

In this part . . .

As nice as it is to be able to set your D3100 to automatic mode and let the camera handle most of the photographic decisions, I encourage you to take creative control and explore the advanced exposure modes (P, S, A, and M). In these modes, you can make your own decisions about the exposure, focus, and color characteristics of your photo, which are key to capturing a compelling image as you see it in your mind's eye. And don't think that you have to be a genius or spend years to be successful — adding just a few simple techniques to your photographic repertoire can make a huge difference in the quality of the pictures you take.

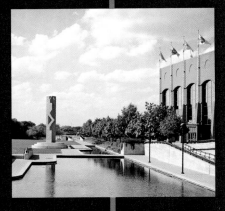

The first two chapters in this part explain everything you need to know to do just that, providing some necessary photography fundamentals as well as details about using the advanced exposure modes. Following that, Chapter 9 helps you draw together all the information presented earlier in the book, summarizing the best camera settings and other tactics to use when capturing portraits, action shots, landscapes, and close-up shots. In short, this part helps you get the most out of your camera, which results in your becoming a better photographer.

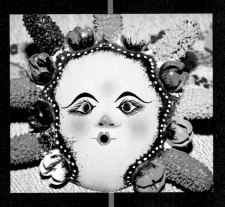

7

Getting Creative with Exposure and Lighting

*U*nderstanding exposure is one of the most intimidating challenges for the new photographer. Discussions of the topic are loaded with technical terms — *aperture, metering, shutter speed, ISO,* and the like. Add the fact that your D3100 offers many exposure controls, all sporting equally foreign names, and it's no wonder that most people throw up their hands and decide that their best option is to simply stick with the Auto exposure mode and let the camera take care of all exposure decisions.

You can, of course, turn out super shots in Auto mode. And I fully relate to the exposure confusion you may be feeling — I've been there. But I can also promise that when you take things nice and slow, digesting just a piece of the exposure pie at a time, the topic is not nearly as complicated as it seems on the surface. And I guarantee that the payoff will be well worth your time and brain energy. You'll not only gain the power to resolve just about any exposure problem, but also discover ways to use exposure to put your own creative stamp on a scene.

To that end, this chapter provides everything you need to know to really exploit your D3100's exposure options, from a primer in exposure science (it's not as bad as it sounds) to explanations of all the camera's exposure controls. In addition, because some controls aren't accessible in the fully automatic exposure modes, this chapter also provides more details about the four advanced modes, P, S, A, and M, first introduced in Chapter 2.

Introducing the Exposure Trio: Aperture, Shutter Speed, and ISO

Any photograph, whether taken with a film or digital camera, is created by focusing light through a lens onto a light-sensitive recording medium. In a film camera, the film negative serves as that medium; in a digital camera, it's the image sensor, which is an array of light-responsive computer chips.

Between the lens and the sensor are two barriers, known as the *aperture* and *shutter,* which together control how much light makes its way to the sensor. The actual design and arrangement of the aperture, shutter, and sensor vary depending on the camera, but Figure 7-1 offers an illustration of the basic concept.

The aperture and shutter, along with a third feature known as *ISO,* determine *exposure* — what most would describe as the picture's overall brightness and contrast. This three-part exposure formula works as follows:

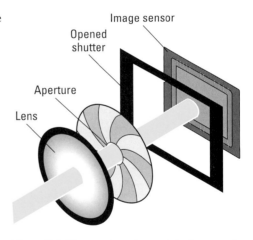

Figure 7-1: The aperture size and shutter speed determine how much light strikes the image sensor.

✔ **Aperture (controls amount of light):** The *aperture* is an adjustable hole in a diaphragm set just behind the lens. By changing the size of the aperture, you control the size of the light beam that can enter the camera. Aperture settings are stated as *f-stop numbers,* or simply *f-stops,* and are expressed with the letter *f* followed by a number: f/2, f/5.6, f/16, and so on. The lower the f-stop number, the larger the aperture, and the more light is permitted into the camera, as illustrated by Figure 7-2.

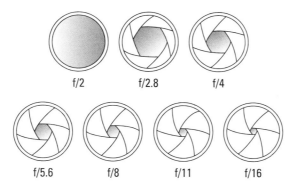

f/2 f/2.8 f/4

f/5.6 f/8 f/11 f/16

Figure 7-2: A lower f-stop number means a larger aperture, allowing more light into the camera.

The range of possible f-stops depends on your lens and, if you use a zoom lens, on the zoom position (focal length) of the lens. When you use the 18–55mm lens that Nikon bundles in the D3100 kit, you can select apertures from f/3.5–f/22 when zoomed all the way out to the shortest focal length, 18mm. When you zoom in to the maximum focal length, 55mm, the aperture range is f/5.6–f/36. (See Chapter 8 for a discussion of focal lengths.)

✔ **Shutter speed (controls duration of light):** Set behind the aperture, the shutter works something like, er, the shutters on a window. When you aren't taking pictures, the camera's shutter stays closed, preventing light from striking the image sensor, just as closed window shutters prevent sunlight from entering a room. When you press the shutter button, the shutter opens briefly to allow light that passes through the aperture to hit the image sensor.

The length of time that the shutter is open is called the *shutter speed* and is measured in seconds: 1/60 second, 1/250 second, 2 seconds, and so on. Shutter speeds on the D3100 range from 30 seconds to 1/4000 second when you shoot without the built-in flash. If you do use the built-in flash, the range is more limited. See the sidebar "In sync: Flash timing and shutter speed," later in this chapter, for information.

Should you want a shutter speed longer than 30 seconds, manual (M) exposure mode also provides a feature called *bulb* exposure. At this setting, the shutter stays open indefinitely as long as you press the shutter button.

✔ **ISO (controls light sensitivity):** ISO, which is a digital function rather than a mechanical structure on the camera, enables you to adjust how responsive the image sensor is to light. The term ISO is a holdover from film days, when an international standards organization rated each film stock according to light sensitivity: ISO 200, ISO 400, ISO 800, and so on.

On a digital camera, the sensor itself doesn't actually get more or less sensitive when you change the ISO — rather, the light "signal" that hits the sensor is either amplified or dampened through electronics wizardry, sort of like how raising the volume on a radio boosts the audio signal. But the upshot is the same as changing to a more light-reactive film stock: A higher ISO means that less light is needed to produce the image, enabling you to use a smaller aperture, faster shutter speed, or both. (In other words, from now on, don't worry about the technicalities and just remember that ISO equals light sensitivity.)

On the D3100, you can select ISO settings ranging from 100 to a whopping 12800. The 12800 setting bears the name Hi 2, while the next lower setting, ISO 6400, is named Hi 1. The special names clue you into the fact that Nikon doesn't suggest using these two highest ISO settings on a regular basis, for reasons you can explore in the upcoming section "ISO affects image noise."

Distilled to its essence, the image-exposure formula is just this simple:

✔ Aperture and shutter speed together determine the quantity of light that strikes the image sensor.

✔ ISO determines how much the sensor reacts to that light and, therefore, how much light you need to expose the picture.

The tricky part of the equation is that aperture, shutter speed, and ISO settings affect your pictures in ways that go *beyond* exposure. You need to be aware of these side effects, explained in the next section, to determine which combination of the three exposure settings will work best for your picture.

Understanding exposure-setting side effects

You can create the same exposure with many combinations of aperture, shutter speed, and ISO. You're limited only by the aperture range allowed by the lens and the shutter speeds and ISO range offered by the camera.

But the settings you select impact your image beyond mere exposure, as follows:

- Aperture affects *depth of field,* or the zone of sharp focus.

- Shutter speed determines whether moving objects appear blurry or sharply focused.

- ISO affects the amount of image *noise,* which is a defect that looks like tiny specks of sand.

As you can imagine, understanding how aperture, shutter speed, and ISO affect your image enables you to have much more creative control over your photographs — and, in the case of ISO, to also ensure the quality of your images. (Chapter 2 discusses other factors that affect image quality.)

The next three sections explore the details of each exposure side effect.

Aperture affects depth of field

The aperture setting, or f-stop, affects *depth of field,* which is the range of sharp focus in your image. I introduce this concept in Chapter 3, but here's a quick recap: With a shallow depth of field, your subject appears more sharply focused than faraway objects; with a large depth of field, the sharp-focus zone spreads over a greater distance.

As you reduce the aperture size — or *stop down the aperture,* in photo lingo — by choosing a higher f-stop number, you increase depth of field. As an example, take a look at the two images in Figure 7-3. For both shots, I established focus on the female statue atop the fountain. Notice that the background in the first image, taken at an aperture setting of f/14, is softer than in the right example, taken at f/29. Aperture is just one contributor to depth of field, however; the focal length of your lens and the distance between that lens and your subject also affect how much of the scene stays in focus. See Chapter 8 for the complete story.

One way to remember the relationship between f-stop and depth of field is to think of the *f* as standing for *focus.* A higher f-stop number produces a larger depth of field, so if you want to extend the zone of sharp focus to cover a greater distance from your subject, you set the aperture to a higher f-stop. Higher *f*-stop number, greater zone of sharp *f*ocus. (Please *don't* share this tip with photography elites, who will roll their eyes and inform you that the *f* in *f-stop* most certainly does *not* stand for focus but for the ratio between the aperture size and lens focal length — as if *that's* helpful to know if you're not an optical engineer. Again, Chapter 8 explains focal length, which *is* helpful to know.)

f/14, 1/80 second, ISO 100   f/29, 1/20 second, ISO 100

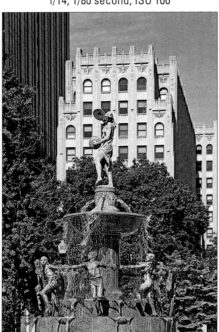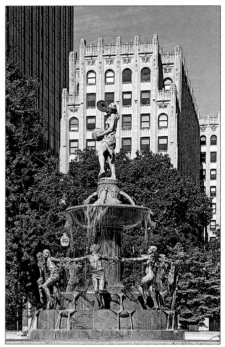

Figure 7-3: Stopping down the aperture (by choosing a higher f-stop number) increases depth of field, or the zone of sharp focus.

Shutter speed affects motion blur

At a slow shutter speed, moving objects appear blurry, whereas a fast shutter speed captures motion cleanly. This phenomenon has nothing to do with the actual focus point of the camera but rather on the movement occurring — and being recorded by the camera — during the time that the shutter is open.

Compare the photos in Figure 7-3, for example. The static elements are perfectly focused in both images, although the background in the right photo appears slightly sharper because I shot that image using a higher f-stop, increasing the zone of sharp focus. But the way the camera rendered the moving portion of the scene — the fountain water — was determined by the shutter speed. At a shutter speed of 1/20 second (right photo), the water blurs, giving it a misty look. At 1/80 second (left photo), the droplets appear more sharply focused. How high a shutter speed you need to freeze action depends on the speed of your subject.

Handholding the camera: How low can you go?

My students often ask how slow they can set the shutter speed and still handhold the camera instead of using a tripod. Unfortunately, there's no one-size-fits-all answer to this question.

The slow-shutter safety limit varies depending on a couple factors, including your physical capabilities and your lens — the heavier the lens, the harder it is to hold steady. For reasons that are too technical to get into, camera shake also affects your picture more when you shoot with a lens that has a long focal length. So you may be able to use a much slower shutter speed when you shoot with a lens that has a maximum focal length of 55mm, like the kit lens, than if you switch to a 200mm telephoto lens. (Chapter 8 explains focal length, if the term is new to you.)

A standard photography rule is to use the inverse of the lens focal length as the minimum handheld shutter speed. For example, with a 50mm lens, use a shutter speed no slower than 1/50 second. But that rule was developed before the advent of today's modern lenses, which tend to be significantly lighter and smaller than older lenses, as do cameras themselves. I have a very light, super-zoom lens that I can handhold at speeds as low as 1/80 second even when I zoom to focal lengths way beyond 80mm, for example.

So the best idea is to do your own tests to see where your handholding limit lies. Start with a slow shutter speed — say, in the 1/40 second neighborhood, and then click off multiple shots, increasing the shutter speed for each picture. If you have a zoom lens, run the test first at the minimum focal length (widest angle) and then zoom to the maximum focal length for another series of shots. Then it's simply a matter of comparing the images in your photo editing program. (You may not be able to accurately judge the amount of blur on the camera monitor.) See Chapter 5 to find out how to see the shutter speed you used for each picture when you view your images. That information, along with other camera settings, appears in the file *metadata*, which you can display in Nikon ViewNX 2 and many other programs.

Remember, too, that if your lens offers Vibration Reduction (as does the D3100 kit lens), enabling that feature can compensate for small amounts of camera shake, enabling you to capture sharp images at slightly slower shutter speeds than normal when handholding the camera. Again, your mileage may vary, but most people can expect to go at least two or three notches down the shutter-speed ramp. See Chapter 1 for more information about this feature.

If your picture suffers from overall blur, where even stationary objects appear out of focus, the camera itself moved during the exposure, which is always a danger when you handhold the camera. The slower the shutter speed, the longer the exposure time and the longer you have to hold the camera still to avoid the blur that's caused by camera shake. For example, I was able to successfully handhold the 1/80 second exposure you see on the left in Figure 7-3, but at 1/20 second, there was enough camera movement to result in the blurry shot shown in Figure 7-4. I mounted the camera on the tripod to get the shake-free version shown on the right in Figure 7-3.

Keep in mind that freezing action isn't the only way to use shutter speed to creative effect. When shooting waterfalls, for example, most photographers use a very slow shutter speed to give the water even more of a flowing, romantic look than you see in my fountain example. With colorful moving subjects, a slow shutter can produce some cool abstract effects and create a heightened sense of motion. Chapter 9 offers examples of both effects.

ISO affects image noise

As ISO increases, making the image sensor more reactive to light, you increase the risk of producing *noise*. Noise is a defect that looks like sprinkles of sand and is similar in appearance to film *grain*, a defect that often mars pictures taken with high ISO film. Noise can also be caused by very long exposure times.

Ideally, then, you should always use the lowest ISO setting on your camera to ensure top image quality. But

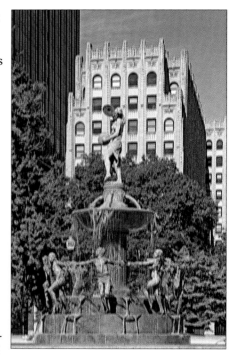

Figure 7-4: If both stationary and moving objects are blurry, camera shake is the usual cause.

sometimes, the lighting conditions simply don't permit you to do so and still use the aperture and shutter speeds you need. Take the photos in Figure 7-5, for example. I wanted to use an aperture that would keep both the front and middle of the flower in focus, leaving only the very back leaves a little soft. Given the focal length of the lens (55mm) and my close proximity to the flower, the f-stop that achieved my depth of field goal was f/8. (See Chapter 8 to find out exactly how focal length and subject distance affect the depth-of-field calculation.)

At f/8, I needed a shutter speed of 1/40 second to expose the image at ISO 100. I had a tripod, so camera shake wasn't an issue, but the weather was: The wind was blowing just enough to make the flower appear blurry at that shutter speed, as shown on the left in Figure 7-5. So I raised the ISO to 400, which enabled me to use a much faster shutter speed (1/125 second) and compensate for the movement of the flower, resulting in a sharp image of the petals. (The background blurs in both images because of the short depth of field.)

Fortunately, you don't encounter serious noise on the D3100 until you really crank up the ISO. In fact, you may even be able to get away with a fairly high ISO if you keep your print or display size small. But as with other image defects, noise becomes more apparent as you enlarge the photo. Noise is also easier to spot in shadow areas of your picture and in large areas of solid color. To give you an idea of how ISO affects noise, Figure 7-6 shows you magnified views of a portion of the rose scene captured at ISO 100, 200, 400, and 800. Even at ISO 800, noise isn't horrible, although that's a relative term, I guess — even a little noise isn't acceptable for pictures that require the highest quality, such as images for a product catalog or a travel shot that you want to blow up to poster size.

ISO 100, f/8, 1/40 second   ISO 400, f/8, 1/125 second

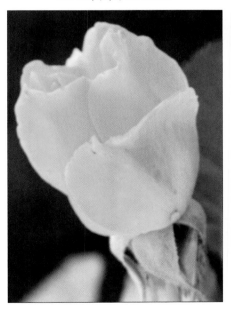 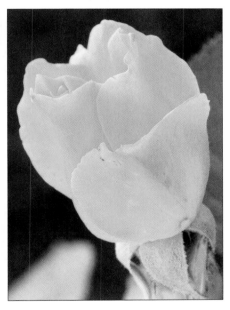

Figure 7-5: Raising the ISO enabled me to bump the shutter speed up enough to permit a blur-free shot on a windy day.

ISO 100 ISO 200

ISO 400 ISO 800

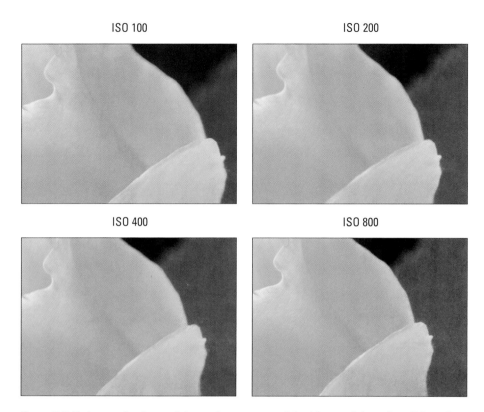

Figure 7-6: To keep noise from ruining a picture, try to stick with one of these four ISO settings.

Jump past ISO 800, though, and things start to degrade pretty quickly, as you can see in Figure 7-7. Even at a small print size, ISO 1600 produces visible noise, and things get progressively ugly from there. Now you have a better idea why Nikon gave the two highest ISO settings their special labels, Hi 1 and Hi 2 — it's a way to let you know that you should use these settings only if the light is so bad that you have no other way to get the shot.

Doing the exposure balancing act

As you change any of the three exposure settings — aperture, shutter speed, and ISO — one or both of the others must also shift in order to maintain the same image brightness. Say that you're shooting a soccer game, for example, and you notice that although the overall exposure looks great, the players appear slightly blurry at your current shutter speed. If you raise the shutter speed, you have to compensate with either a larger aperture, to allow in more light during the shorter exposure, or a higher ISO setting, to make the camera more sensitive to the light — or both.

ISO 1600   ISO 3200

Hi 1 (ISO 6400)   Hi 2 (ISO 12800)

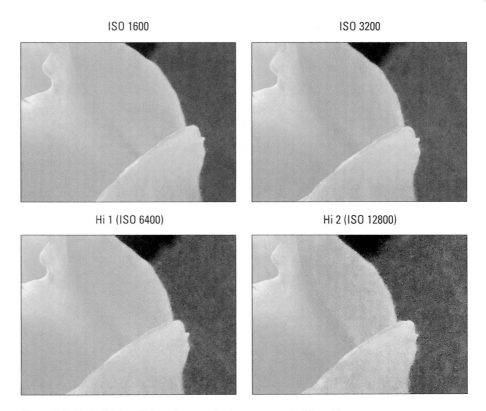

Figure 7-7: At the higher ISO settings, noise becomes a significant issue.

As the previous sections explain, changing these settings impacts your image in ways beyond exposure. As a quick reminder:

- Aperture affects depth of field, with a higher f-stop number producing a greater zone of sharp focus.

- Shutter speed affects whether motion of the subject or camera results in a blurry photo. A faster shutter "freezes" action and also helps safeguard against allover blur that can result from camera shake when you're handholding the camera.

- ISO affects the camera's sensitivity to light. A higher ISO makes the camera more responsive to light but also increases the chance of image noise.

So when you boost that shutter speed to capture your soccer subjects, you have to decide whether you prefer the shorter depth of field that comes with a larger aperture or the increased risk of noise that accompanies a higher ISO.

Everyone has their own approach to finding the right combination of aperture, shutter speed, and ISO, and you'll no doubt develop your own system as you become more practiced at using the advanced exposure modes. In the meantime, here's how I handle things:

- I always use the lowest possible ISO setting unless the lighting conditions are so poor that I can't use the aperture and shutter speed I want without raising the ISO.

- If my subject is moving (or might move, as with a squiggly toddler or antsy pet), I give shutter speed the next highest priority in my exposure decision. I might choose a fast shutter speed to ensure a blur-free photo or, on the flip side, select a slow shutter to intentionally blur that moving object, an effect that can create a heightened sense of motion.

- For images of non-moving subjects, I make aperture a priority over shutter speed, setting the aperture according to the depth of field I have in mind. For portraits, for example, I use the largest aperture (the lowest f-stop number, known as shooting *wide open,* in photographer speak) so that I get a short depth of field, creating a nice, soft background for my subject. For landscapes, I usually go the opposite direction, stopping down the aperture as much as possible to capture the subject at the greatest depth of field.

I know that keeping all this straight is a little overwhelming at first, but the more you work with your camera, the more the whole exposure equation will make sense to you. You can find tips for choosing exposure settings for specific types of pictures in Chapter 9; keep moving through this chapter for details on how to actually monitor and adjust aperture, shutter speed, and ISO settings on the D3100.

Exploring the Advanced Exposure Modes

In the automatic modes described in Chapter 3, you have very little control over exposure. Some modes let you choose from a couple Flash modes, and the Scene modes (Portrait, Landscape, Sports, and so on) let you control ISO setting. Through the Advanced Operation options available in Guide mode, also detailed in Chapter 3, you can play with f-stop and shutter speed to affect depth of field and motion blur, too.

But to gain full control over exposure, set the Mode dial to one of the advanced modes highlighted in Figure 7-8: P, S, A, or M. You also need to shoot in these modes to use certain other features, such as manual white balancing, a color control that you can explore in Chapter 8.

The major difference between the four advanced modes is the level of control over aperture and shutter speed, as follows:

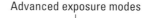

Advanced exposure modes

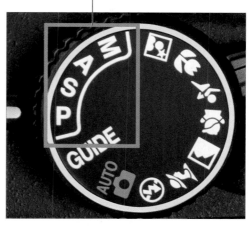

- ✔ **P (programmed autoexposure):** In this mode, the camera selects both aperture and shutter speed. But you can choose from different combinations of the two for creative flexibility.

- ✔ **S (shutter-priority auto-exposure):** In this mode, you select a shutter speed, and the camera chooses the aperture setting that produces a good exposure at your selected ISO setting.

Figure 7-8: You can control exposure and certain other picture properties fully only in P, S, A, or M mode.

- ✔ **A (aperture-priority autoexposure):** The opposite of shutter-priority autoexposure, this mode asks you to select the aperture setting. The camera then selects the appropriate shutter speed to properly expose the picture.

- ✔ **M (manual exposure):** In this mode, you specify both shutter speed and aperture.

To sum up, the first three modes are semi-automatic exposure modes that are designed to help you get a good exposure while still providing you with some photographic flexibility. Note one important point about the semi-auto modes, however: In extreme lighting conditions, the camera may not be able to select settings that will produce a good exposure. The camera will warn you about the potential problem but doesn't prevent you from capturing the shot. Manual mode puts all exposure control in your hands. But even in Manual mode, you're never really flying without a net — the camera assists you by displaying the exposure meter, explained next.

Reading (And Adjusting) the Meter

To help you determine whether your exposure settings are on cue in M (manual) exposure mode, the camera displays an *exposure meter* in the viewfinder and Shooting Info display. The *meter* is a little linear graphic that indicates whether your current settings will properly expose the image.

Figure 7-9 shows the exposure meter as viewed in the Shooting Info display. In the viewfinder, the meter appears to the right of the f-stop and looks similar to the examples shown in Figure 7-10.

The minus-sign end of the meter represents underexposure; the plus sign, overexposure. So if the little notches on the meter fall to the right of 0, as shown in the first example in Figure 7-10, the image will be underexposed. If the indicator moves to the left of 0, as shown in the second example, the image will be overexposed. The farther the indicator moves toward the plus or minus sign, the greater the potential problem. When the meter shows a balanced exposure, as in the third example, you're good to go.

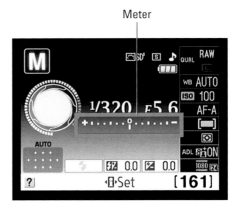

Meter

Figure 7-9: You can view the exposure meter in the Shooting Information display.

Underexposure   Overexposure   Good exposure

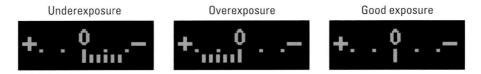

Figure 7-10: The exposure meter indicates whether your exposure settings are on target.

In the other exposure modes, the meter appears in the viewfinder and Shooting Info screen if the camera anticipates an exposure problem. The word Lo at the end of the meter tells you that the photo may be seriously underexposed; the word Hi indicates severe overexposure. In dim lighting, you may also see a blinking flash symbol. It's a not-so-subtle suggestion to add some light to the scene. A blinking question mark tells you that you can press the Zoom Out button to display a Help screen with more information.

Keep in mind that the meter's suggestion on exposure may not always be the one you want to follow. For example, you may want to shoot a backlit subject in silhouette, in which case you *want* that subject to be underexposed. In other words, the meter is a guide, not a dictator. In addition, remember that the exposure information the meter reports is based on the *exposure metering mode,* which determines which part of the frame the camera considers when calculating exposure. At the default setting, exposure is based on the entire frame, but you can select two other metering modes. See the upcoming section "Choosing an Exposure Metering Mode" for details.

One final meter-related tip: The meter turns off automatically if you don't press the shutter button for a period of time — 8 seconds, by default. You can adjust the shut-off timing by taking these steps:

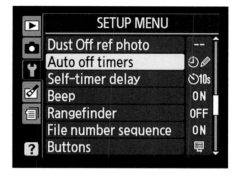

Figure 7-11: You can adjust the timing of the meter's automatic shutdown.

1. **Display the Setup menu, choose the Auto Off Timers option, as shown on the left in Figure 7-11, and press OK.**

2. **Select Custom, as shown on the left in Figure 7-12, and press OK again.**

   The Custom choice enables you to adjust the meter shutdown without also affecting the shutoff timing of the image-review and playback/menu displays, both covered in Chapter 5.

3. **Highlight Auto Meter-Off, as shown on the right in Figure 7-12, and press OK.**

   You see the screen listing the available settings, which range from 4 seconds to 30 minutes.

4. **Select the timing option you want to use and press OK.**

   Keep in mind that shorter delay times conserve battery power.

5. **Highlight Done and press OK.**

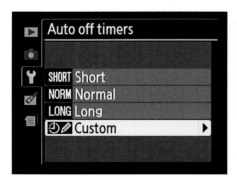
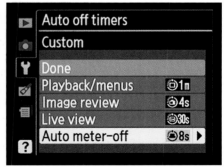

Figure 7-12: To conserve battery power, choose a shorter meter-off delay.

Setting ISO, Aperture, and Shutter Speed

The next sections detail how to view and adjust these three critical exposure settings. Remember, you can adjust ISO in any exposure mode except Auto and Auto Flash Off. But to control aperture (f-stop) or shutter speed, you must switch to one of the four advanced exposure modes (P, S, A, or M) or use the Advanced Operation feature of Guide mode, as outlined in Chapter 3. As I state in that chapter, after you understand the role of aperture and shutter speed in exposure, you can save time by using the P, S, A, or M modes, which let you more quickly dial in the settings you want than Guide mode. (For that reason, this paragraph is the last you'll hear of Guide mode in this chapter, save for a few tidbits that may cause confusion if I ignore them completely.)

Adjusting aperture and shutter speed

You can view the current aperture (f-stop) and shutter speed in the Shooting Info display and viewfinder, as shown in Figure 7-13.

Shutter speed   Aperture (f-stop)

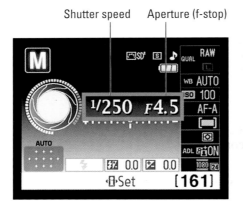 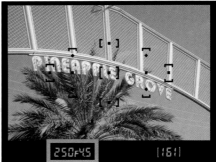

Figure 7-13: Look for the current f-stop and shutter speed here.

In the viewfinder, shutter speeds are presented as whole numbers, even if the shutter speed is set to a fraction of a second. For example, the number 250 indicates a shutter speed of 1/250 second. When the shutter speed slows to 1 second or more, quote marks appear after the number — 1" indicates a shutter speed of 1 second, 4" means 4 seconds, and so on.

To select aperture and shutter speed, start by pressing the shutter button halfway to kick the exposure system into gear. You can then release the button if you want. The next step depends on the exposure mode, as follows:

- ✔ **P (programmed autoexposure):** In this mode, the camera shows you its recommended f-stop and shutter speed when you press the shutter button halfway. But you can rotate the Command dial to select a different combination of settings. The number of possible combinations depends upon the aperture settings the camera can select, which in turn depend on the lighting conditions and your lens.

An asterisk (*) appears next to the P exposure mode symbol in the upper-left corner of the Shooting Information display if you rotate the Command dial to adjust the aperture/shutter speed settings. You see a tiny P* symbol at the left end of the viewfinder display as well. To get back to the initial combo of shutter speed and aperture, rotate the Command dial until the asterisk disappears from the Shooting Info display and the P* symbol turns off in the viewfinder.

- ✔ **S (shutter-priority autoexposure):** In this mode, you select the shutter speed. Just rotate the Command dial to get the job done.

As you change the shutter speed, the camera automatically adjusts the aperture as needed to maintain what it considers the proper exposure. Remember that as the aperture shifts, so does depth of field — so even though you're working in shutter-priority mode, keep an eye on the f-stop, too, if depth of field is important to your photo. Also note that in extreme lighting conditions, the camera may not be able to adjust the aperture enough to produce a good exposure at your current shutter speed — again, possible aperture settings depend on your lens. So you may need to compromise on shutter speed (or in dim lighting, raise the ISO).

- ✔ **A (aperture-priority autoexposure):** In this mode, you control aperture, and the camera adjusts shutter speed automatically. To set the aperture (f-stop), rotate the Command dial.

When you stop down the aperture (raise the f-stop value), be careful that the shutter speed doesn't drop so low that you run the risk of camera shake if you handhold the camera — unless you have a tripod handy, of course. And if your scene contains moving objects, make sure that when you dial in your preferred f-stop, the shutter speed that the camera selects is fast enough to stop action (or slow enough to blur it, if that's your creative goal). These same warnings apply when you use P mode, by the way.

✔ **M (manual exposure):** In this mode, you select both aperture and shutter speed, like so:

- *To adjust shutter speed:* Rotate the Command dial.

- *To adjust aperture:* Press the Exposure Compensation button while simultaneously rotating the Command dial. Notice the little aperture-like symbol that lies next to the button, on the top of the camera? That's your reminder of the button's role in setting the f-stop in Manual mode.

Keep in mind that when you use P, S, or A modes, the settings that the camera selects are based on what it thinks is the proper exposure. If you don't agree with the camera, you have two options: You can switch to manual exposure mode and simply dial in the aperture and shutter speed that deliver the exposure you want; or if you want to stay in P, S, or A mode, you can tweak exposure using the Exposure Compensation feature, explained later in this chapter.

When you view the f-stop and shutter speed in the Shooting Info display, by the way, remember that the camera continues to meter and adjust exposure up to the time you take the shot. (The exception is when you use the autoexposure lock feature, explained later in this chapter.) So if you frame the shot and then move the camera to better see the display, the exposure settings no longer reflect the ones the camera chose for your subject — instead, they show the settings for whatever is now in front of the lens. And if you (like most people) hold the camera with the lens pointing down to view the monitor, the camera begins calculating the correct settings to use to photograph the ground.

The best practice is to use the Shooting Info display to select your initial shutter speed, or aperture, or both, if necessary. Then frame the shot in the viewfinder, press the shutter button halfway to meter the scene in front of the lens, and then, if the viewfinder exposure meter indicates a problem, adjust the exposure settings as necessary without taking your eye away from the viewfinder. (After you get familiar with the operation of the camera, this technique won't be as hard as it first seems, I promise.)

Controlling ISO

The ISO setting, introduced at the start of this chapter, adjusts the camera's sensitivity to light. At a higher ISO, you can use a faster shutter speed or a smaller aperture (higher f-stop number) because less light is needed to expose the image.

You can't adjust ISO in Auto and Auto Flash Off exposure modes, and in Guide mode, you can access the ISO setting only if you select certain options as you work through the Guided Menu screens. (Suffice it to say, if you want to play with ISO, switch out of Guide mode.)

In any other exposure mode, adjust ISO as follows:

✓ **Press the Fn (Function) button while rotating the Command dial.** By default, the Fn button on the side of the camera is set to provide quick access to the ISO setting. Just press and hold the button to highlight the ISO setting in the Shooting Info display, as shown in Figure 7-14, and then rotate the Command dial to adjust the setting. Chapter 11 shows you how to choose a different function for the button if you don't frequently adjust ISO.

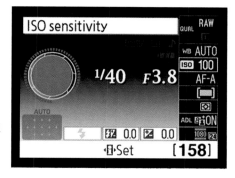

Figure 7-14: By default, pressing the Fn button triggers the ISO adjustment screen; rotate the Command dial to change the setting.

✓ **Quick Settings screen:** Press the Info Edit button to shift from the Shooting Info display to the Quick Settings display. Highlight the ISO setting, as shown on the left in Figure 7-15 and press OK to display the options shown on the right. Choose the desired ISO setting and press OK.

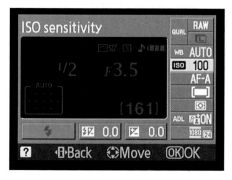 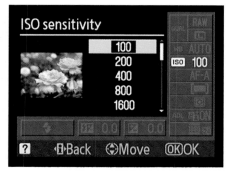

Figure 7-15: You can adjust ISO easily through the Quick Settings screen.

✔ **Shooting menu:** As shown in Figure 7-16, you also can adjust the ISO through the Shooting menu. Note that the second screen in the figure shows options available in the P, S, A, and M modes; you can access only the top option in the other exposure modes.

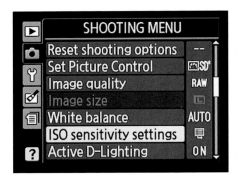 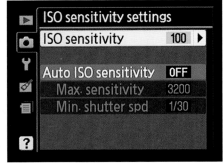

Figure 7-16: You can access additional ISO options through the Shooting menu.

Keep these additional ISO factoids in mind:

✔ **Auto ISO in the fully automatic exposure modes:** In Auto and Auto Flash Off mode, the camera uses the Auto ISO setting and selects the ISO setting for you. In the Scene modes, you can stick with Auto ISO (the default setting) or select a specific ISO value.

✔ **Auto ISO in P, S, A, and M modes:** Auto ISO doesn't appear on the ISO settings list, but you still can enable Auto ISO as sort of a safety net. Here's how it works: You dial in a specific ISO setting — say, ISO 100. If the camera decides that it can't properly expose the image at that ISO given your current aperture and shutter speed, it automatically adjusts ISO as necessary.

To get to this option, select ISO Sensitivity Settings on the Shooting menu, as shown on the left in Figure 7-17, and press OK. On the next screen, turn the Auto ISO Sensitivity option to On, as shown on the right in the figure. The camera will now override your ISO choice when it thinks a proper exposure is not possible with the settings you've specified.

Next, use the two options under the Auto ISO Sensitivity setting to tell the camera exactly when it should step in and offer ISO assistance:

• *Max. Sensitivity:* Specify the highest ISO setting — maximum ISO sensitivity — the camera may select when it overrides your ISO decision. For example, the value in Figure 7-17 is set to ISO 800.

• *Min. Shutter Spd:* Set the minimum shutter speed at which the ISO override engages when you use the P and A exposure modes. For example, you can specify that you want the camera to amp up ISO if needed to prevent the shutter speed from dropping below 1/60 second, as shown in the figure.

If the camera is about to override your ISO setting, it alerts you by blinking the ISO Auto label in the viewfinder. The message "ISO-A" blinks at the top of the Shooting Info screen as well. And in playback mode, the ISO value appears in red if you view your photos in a display mode that includes the ISO value. (Chapter 5 has details.)

To disable Auto ISO override, just reset the Auto ISO Sensitivity option to Off.

✓ **ISO value display:** Although the Shooting Info screen always displays the current ISO setting, the viewfinder reports the ISO value only when the option is set to Auto. Otherwise, the ISO area of the viewfinder is empty.

✓ **Hi 1 and Hi 2:** The specific ISO values presented to you range from 100 to 3200. But if you scroll past 3200, you discover two additional settings, Hi 1 and Hi 2, which translate to ISO values of 6400 and 12800, respectively. Choosing ISO 3200 pretty much ensures a noisy image (refer to Figure 7-7), and shifting to the Hi settings just makes things worse. If cranking up ISO is the only way to capture the image, and you'd rather have a noisy picture than no picture, go for it. Otherwise, adjust shutter speed and aperture to get the exposure you want instead. You can always mount the camera on a tripod if the shutter speed is too slow for using the camera handheld, although you should keep in mind that a long exposure time also can produce added noise.

Also check out the nearby sidebar "Dampening noise" for a feature that may help calm noise somewhat.

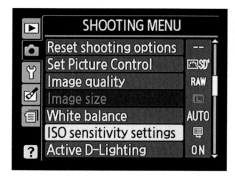
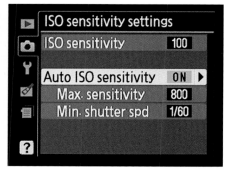

Figure 7-17: In P, S, A, and M modes, you can set limits for Auto ISO override.

Dampening noise

Noise, the digital defect that gives your pictures a speckled look (refer to Figure 7-7), can occur for two reasons: a high ISO speed and a long exposure time.

The D3100 offers a tool for dealing with both cause of noise. If you visit the Setup menu and enable the Noise Reduction feature, as shown here, the camera applies a filter designed to soften the appearance of noise. A couple issues to note:

✔ The filter is applied only to pictures taken at shutter speeds of longer than 8 seconds or ISO settings the camera thinks may be problematic. The filter is applied after you take the picture, as the camera processes the image data. When you use a slow shutter speed, the message "Job Nr" may appear in the viewfinder while the noise removal takes place, and you can't take another picture until the message disappears.

✔ If you choose Off, the camera actually still applies a tiny amount of noise removal, but only at high ISO settings. This camera doesn't apply this automatic noise removal when you use a slow shutter speed, however. Nor do you typically experience any camera slowdown or see the Job Nr symbol.

Perhaps most important, you should know that although long-exposure noise reduction filters can work fairly well, those that attack high ISO noise work primarily by applying a slight blur to the image. Don't expect this process to totally eliminate noise, and do expect some resulting image softness. You may be able to get better results by using the blur tools or noise-removal filters found in many photo editors because you can blur just the parts of the image where noise is most noticeable — usually in areas of flat color or little detail, such as skies. I prefer this option and so typically leave the camera's Noise Reduction feature turned Off.

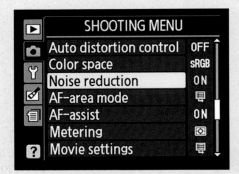

Choosing an Exposure Metering Mode

To fully interpret what your exposure meter tells you, you need to know which *metering mode* is active. The metering mode determines which part of the frame the camera analyzes to calculate the proper exposure. The metering mode affects the exposure-meter reading as well as the exposure settings that the camera chooses in the fully automatic shooting modes (Auto, Portrait, and so on) as well as in the semi-auto modes (P, S, and A).

Your D3100 offers three metering modes, described in the following list and represented on the Shooting Information display by the icons you see in the margins:

✔ **Matrix:** The camera analyzes the entire frame and then selects an exposure that's designed to produce a balanced exposure.

Your camera manual refers to this mode as 3D Color Matrix II, which is simply the label that Nikon created to describe the specific technology used in this mode.

✔ **Center-weighted:** The camera bases exposure on the entire frame but puts extra emphasis — or *weight* — on the center of the frame.

✔ **Spot:** In this mode, the camera bases exposure entirely on a circular area that's about 3.5mm in diameter, or about 2.5 percent of the frame. The exact location used for this pin-point metering depends on an autofocusing option called the AF-area mode. Detailed in Chapter 8, this option determines which of the camera's 11 focus points the autofocusing system uses to establish focus. Here's how the setting affects exposure:

  • *If you choose the Auto-area mode,* in which the camera chooses the focus point for you, exposure is based on the center focus point.

  • *If you use any of the other AF-area modes,* which enable you to select a specific focus point, the camera bases exposure on that point.

Because of this autofocus/autoexposure relationship, it's best to switch to one of the AF-area modes that allow focus-point selection when you want to use spot metering. In the Auto-area mode, exposure may be incorrect if you compose your shot so that the subject isn't at the center of the frame.

As an example of how metering mode affects exposure, Figure 7-18 shows the same image captured at each mode. In the matrix example, the bright background caused the camera to select an exposure that left the statue quite dark. Switching to center-weighted metering helped somewhat, but didn't quite bring the statue out of the shadows. Spot metering produced the best result as far as the statue goes, although the resulting increase in exposure left the sky a little washed out.

Matrix metering 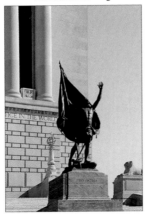 Center-weighted metering 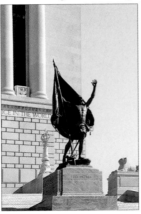 Spot metering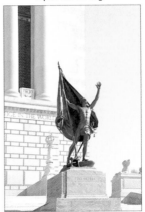

Figure 7-18: The metering mode determines which area of the frame the camera considers when calculating exposure.

You don't have a choice of metering modes in any of the fully automatic exposure modes, including Guide mode; the camera automatically uses matrix mode for all shots. But in P, A, S, or M modes, you can specify which metering mode you prefer by using either of these techniques:

✔ **Quick Settings display:** Bring up the Shooting Info screen and then press the Info Edit button to shift to the Quick Settings display. Highlight the Metering icon, as shown on the left in Figure 7-19, and press OK to display the second screen in the figure. Select the desired mode and press OK again.

✔ **Shooting menu:** Select Metering, as shown on the left in Figure 7-20, to access the available settings, shown on the right.

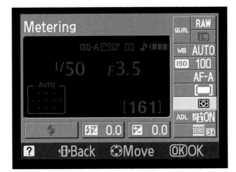 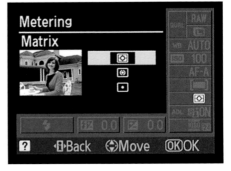

Figure 7-19: The Quick Settings display offers the fastest route to changing the metering mode.

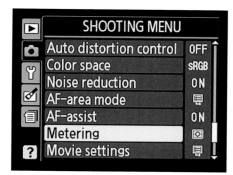 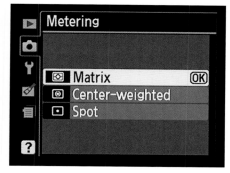

Figure 7-20: But you also can change the metering mode through the Shooting menu.

The metering mode you choose stays in effect when shooting in P, S, A, and M modes, even when you turn off the camera. Remember to change the metering mode when taking a picture under different lighting conditions.

In theory, the best practice is to check the metering mode before you shoot and choose the one that best matches your exposure goals. But in practice, that's a bit of a pain, not just in terms of having to adjust yet one more capture setting but in terms of having to *remember* to adjust one more capture setting. So here's my advice: Until you're really comfortable with all the other controls on your camera, just stick with the default setting, which is matrix metering. That mode produces good results in most situations, and after all, you can see in the monitor whether you disagree with how the camera metered or exposed the image and simply reshoot after adjusting the exposure settings to your liking. This option, in my mind, makes the whole metering mode issue a lot less critical than it is when you shoot with film.

The one exception to this advice might be when you're shooting a series of images in which a significant contrast in lighting exists between subject and background, as in Figure 7-18. Then, switching to center-weighted metering or spot metering may save you the time of having to adjust the exposure for each image. You may also want to investigate the section "Expanding Tonal Range with Active D-Lighting," which tells you about a camera feature that can help you record brighter shadows without losing highlights.

Applying Exposure Compensation

When you set your camera to the P, S, or A modes, you can enjoy autoexposure support but still retain some control over the final exposure. If you think that the image the camera produced is too dark or too light, you can use *Exposure Compensation.* You also can access Exposure Compensation if you use the Advanced Operation setting of Guide mode — but again, using Guide mode makes life more difficult because you have to paw through lots more screens to get to the setting.

At any rate, Exposure Compensation enables you to tell the camera to produce a darker or lighter exposure than what its autoexposure mechanism thinks is appropriate. Best of all, this feature is probably one of the easiest on the whole camera to understand. Here's all there is to it:

- ✔ Exposure compensation settings are stated in terms of Exposure Compensation values, as in EV +2.0. Possible values range from EV +5.0 to EV –5.0. (*EV* stands for *exposure value.*)

  Each full number on the EV scale represents an exposure shift of one *stop.* In plain English, that means that if you change Exposure Compensation from EV 0.0 to EV –1.0, the resulting exposure is equivalent to adjusting the aperture or shutter speed to allow half as much light into the camera as at the current setting. If you instead raise the value to EV +1.0, the exposure is equivalent to adjusting the settings to allow twice the light.

- ✔ A setting of EV 0.0 results in no exposure adjustment.

- ✔ For a brighter image, raise the Exposure Compensation value. The higher you go, the brighter the image becomes.

- ✔ For a darker image, lower the EV.

As an example, take a look at the first image in Figure 7-21. The initial exposure selected by the camera left the balloon a tad too dark for my taste. So I just amped the Exposure Compensation setting to EV +1.0, which produced the brighter exposure on the right.

You can view the current Exposure Compensation setting in the Shooting Info screen; look for it in the area highlighted in the left screen in Figure 7-22. To change the setting, you have two options:

- ✔ **Press the Exposure Compensation button while rotating the Command dial.** As soon as you press the button, the Shooting Info display appears as shown on the right in Figure 7-22. If you're looking through the viewfinder, the frames-remaining value is temporarily replaced by the Exposure Compensation value when you press the Exposure Compensation button.

  While holding the Exposure Compensation button, rotate the Command dial to adjust the EV. As you change the setting, the exposure meter in the viewfinder and Shooting Information display updates to show you the degree of adjustment you're making. Each bar that appears under the meter equals an adjustment of 1/3 stop (EV +/–0.3).

EV 0.0   EV +1.0

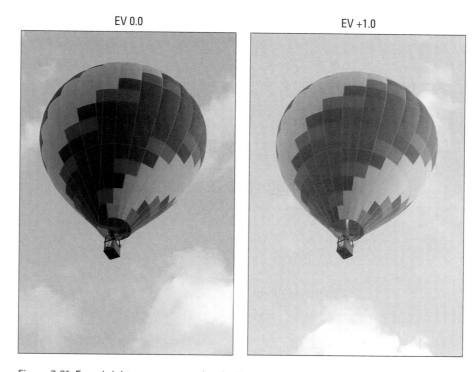

Figure 7-21: For a brighter exposure, raise the Exposure Compensation value.

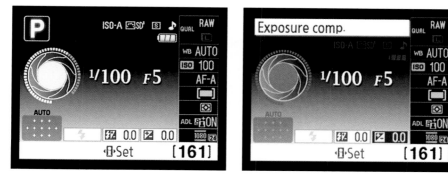

Figure 7-22: Press the Exposure Compensation button and rotate the Command dial to quickly adjust the setting.

After you release the button, the Shooting Info screen goes back to normal, and the frames-remaining value returns to the viewfinder.

✔ **Use the Quick Settings display:** You also can adjust the Exposure Compensation setting via the Quick Settings display, as shown in Figure 7-23. Remember, you can shift from the Shooting Info screen to the Quick Settings display by pressing the Info Edit button.

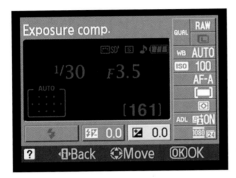 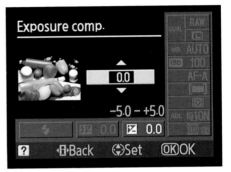

Figure 7-23: You also can raise or lower Exposure Compensation through the Quick Settings screen.

 Your Exposure Compensation setting remains in force until you change it, even if you power off the camera. So you may want to make a habit of checking the setting before each shoot or always setting the value back to EV 0.0 after taking the last shot for which you want to apply compensation.

Here are a few other tips about Exposure Compensation:

✔ How the camera arrives at the brighter or darker image you request through your Exposure Compensation setting depends on the exposure mode:

• In A (aperture-priority autoexposure) mode, the camera adjusts the shutter speed but leaves your selected f-stop in force. Be sure to check the resulting shutter speed to make sure that it isn't so slow that camera shake or blur from moving objects is problematic.

• In S (shutter-priority autoexposure) mode, the opposite occurs: The camera opens or stops down the aperture, leaving your selected shutter speed alone.

• In P (programmed autoexposure) mode, the camera decides whether to adjust aperture, shutter speed, or both.

• In all three modes, the camera may also adjust ISO if you have Auto ISO enabled.

Keep in mind that the camera can adjust f-stop only so much, according to the aperture range of your lens. And the range of shutter speeds, too, is limited by the camera itself. So if you reach the ends of those ranges, you either have to compromise on shutter speed or aperture or adjust ISO.

✔ Finally, if you don't want to fiddle with Exposure Compensation, just switch to Manual exposure mode — M, on the Mode dial — and select whatever aperture and shutter speed settings produce the exposure you're after. Exposure compensation has no effect on manual exposures; again, that adjustment is made only in the P, S, and A modes.

Using Autoexposure Lock

To help ensure a proper exposure, your camera continually meters the light in a scene until the moment you depress the shutter button fully and capture the image. In autoexposure modes — that is, any mode but M — it also keeps adjusting exposure settings as needed to maintain a good exposure.

For example, say that you set your camera to shutter-priority autoexposure (S) mode and set the shutter speed to 1/125 second. The camera immediately reports the f-stop that it considers appropriate to expose the scene at that shutter speed. But if the light in the scene changes or you reframe your shot before snapping the picture, the camera may shift the f-stop automatically to make sure that the exposure remains correct.

For most situations, this approach works great, resulting in the right settings for the light that's striking your subject at the moment you capture the image. But on occasion, you may want to lock in a certain combination of exposure settings. For example, perhaps you want your subject to appear at the far edge of the frame. If you were to use the normal shooting technique, you'd place the subject under a focus point, press the shutter button halfway to lock focus and set the initial exposure, and then reframe to your desired composition to take the shot. The problem is that exposure is then recalculated based on the new framing, which can leave your subject under- or overexposed.

The easiest way to lock in exposure settings is to switch to M (manual) exposure mode and use the f-stop, shutter speed, and ISO settings that work best for your subject. But if you prefer to stay in P, S, or A mode, you can press the AE-L/AF-L button to lock exposure and focus simultaneously. Here's the technique I recommend:

1. **Set the metering mode to spot metering.**

   See the section "Choosing an Exposure Metering Mode," earlier in this chapter, if you need help changing the metering mode. You can select a metering mode through the Shooting menu or Quick Settings display.

2. **Set the AF-area mode option to the Single Point setting and then use the Multi Selector to select your desired focus point.**

   This step tells the camera which part of the frame you want to use for establishing focus and, if you use spot metering, also determines which part of the frame the camera uses to calculate exposure. (You sometimes need to press the shutter button halfway and release it before you can do so.)

   You can set the AF-area mode through the Shooting menu or the Quick Settings display; see Chapter 8 for details. After you select the Single Point option, you can use the Multi Selector to choose a focusing point.

3. **Frame your shot so that the subject appears under the selected focus point and then press the shutter button halfway to set focus.**

4. **Press and hold the AE-L/AF-L button.**

   The button's just to the right of the viewfinder.

   While the button is pressed, the letters AE-L appear at the left end of the viewfinder to remind you that exposure lock is applied.

5. **Reframe the shot if desired and take the photo.**

   Be sure to keep holding the AE-L/AF-L button until you release the shutter button!

By default, this step locks both exposure and focus for as long as you press the AE-L/AF-L button, even if you release the shutter button. (*AE-L* stands for autoexposure lock; *AF-L,* for autofocus lock.) But if you dig into the Setup menu, you can change the button's function. You can set the button to lock only exposure, for example, or only focus, instead of locking both as it does by default. Chapter 11 offers details.

One more tidbit: Matrix metering doesn't produce good results with the autoexposure lock feature. However, you usually can use center-weighted metering successfully instead of spot metering if you prefer. In that case, compose the picture initially so that your subject appears in the center of the frame; then recompose after locking exposure and focus. I prefer to use spot metering, however, because it sets exposure on a more precise area of the frame.

Expanding Tonal Range with Active D-Lighting

A high-contrast scene — one that features both very bright and very dark areas — presents the classic photographer's challenge: Choosing exposure settings that capture the darkest parts of the subject appropriately causes the brightest areas to be overexposed. And if you instead *expose for the highlights* — that is, set the exposure settings to capture the brightest regions properly — the darker areas are underexposed. The left photo in Figure 7-24 offers an example.

Active D-Lighting Off   Active D-Lighting On

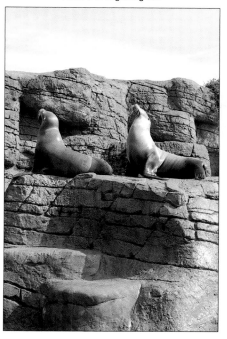 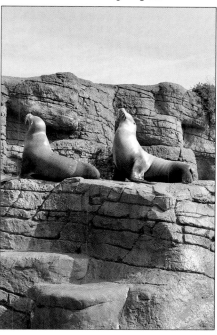

Figure 7-24: Active D-Lighting enabled me to capture the shadows without blowing out the highlights.

In the past, you had to choose between favoring the highlights or the shadows. But thanks to the Active D-Lighting feature on your camera, you have a better chance of keeping your highlights intact while better exposing the darkest areas. In my seal scene, turning on Active D-Lighting produced a

brighter rendition of the darkest parts of the rocks and the seals, for example, and yet the color in the sky didn't get blown out as it did when I captured the image with Active D-Lighting turned off. The highlights in the seal
and in the rocks on the lower-right corner of the image also are toned down
a tad in the Active D-Lighting version.

Active D-Lighting actually does its thing in two stages. First, it selects exposure settings that result in a slightly darker exposure than normal. This half
of the equation guarantees that you retain details in your highlights. Without
that adjustment, the brightest areas of the image might be overexposed, leaving you with a batch of all-white pixels that really should contain a range of
tones from light to lighter to white. So a cloud, for example, would appear as
a big white blob, with no subtle tonal details to give it form. After you snap
the photo, the second part of the process occurs. During this phase, the
camera applies an internal software filter to brighten only the darkest areas
of the image. This adjustment rescues shadow detail so that you wind up
with a range of dark tones instead of a big black blob.

For best results, pair Active D-Lighting with the matrix metering mode so
that the camera takes brightness values throughout the frame into consideration when producing the exposure. (See the earlier section "Choosing an
Exposure Metering Mode" for details.) After setting the metering mode, turn
Active D-Lighting on and off using any of these methods:

✔ **Quick Settings display:** After displaying the Shooting Information
  screen, press the Info Edit button to shift to Quick Settings mode. Then
  highlight the Active D-Lighting option, as shown on the left in Figure
  7-25, and press OK to get to the screen shown on the right in the figure.
  Select the setting you want to use and press OK.

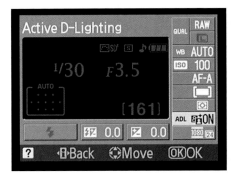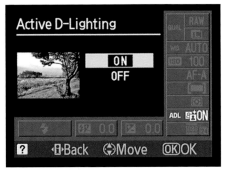

Figure 7-25: You can change the Active D-Lighting setting easily via the Quick Settings screen.

✔ **Shooting menu:** If you prefer menus to the Quick Settings display, you can enable and disable the Active D-Lighting adjustment from the Shooting menu, as shown in Figure 7-26.

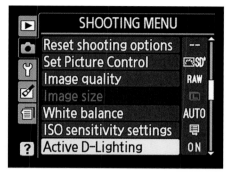

Figure 7-26: Or enable the adjustment through the Shooting menu.

✔ **Fn button plus Command dial:** You also can set the Fn (Function button) to immediately call up the Active D-Lighting setting instead of performing its default role, which is to offer quick access to the ISO Sensitivity option. Chapter 11 shows you how. If you make the change, rotate the Command dial while pressing the Fn button to change the Active D-Lighting setting.

Active D-Lighting does have a couple drawbacks. First, the camera takes longer to record your shot because it needs time to apply the exposure adjustment. For rapid-fire action shooting, it's best to disable the feature.

Second, you may notice increased noise in your photos when you combine Active D-Lighting with a higher ISO setting. The extra noise is usually most apparent in the shadow areas of the picture.

If you opt out of Active D-Lighting, remember that the camera's Retouch menu offers a D-Lighting filter that applies a similar adjustment to existing pictures. (See Chapter 10 for help.) Some photo-editing programs, such as Adobe Photoshop Elements and Photoshop, also have good shadow and highlight recovery filters. In either case, when you shoot with Active D-Lighting disabled, you're better off setting the initial exposure settings to record the highlights as you want them. It's very difficult to bring back lost highlight detail after the fact, but you typically can unearth at least a little bit of detail from the darkest areas of the image.

Investigating Advanced Flash Options

Sometimes, no amount of fiddling with aperture, shutter speed, and ISO produces a bright enough exposure — in which case, you simply have to add more light. The built-in flash on your D3100 offers the most convenient solution, but you also can attach an external flash head to the camera.

Chapter 2 provides a basic introduction to using flash, and Chapter 3 details the flash settings available in the fully automatic exposure modes (Auto, Auto Flash Off, Scene, and Guide modes). In all those exposure modes, your flash options are pretty limited, though. You may be able to choose from a couple Flash modes, such as regular flash or red-eye reduction flash, and a few of the modes let you disable flash altogether.

When you shoot in the advanced exposure modes (P, S, A, and M), you gain a whole new level of flash control. For example, you gain access to Flash modes not available in the full-auto modes, and you decide when the flash fires — the camera doesn't make that call for you. Additionally, you can adjust the flash power through Flash Compensation.

The rest of this chapter details the advanced flash options and offers some tips on getting better results in your flash pictures. Be sure to also visit Chapter 9, where you can find more flash and lighting tips related to specific types of photographs.

One important note before you dive in: Because the features available with external flash units vary depending on the specific flash, this book concentrates on using the built-in flash. However, note that some camera settings, such as the Flash mode, affect the performance of an external flash as well as the built-in flash. Check your flash user guide to find out which settings you can adjust via the camera and which you establish via controls on the flash head itself.

Enabling flash in P, S, A, and M modes

In the advanced exposure modes, the camera hands over all flash control to you — it doesn't raise the flash automatically in dim light or prevent the flash from firing in bright light.

Enabling and disabling flash is easy:

✔ To raise the built-in flash, press the Flash button on the front-left side of the camera, labeled in Figure 7-27.

✔ To disable the built-in flash, just press down gently on the top of the flash to close it.

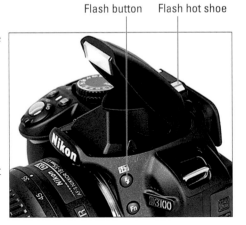

Flash button   Flash hot shoe

Figure 7-27: In the P, S, A, and M exposure modes, just press the Flash button to use flash.

Pay careful attention to your results when you use the built-in flash with a tele-photo lens that's very long. You may find that the flash casts an unwanted shadow when it strikes the lens. Unfortunately, the only way to avoid the problem is to use an external flash, which raises the light source farther above the lens and, on most flash units, enables you to angle the flash head.

Choosing the right Flash mode

Chapter 2 details the art of setting the Flash mode, but here's a quick recap. You can view the current mode in the Shooting Info display, in the area labeled in Figure 7-28. (The viewfinder doesn't display any mode information; you simply see the little lightning-bolt icon to tell you that flash is enabled.)

To change the Flash mode, use either of these two techniques:

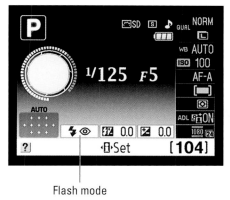

Flash mode

Figure 7-28: The current Flash mode appears in the Shooting Info display.

- ✔ **Press the Flash button as you rotate the Command dial.** As soon as you press the button, the Shooting Info screen changes to display the Flash mode flag, as shown in Figure 7-29. Keep the button pressed while rotating the dial to cycle through the available Flash modes.

- ✔ **Use the Quick Settings display.** Alternatively, you can set the Flash mode through the Quick Settings screen, as shown in Figure 7-30. After highlighting the Flash mode icon, press OK to access the available settings. Highlight the desired mode and press OK.

Your Flash mode choices break down into three basic categories, described in the next sections: fill flash; red-eye reduction flash; and the sync modes, slow-sync and rear-sync, which are special-purpose flash options. Note

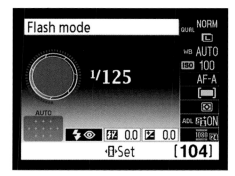

Figure 7-29: After raising the flash, press the Flash button while rotating the Command dial to change the Flash mode.

that the list of available Flash modes doesn't include three options available in the fully automatic exposure modes: Auto, in which the camera makes the decisions about when to fire the flash; its companion, Auto with Red-Eye Reduction; and Off. Instead, if you don't want the flash to fire, simply keep the flash unit closed.

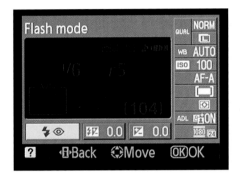 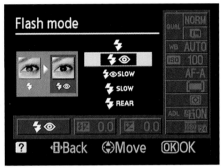

Figure 7-30: You also can adjust the Flash mode through the Quick Settings display.

The camera does give you a little auto-flash input though: You see a blinking question mark, flash symbol, or both in the viewfinder in the P, S, and A modes if the camera thinks you need flash, and the Shooting Info display also tells you that the scene is too dark. Press the Zoom Out button (the one with the question mark above it), and a message appears recommending that you use flash.

Fill flash

 The fill flash setting is represented by the plain-old lightning-bolt symbol you see in the margin here. You can think of this setting as "normal flash" — at least in the way that most think of using a flash.

You may also hear this mode called *force* flash because the flash fires no matter what the available light, unlike in the Auto Flash mode provided for the fully automatic exposure modes, in which the camera decides when flash is needed. In fill Flash mode, the flash fires even in the brightest daylight — which, by the way, is often an excellent idea.

 Yep, you read me correctly: Adding a flash can really improve outdoor photos, even when the sun is at its sunniest. Just as an example, Figure 7-31 shows a floral image taken both with and without a flash. The small pop of light provided by the built-in flash is also extremely beneficial when shooting subjects that happen to be slightly shaded, such as the carousel horses featured in the next section. For outdoor portraits, a flash is even more important; the section on shooting still portraits in Chapter 9 discusses that subject and offers a look at the difference a flash can make.

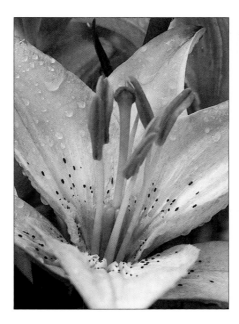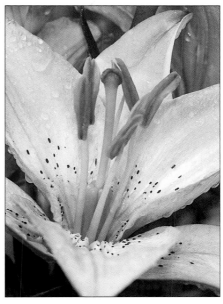

Figure 7-31: Adding flash resulted in better illumination and a slight warming effect.

You do need to beware of a couple complications of using fill flash:

- **Colors may need tweaking when you mix light sources.** When you combine multiple light sources, such as flash with daylight, colors may appear slightly warmer or cooler than neutral. In Figure 7-31, colors became warmer with the addition of flash, for example. For outdoor portraits, the warming effect is usually flattering to skin tones, and I usually like the result with nature shots as well. But if you prefer a neutral color rendition, see the Chapter 8 section related to the White Balance control to find out how to address this issue.

- **Keep an eye on shutter speed.** Because of the way the camera needs to synchronize the firing of the flash with the opening of the shutter, the fastest shutter speed you can use with the built-in flash is 1/200 second. In bright sun, you may need to stop down the aperture significantly or lower ISO, if possible, to avoid overexposing the image even at 1/200 second. As another option, you can place a neutral density filter over your lens; this accessory reduces the light that comes through the lens without affecting colors. Of course, if possible, you can simply move your subject into the shade.

On the flip side, the camera may select a shutter speed as slow as 1/60 second in the P and A modes, depending on the lighting conditions. So if your subject is moving, it's a good idea to work in the S or M modes so that you control shutter speed.

Adjusting flash power through Flash Compensation, explained later in this chapter, is still another way to modify exposure in flash pictures.

Red-eye reduction flash

Red-eye is caused when flash light bounces off a subject's retinas and is reflected back to the camera lens. Red-eye is a human phenomenon, though; with animals, the reflected light usually glows yellow, white, or green, producing an image that looks like your pet is possessed by some demon.

Man or beast, this issue isn't nearly the problem with the type of pop-up flash found on your D3100 as it is on non-SLR cameras. The D3100's flash is positioned in such a way that the flash light usually doesn't hit a subject's eyes straight on, which lessens the chances of red-eye. However, red-eye may still be an issue when you use a lens with a long focal length (a telephoto lens) or you shoot subjects from a distance. Even then, the problem usually crops up only in dark settings — in outdoor shots and other brightly lit scenes, the pupils constrict in reaction to the light, lessening the chance of red-eye. And because of the bright light, the flash power needed to expose the picture is lessened, also helping eliminate red-eye.

 If you do notice red-eye, you can try the red-eye reduction mode, represented by the icon shown in the margin here. In this mode, the AF-assist lamp on the front of the camera lights up briefly before the flash fires. The subject's pupils constrict in response to the light, allowing less flash light to enter the eye and cause that glowing red reflection. Be sure to warn your subjects to wait for the flash, or they may step out of the frame or stop posing after they see the light from the AF-assist lamp.

For an even better solution, try the flash-free portrait tips covered in Chapter 9. If you do a lot of portrait work that requires flash, you may also want to consider an external flash unit, which enables you to aim the flash light in ways that virtually eliminate red-eye.

If all else fails, check out Chapter 10, which shows you how to use the built-in red-eye removal tool on your camera's Retouch menu. Sadly, though, this feature removes only red-eye, not the yellow/green/white eye that you get with animal portraits.

Slow-sync and rear-sync flash

In fill flash and red-eye reduction Flash modes, the flash and shutter are synchronized so that the flash fires at the exact moment the shutter opens.

Technical types refer to this flash arrangement as *front-curtain sync*.

Your D3100 also offers four special-sync modes, which work as follows:

✔ **Slow-Sync:** This mode, available only in the P and A exposure modes, also uses front-curtain sync but allows a shutter speed slower than the 1/60 second minimum that's in force when you use fill flash and red-eye reduction flash.

   The benefit of this longer exposure is that the camera has time to absorb more ambient light, which in turn has two effects: Background areas that are beyond the reach of the flash appear brighter; and less flash power is needed, resulting in softer lighting.

   The downside of the slow shutter speed is, well, the slow shutter speed. As discussed earlier in this chapter, the longer the exposure time, the more you have to worry about blur caused by movement of your subject or your camera. A tripod is essential to a good outcome, as are subjects that can hold very, very still. I find that the best practical use for this mode is shooting nighttime still-life subjects like the one you see in Figure 7-32. However, if you're shooting a nighttime portrait and you have a subject that *can* maintain a motionless pose, slow-sync flash can produce softer, more flattering light. Again, the portrait section of Chapter 9 offers an example.

   Some photographers, on the other hand, turn the downside of slow-sync flash to an upside, using it to purposely blur their subjects. The idea is to use the blur to emphasize motion.

   Note that even though the official Slow-Sync mode appears only in the P and A exposure modes, you can get the same result in the M and S modes by simply using a slow shutter speed and the normal, fill flash mode. You can use a shutter speed as slow as 30 seconds when using flash in those modes.

Normal flash Slow-sync flash

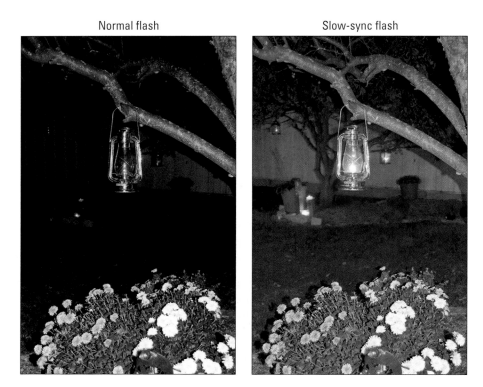

Figure 7-32: Slow-sync flash produces softer, more even lighting than normal flash in nighttime pictures.

✐ **Rear-Curtain Sync:** In this mode, available only in shutter-priority (S) and manual (M) exposure modes, the flash fires at the very end of the exposure, just before the shutter closes. The classic use of this mode is to combine the flash with a slow shutter speed to create trailing-light effects like the one you see in Figure 7-33. With Rear-Curtain Sync, the light trails extend behind the moving object (my hand, and the match, in this case), which makes visual sense. If instead you use slow-sync flash, the light trails appear in front of the moving object.

You can set the shutter speed as low as 30 seconds and as high as 1/200 second in this Flash mode.

✐ **Slow-Sync with Rear-Curtain Sync:** Hey, not confusing enough for you yet? This mode enables you to produce the same motion trail effects as with Rear-Curtain Sync, but in the P and A exposure modes. The camera automatically chooses a slower shutter speed than normal after you set the f-stop, just as with regular Slow-Sync mode.

Note that as you scroll through the available Flash modes, the symbol for this mode initially shows just the flash symbol and the word Rear; after you finish selecting the setting, the label changes to Slow Rear.

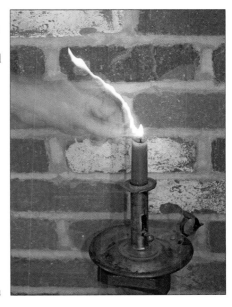

Figure 7-33: I used rear-curtain flash to create this candle-lighting image.

✓ **Slow-Sync with Red-Eye Reduction:** In P and A exposure modes, you can also combine a slow-sync flash with the red-eye reduction feature. Given the potential for blur that comes with a slow shutter, plus the potential for subjects to mistake the pre-light from the AF-assist lamp for the real flash and walk out of the frame before the image is actually recorded, I vote this Flash mode as the most difficult to pull off successfully.

All these modes are somewhat tricky to use successfully, however. So have fun playing around, but at the same time, don't feel too badly if you don't have time right now to master these modes plus all the other exposure options presented to you in this chapter. In the meantime, do a Web search for slow-sync and rear-sync image examples if you want to get a better idea of the special effects that other photographers create with these Flash modes.

Adjusting flash output

When you shoot with your built-in flash, the camera attempts to adjust the flash output as needed to produce a good exposure. But if you shoot in the P, S, A, or M exposure modes and you want a little more or less flash light than the camera thinks is appropriate, you can adjust the flash output by using *Flash Compensation.*

This feature works just like Exposure Compensation, discussed earlier in the chapter, except that it enables you to override the camera's flash-power decision instead of its autoexposure decision. As with Exposure Compensation, the Flash Compensation settings are stated in terms of EV *(exposure value)* numbers. A setting of 0.0 indicates no flash adjustment; you can increase the flash power to EV +1.0 or decrease it to EV –3.0.

As an example of the benefit of this feature, look at the carousel images in Figure 7-34. The first image shows you a flash-free shot. Clearly, I needed a flash to compensate for the fact that the horses were shadowed by the roof of the carousel. But at normal flash power, as shown in the middle image, the flash was too strong, creating glare in some spots and blowing out the highlights in the white mane. By dialing the flash power down to EV –0.7, I got a softer flash that straddled the line perfectly between no flash and too much flash.

No flash

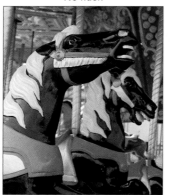

Flash EV 0.0

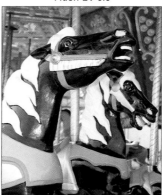

Flash EV –0.7

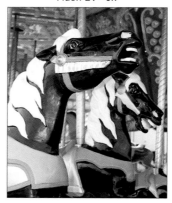

Figure 7-34: When normal flash output is too strong, dial in a lower Flash Compensation setting.

In sync: Flash timing and shutter speed

To properly expose flash pictures, the camera has to synchronize the timing of the flash output with the opening and closing of the shutter. For this reason, the range of shutter speeds available to you is more limited when you use flash than when you go flash-free.

When you use flash, the maximum shutter speed is 1/200 second. The minimum shutter speed varies depending on your exposure mode, as follows:

- **Auto, Child, Close-Up:** 1/60 second
- **Nighttime Portrait mode:** 1 second

- **Portrait, S mode:** 30 seconds
- **P, A modes:** 1/60 second (unless you use one of the slow-sync Flash modes, which permit a slower shutter speed)
- **M mode:** 30 seconds (unless you use bulb mode, in which the shutter stays open as long as you press the shutter button)

These same shutter-speed requirements apply to both the built-in flash and an external flash head.

As for boosting the flash output, well, you may find it necessary on some occasions, but don't expect the built-in flash to work miracles even at a Flash Compensation of +1.0. Any built-in flash has a limited range, and you simply can't expect the flash light to reach faraway objects. In other words, don't even try taking flash pictures of a darkened recital hall from your seat in the balcony — all you'll wind up doing is annoying everyone.

The current Flash Compensation setting appears in the Shooting Info display, in the area highlighted in Figure 7-35. Don't confuse the setting with the neighboring Exposure Compensation setting, also labeled in the figure. (The flash symbol in the Flash Compensation icon is the key reminder to which setting does what.)

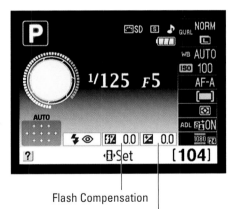

Flash Compensation

Exposure Compensation

Figure 7-35: The Flash Compensation setting lives just next door to the Exposure Compensation setting.

To adjust the amount of Flash Compensation, you have two options:

✔ **Use the two-button plus Command dial maneuver.** First, press the Flash button to pop up the built-in flash. Then press and hold the Flash button and the Exposure Compensation button simultaneously. When you press the buttons, you see the screen shown in Figure 7-36. In the view-finder, the current setting takes the place of the usual frames-remaining value. While keeping both the buttons pressed, rotate the Command dial to adjust the setting. I find that any technique that involves coordinating this many fingers a little complex, but you may find it easier than I do.

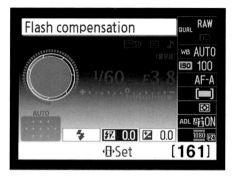

Figure 7-36: Rotate the Command dial while pressing the Flash and Exposure Compensation buttons to adjust flash power.

✔ **Use the Quick Settings screen.** Just bring up the Shooting Info display, press the Info Edit button to shift to Quick Settings mode, and highlight the Flash Compensation setting, as shown on the left in Figure 7-37. Press OK to display a screen where you can set the flash power, as shown in the second screen of the figure. Press the Multi Selector up or down to change the setting and then press OK.

As with Exposure Compensation, any flash-power adjustment you make remains in force, even if you turn off the camera, until you reset the control. So be sure to check the setting before you next use your flash.

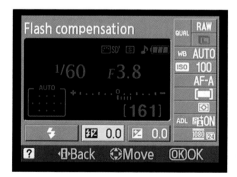
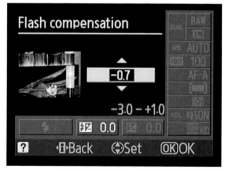

Figure 7-37: For a less cumbersome way to adjust flash power, use the Quick Settings screen.

Controlling Flash Output Manually

If you're experienced in the way of the flash, you can manually set the flash output by taking these steps:

1. **Display the Shooting menu and select Built-in Flash.**

2. **Press OK.**

   The options shown on the right in Figure 7-38 appear.

   The TTL setting is the default flash setting, in which the camera sets the proper flash power for you. *TTL* stands for *through the lens.*

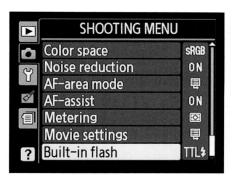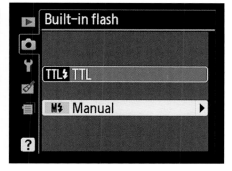

Figure 7-38: Through this option, you can control the flash output manually.

3. **Highlight Manual and press OK.**

   The menu shown in Figure 7-39 appears.

4. **Highlight the desired flash output and press OK.**

   Your options are from Full power to 1/32 power. The next time you use the built-in flash, it emits a burst of light at the power you specify. While manual flash control is enabled, an icon that looks like the Shooting Info screen's Flash Compensation icon (lightning bolt with a plus-minus sign) blinks in the viewfinder. If you want to get really tricky, you can employ Flash Compensation even with manual flash control.

Figure 7-39: Specify the amount of light you want the flash to emit.

Becoming a flash master

Although this chapter covers a lot of flash information, what I have room to present in this book still provides just the most basic introduction to flash photography. So I urge you to check out the many great books on the subject to gain a better understanding of how to take truly great flash pictures — there's a lot more to this particular photographic art than you may imagine.

Also take a look at two of my favorite online resources for finding out more about flash photography:

✔ www.strobist.com: This Web site is completely dedicated to flash photography, enabling you to learn from and share with other photographers.

✔ www.nikon.com: Nikon's Web site also offers some great tutorials on flash photography (as well as other subjects). Start in the Learn and Explore section of the site, and also seek out pages related to the Nikon Creative Lighting System (CLS). In a nutshell, the CLS enables you to light a subject using multiple flash units, which is a great alternative to using old-style studio lights, which can be bulky and, depending on the bulbs used, very hot.

Manipulating Focus and Color

*T*o many people, the word *focus* has just one interpretation when applied to a photograph: Either the subject is in focus or it's blurry. And it's true — this characteristic of your photographs is an important one. There's not much to appreciate about an image that's so blurry that you can't make out whether you're looking at Peru or Peoria. But an artful photographer knows that there's more to focus than simply getting a sharp image of a subject. You also need to consider *depth of field,* or the distance over which objects remain sharply focused.

This chapter explains all the ways to control depth of field and also explains how to use your D3100's advanced focusing options. Note, however, that the autofocusing features covered here relate only to regular, through-the-viewfinder photography; Chapter 4 focuses (yuk yuk) on Live View and movie autofocusing, which involves a different set of features and techniques.

This chapter also dives into the topic of color, explaining your camera's White Balance control, which compensates for the varying color casts created by different light sources. You also can get my take on the other advanced color options on your D3100, including the Color Space option and Picture Controls, in this chapter.

Mastering the Autofocus System

The D3100, like its siblings in the Nikon dSLR line, offers a fast and trustworthy autofocusing system — you can rely on it for tack-sharp images 99 percent of the time, in my experience. But to get the best autofocusing performance, you need to understand which autofocus settings work best for different types of subjects. The default settings usually work fine for portraits, for example, but for sports photography, adjusting the settings typically produces more reliable results.

On the D3100, you can control the following two aspects of the camera's autofocusing behavior:

- **Which focus points are used to establish focus (AF-area mode):** You can tell the camera to consider all 11 autofocus points or to base focus on a single point that you select.

- **When the final focusing distance is set (Focus mode):** You can set the camera to lock focus when you press the shutter button halfway or adjust focus continually up to the moment you depress the button fully to take the picture.

The next several sections provide the background you need to master autofocusing, starting with a quick review of the proper focusing technique and then digging into specific autofocus options.

Reviewing autofocus basics

The Chapter 3 section on taking your first pictures in the Auto and Auto Flash Off exposure modes provides an introduction to the process of autofocusing with the D3100. But in case you haven't dug into that chapter, the following steps get you up to speed.

Auto/Manual focus switch

These steps apply to any exposure mode, not just Auto or Auto Flash Off. However, they *don't* apply to Live View photography or movie recording; again, check Chapter 4 for information on autofocusing in those modes.

1. **Set the focusing switch on the lens to A (autofocus), as shown in Figure 8-1.**

   These directions are specific to the kit lens sold with the D3100. Other lenses may have a different sort of switch or no switch at all, so check the product manual. And note that not all lenses

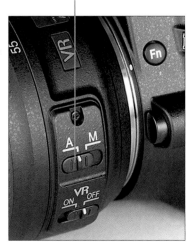

Figure 8-1: Set the lens switch to the A position to use autofocusing.

provide autofocusing when paired with the D3100; the camera manual provides information on compatible lenses.

2. **Frame the picture so that your subject falls under one of the 11 focus points.**

   The focus points are represented by the little black markings in the viewfinder. Note that the brackets are there simply to help you see the focus points — they don't indicate any special focusing purpose.

   For most exposure modes, all 11 focus points are active by default, which means that the camera considers all points when deciding where to set focus. But in Close Up mode and Sports mode, the camera bases focus only on the center point by default, so be sure to frame your subject under that point. To find out how to modify this autofocus behavior, see the next section.

3. **Press and hold the shutter button halfway down.**

   Depending on the lighting conditions, the AF-assist lamp on the front of the camera may emit a beam to help the autofocus system find its target. (If the light becomes a distraction, you can disable it through the AF-assist option on the Shooting menu. But the camera may have trouble locking focus, so you may need to focus manually.)

   As soon as you press the button halfway, one or more of the focus points flashes red, as shown in Figure 8-2, to let you know which points the camera will use to establish focus.

   Your half-press of the shutter button also kicks the exposure metering system into gear. And the shots remaining value in the viewfinder changes to show the number of frames that will fit in the camera's buffer. For more on exposure, travel back to Chapter 7; information about the buffer awaits in Chapter 2.

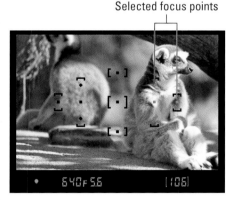

Selected focus points

Figure 8-2: The red dots indicate active focus points.

4. **Pause for a second to allow the camera to establish focus.**

   Don't just jab the shutter button all the way down in one step — otherwise, the autofocusing system doesn't have time to do its thing.

   The camera signals you that it set focus successfully differently depending on whether your subject is moving:

   • *For stationary subjects:* The green focus dot lights in the lower-left corner of the viewfinder, as shown in Figure 8-2, and the camera emits a tiny beep. (See Chapter 1 to find out how to disable the beep if you want it to keep quiet.) Focus is now locked as long as you keep the shutter button depressed halfway. That means that you can reframe the picture if desired and still retain focus on the subject.

- *For moving subjects*: If the camera detects movement, it sets the initial focus point and then adjusts focus if the subject moves out of the selected point. You need to reframe the picture as needed to keep the subject within the area covered by the 11 focus points, however. The green focus indicator may flicker on and off as the camera continues to track focus. The beep may or may not sound.

To find out how to adjust this aspect of autofocus behavior, check out the upcoming discussion related to the Focus mode.

5. **Press the button the rest of the way to take the picture.**

For stationary subjects, the camera refuses to release the shutter button and take the picture if it can't lock focus. For moving subjects, on the other hand, the camera may snap the picture before the green focus lamp lights — the thinking is that you're more concerned with capturing a fleeting moment in time than seeing the focus light.

Now that you understand how things work at the default AF-area mode and Focus mode settings, the next several sections explain how to modify the settings to best suit your subject.

Understanding the AF-area mode setting

The AF-area mode option determines which of the 11 focusing points the camera uses to establish focus. (The *AF* in AF-area mode stands for *autofocus*.) You can view the current setting on the Shooting Info display. In fact, the display contains two different icons representing the setting, as shown in Figure 8-3. The one in the lower-left corner is designed to give you a bit more information than the simplified version on the right side of the screen. More about what you can glean from that detailed icon momentarily.

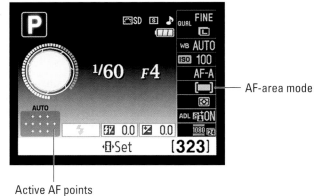

AF-area mode

Active AF points

Figure 8-3: These symbols show the current AF-area mode setting and which focus points are active.

Shutter speed and blurry photos

A poorly focused photo isn't always related to the issues discussed in this chapter. Any movement of the camera or subject can also cause blur. Both of these problems are related to shutter speed, an exposure control that I cover in Chapter 7. Be sure to also visit Chapter 9, which provides some additional tips for capturing moving objects without blur.

You can choose from four settings, which work as described in the following list and are represented in the lower-left corner of the Shooting Info display by the margin icons shown here. (Flip ahead to Figures 8-4 and 8-5 to see the simplified icons, which appear both in the Quick Setting screens and menus.)

✔ **Single Point:** This mode is designed for shooting still subjects. You select one of the 11 focus points, and the camera sets focus on the object that falls within that point. (See the upcoming section "Selecting a single focus point," in this chapter, for specifics on how to designate your chosen point.) The camera uses this mode by default when you shoot in the Close Up Scene mode.

In the lower-left corner of the Shooting Info display, the position of the brackets in the AF-area mode icon show you which point is selected. For example, an icon like the one you see in the margin here tells you that the center point is selected.

✔ **Dynamic Area:** In this mode, designed for shooting moving subjects, you select an initial focus point, just as in Single Point mode. But if the subject within that focus point moves after you press the shutter button halfway to set focus, the camera looks for focus information from the other focus points. The idea is that the subject is likely to wind up within one of the 11 focus areas. Dynamic Area is the default setting when you shoot in the Sports exposure mode.

However — and this is a biggie — for the automatic focus adjustment to occur, you also must set the Focus mode option (explained next) to either AF-A, the default setting, or AF-C. If you instead set that option to AF-S, which is designed for shooting still subjects, the camera sticks with the initial focus point you select, even if the subject moves before you take the picture.

In the lower-left corner of the Shooting Info display, the icon for this mode looks similar to the one in the margin here. Your selected focus point is surrounded by brackets, but you also see little plus signs marking the other points to indicate that they're ready to take over if your subject moves.

- ✔ **Auto Area:** The camera analyzes the objects under all 11 autofocus points and selects the one it deems most appropriate. This mode is the default setting for all exposure modes except Sports and Close Up. Notice that none of the focus points in the detailed icon are surrounded by brackets this time, indicating that any focus point may be used.

- ✔ **3D Tracking:** This one is a variation of Dynamic Area autofocusing — well, sort of. As with Dynamic Area mode, you start by selecting a single focus point and then press the shutter button halfway to set focus. But the goal of this mode is to maintain focus on your subject if you recompose the shot after you press the shutter button halfway to lock focus.

Again, you have to set the Focus mode to AF-A or AF-C for this focus adjustment to occur. In fact, the 3D Tracking option doesn't even appear on the menus or Quick Settings display when the Focus mode is set to AF-S.

The only problem with 3D Tracking is that the way the camera detects your subject is by analyzing the colors of the object under your selected focus point. So if not much difference exists between the subject and other objects in the frame, the camera can get fooled. And if your subject moves out of the frame, you must release the shutter button and reset focus by pressing it halfway again.

The 3D Tracking display icon appears in the lower-left corner of the Shooting Info display as shown in the margin here. As with the Dynamic Area mode, the brackets indicate the focus area you initially select.

If you're feeling overwhelmed by all your autofocus options, Auto-area produces good results for most subjects. Personally, however, I rely on the first two modes because if the Auto-area mode makes the wrong focus assumptions, there's no way to select a different focus point. So for still subjects, I stick with Single Point focus; for moving subjects, I go with Dynamic Area.

Whatever your conclusions on the subject, the next two sections show you how to adjust the AF-area mode and select a specific focus point.

Changing the AF-area mode setting

You can control the AF-area mode setting in any of your camera's exposure modes. Use either of these options:

- ✔ **Quick Settings screen:** If the Shooting Info screen is visible, tap the Info Edit button to shift to Quick Settings mode. Otherwise, press the button twice. Then highlight the AF-area mode icon, as shown on the left in Figure 8-4, and press OK to access the second screen in the figure, where you see the simplified versions of the icons representing the different mode options. From top to bottom, the settings are Single Point, Dynamic Area, Auto Area, and 3D Tracking.

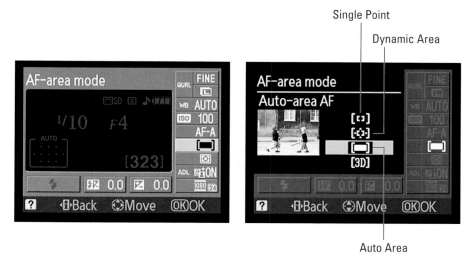

Figure 8-4: The fastest way to adjust the AF-area mode is through the Quick Settings screen.

Don't see the 3D Tracking option on your screen? That happens if the Focus mode is set to AF-S. So if you want to use 3D Tracking, set the Focus mode to AF-C or AF-A — the setting is located directly above the AF-area mode option in the Quick Settings display. Refer to the upcoming section "Changing the Focus mode setting," in this chapter, for more information about this aspect of the focusing system.

✓ **Shooting menu:** Look for the option in the menu position shown in Figure 8-5. After selecting the option, press OK to display the left screen shown in Figure 8-6. Here, you specify whether you want to adjust the setting for viewfinder shooting or Live View and movie shooting. Select Viewfinder and press OK to access the four settings, as shown on the right in Figure 8-6. (See Chapter 4 to find out about the Live View and movie options for this setting.)

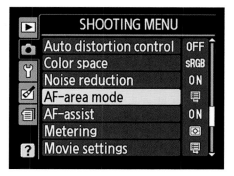

Figure 8-5: You also can adjust the setting through the Shooting menu.

Although going the menu route takes longer, it offers one advantage over using the Quick Settings screen: When you get to the final screen (right screen in Figure 8-6), the option names are spelled out — you don't have to remember what all the icons represent.

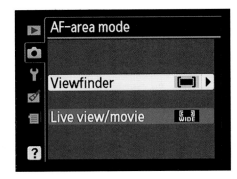
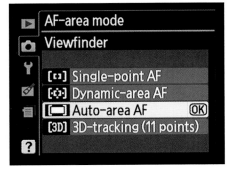

Figure 8-6: Select the Viewfinder option to access AF-area modes for regular photography.

Selecting a single focus point

In the Single Point, Dynamic Area, and 3D Tracking AF-area modes, your first step is to specify which focus point you want the camera to use. For Single Point mode, focus is locked on your selected point. In Dynamic Area and 3D Tracking, focus is initially set on your chosen point, but if your subject moves or you reframe the shot, the camera may automatically shift to a different focus point to keep the subject in focus.

As an aside, selecting a focus point is also a good idea when you focus manually, although not technically required. See the section "Focusing Manually" later in this chapter, for more information.

Take these steps to select a focus point:

1. **Press the shutter button halfway and release it to engage the exposure meters.**

   The currently selected point flashes red. For example, in Figure 8-7, the point directly over the top of the clock tower is selected.

2. **Use the Multi Selector to select a different focus point.**

   As you press the Multi Selector to cycle through the points, the currently selected one flashes red.

To quickly select the center focus point, press OK. No need to cycle your way through all the other focus points to get to the center.

Selected focus point

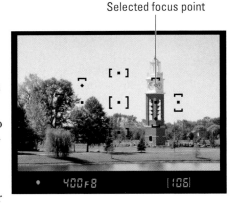

Figure 8-7: Use the Multi Selector to select the focus point that's over your subject.

Changing the Focus mode setting

Throughout this book, I use the term *auto/manual focusing mode* generically to refer to the lens switch that shifts your camera from autofocusing to manual focusing — at least, on the kit lens sold with the D3100. But there is also an official Focus mode setting, which controls another aspect of your camera's focusing behavior. There are four options, which work as follows:

✔ **AF-S (single-servo autofocus):** In this mode, which is geared to shooting stationary subjects, the camera locks focus when you depress the shutter button halfway.

Use this mode if you want to frame your subject so that it doesn't fall under an autofocus point: Compose the scene initially to put the subject under a focus point, press the shutter button halfway to lock focus, and then reframe to the composition you have in mind. As long as you keep the button pressed halfway, focus remains set on your subject. Remember, though, that exposure is adjusted up to the time you take the picture. See Chapter 7 to find out how to use the AE-L/AF-L button to lock exposure instead.

✔ **AF-C (continuous-servo autofocus):** In this mode, which is designed for moving subjects, the camera focuses continuously for the entire time you hold the shutter button halfway down.

When you combine this mode with the Singe Point AF-area mode, be sure to reframe the shot as needed to keep a moving subject under the selected focus point after you initially establish focus. In the other AF-area modes, the camera should track focus as long as the subject stays within one of the 11 focus points.

To lock focus at a certain distance while using AF-C mode, use the technique described in the section, "Using autofocus lock," later in this chapter.

✔ **AF-A (auto-servo autofocus):** This mode is the default setting. The camera analyzes the scene and, if it detects motion, automatically selects continuous-servo mode (AF-C). If the camera instead believes you're shooting a stationary object, it selects single-servo mode (AF-S). This mode works pretty well, but it can get confused sometimes. For example, if your subject is motionless but other people are moving in the background, the camera may mistakenly switch to continuous autofocus. By the same token, if the subject is moving only slightly, the camera may not make the switch.

✔ **MF (manual focus):** If you use a lens that doesn't offer an external switch to shift from auto to manual focus, you need to select this setting to focus manually. You also need to choose this setting if your lens doesn't offer an autofocus motor at all. On the kit lens featured in this book, simply setting the switch on the lens to M automatically sets the Focus mode to MF. However, the opposite isn't true: Choosing the MF setting for the Focus mode does not free the focusing ring so that you can set focus manually; you must set the lens switch to the M position.

You can choose from all four settings only in the P, S, A, and M exposure modes. In the other modes, you can choose between AF-A and MF only.

Assuming that you use a mode that allows full control, which Focus mode should you select? As for the autofocus options, single-servo mode (AF-S) works best for shooting still subjects, and continuous-servo (AF-C) is the right choice for moving subjects. But frankly, auto-servo (AF-A), which is the default setting, does a good job in most cases of making that shift for you. So, in my mind, there's no real reason to fiddle with the setting unless you're having trouble getting the camera to lock onto your subject.

At any rate, change the Focus mode via the Quick Settings display, as shown in Figure 8-8. This setting is one of the few that can be adjusted only through the display and not through the menus.

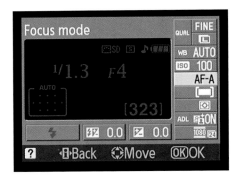 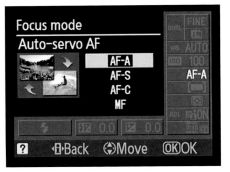

Figure 8-8: The Focus mode determines whether the autofocusing system locks focus when you press the shutter button halfway.

Choosing the right autofocus combo

You get the best autofocus results if you pair your chosen Focus mode with the most appropriate AF-area mode because the two settings work in tandem. Here are the combinations that I suggest for the maximum autofocus control:

✓ **For still subjects, use Single Point as the AF-area mode and AF-S as the Focus mode.** You then select a specific focus point, and the camera locks focus on that point when you press the shutter button halfway. Focus remains locked on your subject even if you reframe the shot after you press the button halfway. (It helps to remember the *s* factor: For *s*till subjects, *S*ingle Point and AF-*S*.)

> ✔ **For moving subjects, set the AF-area mode to Dynamic Area and the Focus mode to AF-C.** You still begin by selecting a focus point, but the camera adjusts focus as needed if your subject moves within the frame after you press the shutter button halfway to establish focus. (Think *motion, dynamic, continuous.*) Remember to reframe as needed to keep your subject within the boundaries of the 11 autofocus points, though.

Again, though, you get full control over the Focus mode only in the P, S, A, and M exposure modes. In the other modes, you have only two choices — either MF (manual focus) or AF-A.

Using autofocus lock

When you set your camera's Focus mode to AF-C (continuous-servo auto-focus), pressing and holding the shutter button halfway initiates autofocus. But focusing is continually adjusted while you hold the shutter button half-way, so the focusing distance may change if the subject moves out of the active autofocus point or you reframe the shot before you take the picture. The same is true if you use AF-A mode (auto-servo autofocus) and the camera senses movement in front of the lens, in which case it shifts to AF-C mode and operates as I just described. Either way, the upshot is that you can't control the exact focusing distance the camera ultimately uses.

Should you want to lock focus at a specific distance, you have a couple options:

✔ **Focus manually.**

✔ **Change the Focus mode to AF-S (single-servo autofocus).** In this mode, focus is locked when you press and hold the shutter button halfway.

✔ **Lock focus with the AE-L/AF-L button.** First set focus by pressing the shutter button halfway. When the focus is established at the distance you want, press and hold the AE-L/AF-L button, located near the view-finder. Focus remains set as long as you hold the button down, even if you release the shutter button.

Keep in mind, though, that by default, pressing the AE-L/AF-L button also locks in autoexposure. (Chapter 7 explains.) You can change this behavior, however, setting the button to lock just one or the other. Chapter 11 explains this option as well as a couple other ways to customize the button's function.

For my money, manual focusing is by far the easiest solution. Yes, it may take you a little while to get comfortable with manual focusing, but in the long run, you really save yourself a lot of time fiddling with the various autofocus settings, remembering which button initiates the focus lock, and so on. See the next section for help with manual focusing.

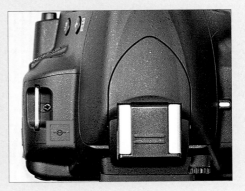

Finding the precise camera-to-subject distance

Should you ever need to know the exact distance between your subject and the camera, the *focal plane position mark* on the top left side of the camera is key. Highlighted in the figure here, the mark indicates the plane at which light coming through the lens is focused onto the negative in a film camera or the image sensor in a digital camera. Basing your measurement on this mark produces a more accurate camera-to-subject distance than using the end of the lens or some other external point on the camera body as your reference point.

Focusing Manually

Some subjects confuse even the most sophisticated autofocusing systems, causing the camera's autofocus motor to spend a long time "hunting" for its focus point. Animals behind fences, reflective objects, water, and low-contrast subjects are just some of the autofocus troublemakers. Autofocus systems also struggle in dim lighting, although that difficulty is often offset on the D3100 by the AF-assist lamp, which shoots out a beam of light to help the camera find its focusing target.

When you encounter situations that cause an autofocus hang-up, you can try adjusting the autofocus options discussed earlier in this chapter. But often, it's simply easier and faster to switch to manual focusing. For best results, follow these manual-focusing steps:

1. **Adjust the viewfinder to your eyesight.**

   Chapter 1 shows you how to take this critical step. If you don't adjust the viewfinder, scenes that are in focus may appear blurry and vice versa.

2. **Set the focus switch on the lens to M, as shown in Figure 8-9.**

   If your lens doesn't have an auto/manual switch, you must set the camera's Focus Mode setting to MF (Manual Focus) The fastest way to access the option is via the Quick Settings screen (refer to Figure 8-8). (The section "Changing the Focus mode setting," earlier in this chapter, has more details about this option.)

With the kit lens, as well as some other compatible lenses, the camera automatically changes this setting for you as soon as you set the lens switch to M.

3. **Select a focus point.**

Use the same technique as when selecting a point during autofocusing: Looking through the viewfinder, press the Multi Selector right, left, up, or down until the point you want to use flashes red.

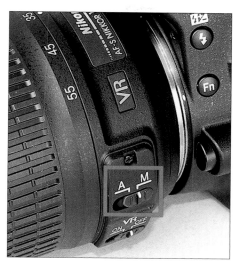

Figure 8-9: Remember to set the lens switch to M before turning the focusing ring.

During autofocusing, the selected focus point tells the camera what part of the frame to use when establishing focus. And technically speaking, you don't *have* to choose a focus point for manual focusing — the camera will set the focus according to the position that you set by turning the focusing ring. However, choosing a focus point is still a good idea, for two reasons: First, even though you're focusing manually, the camera provides some feedback to let you know if focus is correct, and that feedback is based on your selected focus point. Second, if you use spot metering, an exposure option covered in Chapter 7, exposure is based on the selected focus point.

4. **Frame the shot so that your subject is under your selected focus point.**

When the camera thinks focus is set on the object under your focus point, the green focus lamp in the lower-left corner of the viewfinder lights, just as it does during autofocusing.

5. **Press the shutter button halfway to initiate exposure metering.**

Adjust exposure as needed; see Chapter 7 for help.

6. **Press the shutter button the rest of the way to take the shot.**

I know that when you first start working with an SLR-style camera, focusing manually is intimidating. But if you practice a little, you'll find that it's really no big deal and saves you the time and aggravation of trying to bend the autofocus system to your will when it has "issues."

In addition to the green focus lamp, the D3100 offers another manual focusing aid to help you feel more confident, too: You can swap out the viewfinder's exposure meter with a *rangefinder,* which uses a similar, meter-like display, as shown in Figure 8-10, to indicate whether focus is set on the object in the selected focus point. If bars appear to the left of the 0, as shown in the left example in Figure 8-10, focus is set in front of the subject; if the bars are to the right, as in the middle example, focus is slightly behind the subject. The more bars you see, the greater the focusing error. As you twist the focusing ring, the rangefinder updates to help you get focus on track. When you see a single bar on either side of the 0, you're good to go.

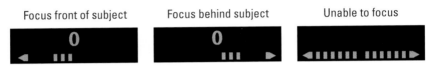

Figure 8-10: The rangefinder offers manual-focusing assistance.

Before I tell you how to activate this feature, I want to point out a couple issues:

- ✔ You can use the rangefinder in any exposure mode except M (manual exposure). In M mode, the viewfinder always displays the exposure meter.

- ✔ In the other exposure modes, you can continue to view the exposure meter in the Shooting Info display, even with the rangefinder enabled.

- ✔ Your lens must offer a maximum aperture (f-stop number) of f/5.6 or lower. To understand f-stops, head back to Chapter 7. The kit lens sold with the D3100 meets this qualification.

- ✔ With subjects that confuse the camera's autofocus system, the rangefinder may not work well either; it's based on the same system. If the system can't find the focusing target, you see the rangefinder display shown on the right in Figure 8-10.

- ✔ The rangefinder is automatically replaced by the normal exposure meter if you switch back to autofocusing, but reappears when you return to manual focus.

Personally, I leave the rangefinder off and just rely on the focus indicator lamp and my eyes to verify focus. I shoot in the S and A exposure modes frequently, and I find it a pain to monitor exposure in the Shooting Info display rather than in the viewfinder. That's not a recommendation to you either way — it's just how I prefer to work. If you want to try the rangefinder, set the Mode dial to any setting but M and then set the Rangefinder option on the Setup menu to On, as shown in Figure 8-11.

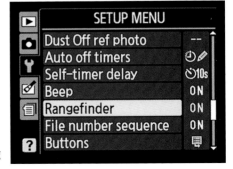

Figure 8-11: Enable the rangefinder via the Setup menu.

Correcting lens distortion

If you take a lot of pictures with wide-angle lenses, you may notice that vertical structures in the scene sometimes appear to bend outward from the center of the image. This is known as *barrel distortion*. On the flip side of the coin, shooting with a long telephoto lens sometimes causes those verticals to bow inward, which is known as *pincushion distortion*.

The Retouch menu on your camera has a post-capture filter you can apply to try to correct both problems. (See Chapter 10 for help.) But the D3100 also has an Auto Distortion Control feature that attempts to correct the image as you're shooting. It only works with certain types of lenses (specifically, those that Nikon classifies as type G and D), but is worth trying if your lens is compatible. To activate the option, just set the Auto Distortion Control on the Shooting Menu to On, as shown in the figure here.

When you use this feature, understand that some of the area you see in your viewfinder may not be visible in the final photo because the anti-distortion manipulation requires some cropping of the scene. So after activating the feature, take some test shots and examine the pictures carefully. If you're not happy with the results, return to the menu and change the setting back to Off.

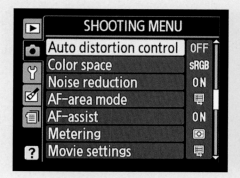
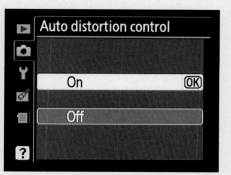

Manipulating Depth of Field

Getting familiar with the concept of *depth of field* is one of the biggest steps you can take to becoming a more artful photographer. I introduce you to depth of field in Chapters 3 and 7; here's a summary in case you missed those pages:

- *Depth of field* refers to the distance over which objects in a photograph appear sharply focused.

- With a shallow, or small, depth of field, distant objects appear more softly focused than the main subject (assuming that you set focus on the main subject, of course).

- With a large depth of field, the zone of sharp focus extends to include objects at a distance from your subject.

Which arrangement works best depends entirely on your creative vision and your subject. In portraits, for example, a classic technique is to use a shallow depth of field, as shown in the photo in Figure 8-12. This approach increases emphasis on the subject while diminishing the impact of the background. But for the photo in Figure 8-13, I wanted to emphasize that the foreground figures were in St. Peter's Square, at the Vatican, so I used a large depth of field, which kept the background buildings sharply focused and gave them equal weight in the scene.

So exactly how do you adjust depth of field? You have three points of control: aperture, focal length, and camera-to-subject distance, as spelled out in the following list:

Aperture, f/5.6; Focal length, 90mm

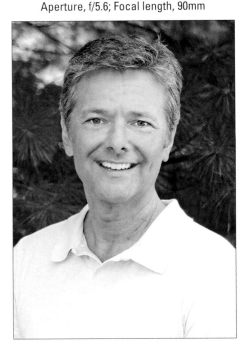

Figure 8-12: A shallow depth of field blurs the background and draws added attention to the subject.

- **Aperture setting (f-stop):** The aperture is one of three exposure settings, all explained fully in Chapter 7. Depth of field increases as you stop down the aperture (by choosing a higher f-stop number). For shallow depth of field, open the aperture (by choosing a lower f-stop number). Figure 8-14 offers an example; in the f/22 version, focus is sharp all the way through the frame; in the f/13 version, focus softens as the distance from the center lure increases. I snapped both images using the same focal length and camera-to-subject distance, setting focus on the center lure.

- **Lens focal length:** In lay terms, *focal length* determines what the lens "sees." As you increase focal length, measured in millimeters, the angle of view narrows, objects appear larger in the frame, and — the important point for this discussion — depth of field decreases. Additionally, the spatial relationship of objects changes as you adjust focal length. As an example, Figure 8-15 compares the same scene shot at a focal length of 127mm and 183mm. I used the same aperture, f/5.6, for both examples.

  Whether you have any focal length flexibility depends on your lens: If you have a zoom lens, you can adjust the focal length — just zoom in or out. (The D3100 kit lens, for example, offers a focal-length range of 18–55mm.) If you don't have a zoom lens, the focal length is fixed, so scratch this means of manipulating depth of field.

For more technical details about focal length and your D3100, see the sidebar "Fun facts about focal length," later in this chapter.

✏ **Camera-to-subject distance:** As you move the lens closer to your subject, depth of field decreases. This assumes that you don't zoom in or out to reframe the picture, thereby changing the focal length. If you do, depth of field is affected by both the camera position and focal length.

Together, these three factors determine the maximum and minimum depth of field that you can achieve, as illustrated by my clever artwork in Figure 8-16 and summed up in the following list:

✏ **To produce the shallowest depth of field:** Open the aperture as wide as possible (the lowest f-stop number), zoom in to the maximum focal length of your lens, and get as close as possible to your subject.

Aperture, f/14; Focal length, 42mm

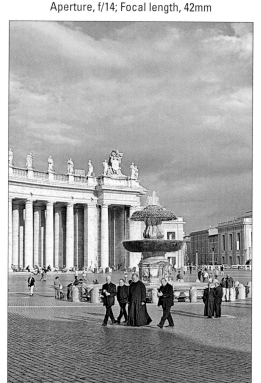

Figure 8-13: A large depth of field keeps both foreground and background subjects in focus.

When you combine a very large aperture — f/2.0, for example — you can wind up with an extremely shallow depth of field if you also use a long focal length, are very close to your subject, or both. In fact, in a portrait in which one subject is only a foot or so in front of the other, the depth of field may not be sufficient to keep both people sharply focused. So always shoot a test image and then use the playback zoom feature to check focus on all subjects in the frame. See Chapter 5 to find out how.

✏ **To produce maximum depth of field:** Stop down the aperture to the highest possible f-stop number, zoom out to the shortest focal length your lens offers, and move farther from your subject.

Just to avoid a possible point of confusion that has arisen in some of the classes I teach: When I say *zoom in,* some students think that I mean to twist the zoom barrel so that it moves *in* toward the camera body. But in fact, the phrase *zoom in* means to zoom to a longer focal length, which produces the visual effect of bringing your subject closer. This requires twisting the zoom barrel of the lens so that it extends farther *out* from the camera. And the phrase *zoom out* refers to the opposite maneuver: I'm talking about widening your view of the subject by zooming to a shorter focal length, which requires moving the lens barrel *in* toward the camera body.

Aperture, f/22; Focal length, 92mm

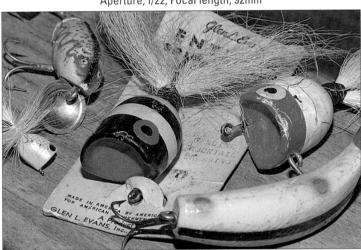

Aperture, f/13; Focal length, 92mm

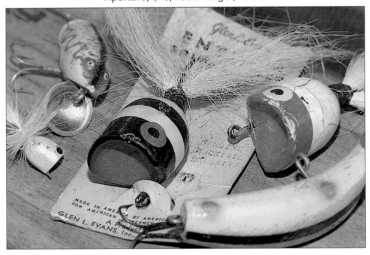

Figure 8-14: A lower f-stop number (wider aperture) decreases depth of field.

Aperture, f/5.6; Focal length, 127mm

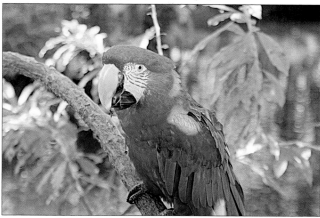

Aperture, f/5.6; Focal length, 183mm

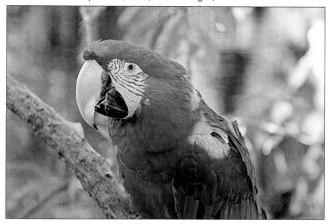

Figure 8-15: Zooming to a longer focal length also reduces depth of field.

Here are a few additional tips and tricks related to depth of field:

✔ **Aperture-priority autoexposure (A) mode enables you to easily control depth of field.** In this mode, detailed fully in Chapter 7, you set the f-stop, and the camera selects the appropriate shutter speed to produce a good exposure. The range of aperture settings you can access depends on your lens.

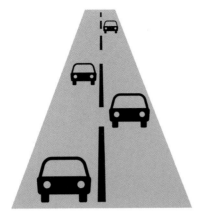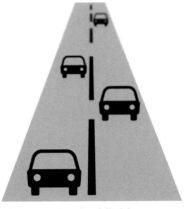

Greater depth of field:
Select higher f-stop
Decrease focal length (zoom out)
Move farther from subject

Shorter depth of field:
Select lower f-stop
Increase focal length (zoom in)
Move closer to subject

Figure 8-16: Your f-stop, focal length, and shooting distance determine depth of field.

Even in aperture-priority mode, keep an eye on shutter speed as well. To maintain the same exposure, shutter speed must change in tandem with aperture, and you may encounter a situation where the shutter speed is too slow to permit hand-holding of the camera. Lenses that offer optical image stabilization, or Vibration Reduction (VR lenses, in the Nikon world), enable most people to use a slower shutter speed than normal, but double-check your results just to be sure. Or use a tripod for extra security. Of course, all this assumes that you have dialed in a specific ISO Sensitivity setting; if you instead are using Auto ISO adjustment, the camera may adjust the ISO setting instead of shutter speed. (Chapter 7 explores the whole aperture/shutter speed/ISO relationship.)

✔ **Portrait and Close Up modes are designed to produce shallow depth of field; Landscape mode is designed for large depth of field.** You can't adjust aperture in these modes, however, so you're limited to the setting the camera chooses. In addition, the extent to which the camera can select an appropriate f-stop depends on the lighting conditions. If you're shooting in Landscape mode at dusk, for example, the camera may have to open the aperture to a wide setting to produce a good exposure.

✔ **For greater background blurring, move the subject farther from the background.** The extent to which background focus shifts as you adjust depth of field also is affected by the distance between the subject and the background. For increased background blurring, move the subject farther in front of the background.

Fun facts about focal length

Every lens can be characterized by its *focal length,* or in the case of a zoom lens, the range of focal lengths it offers. Measured in millimeters, focal length determines the camera's angle of view, the apparent size and distance of objects in the scene, and depth of field. According to photography tradition, a focal length of 50mm is described as a "normal" lens. Most point-and-shoot cameras feature this focal length, which is a medium-range lens that works well for the type of snapshots that users of those kinds of cameras are likely to shoot.

A lens with a focal length under 35mm is characterized as a *wide-angle* lens because at that focal length, the camera has a wide angle of view and produces a large depth of field, making it good for landscape photography. A short focal length also has the effect of making objects seem smaller and farther away. At the other end of the spectrum, a lens with a focal length longer than 80mm is considered a *telephoto* lens and often referred to as a *long lens.* With a long lens, angle of view narrows, depth of field decreases, and faraway subjects appear closer and larger, which is ideal for wildlife and sports photographers.

Note, however, that the focal lengths stated here and elsewhere in the book are so-called *35mm equivalent* focal lengths. Here's the deal: For reasons that aren't really important, when you put a standard lens on most digital cameras, including your D3100, the available frame area is reduced, as if you took a picture on a camera that uses 35mm film negatives (the kind you've probably been using for years) and then cropped it.

This so-called *crop factor* varies depending on the digital camera, which is why the photo industry adopted the 35mm-equivalent measuring stick as a standard. With the D3100, the cropping factor is roughly 1.5. So the 18–55mm kit lens, for example, actually captures the approximate area you would get from a 27–83mm lens on a 35mm film camera. In the figure here, for example, the red outline indicates the image area that results from the 1.5 crop factor.

Note that although the area the lens can capture changes when you move a lens from a 35mm film camera to a digital body, depth of field isn't affected, nor are the spatial relationships between objects in the frame. So when lens shopping, you gauge those two characteristics of the lens by looking at the stated focal length — no digital-to-film conversion math is required.

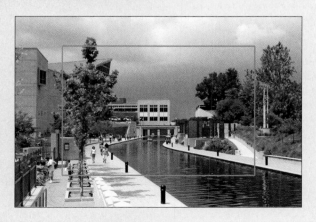

Controlling Color

Compared with understanding some aspects of digital photography — resolution, aperture and shutter speed, depth of field, and so on — making sense of your camera's color options is easy-breezy. First, color problems aren't all that common, and when they are, they're usually simple to fix with a quick shift of your D3100's White Balance control. And getting a grip on color requires learning only a couple new terms, an unusual state of affairs for an endeavor that often seems more like high-tech science than art.

The rest of this chapter explains the aforementioned White Balance control, plus a couple menu options that enable you to fine-tune the way your camera renders colors. For information on how to use the Retouch menu's color options to alter colors of existing pictures, see Chapter 10.

Correcting colors with white balance

Every light source emits a particular color cast. The old-fashioned fluorescent lights found in most public restrooms, for example, put out a bluish-greenish light, which is why we all look so sickly when we view our reflections in the mirrors in those restrooms. And if you think that your beloved looks especially attractive by candlelight, you aren't imagining things: Candlelight casts a warm, yellow-red glow that is flattering to the skin.

Science-y types measure the color of light, officially known as *color temperature,* on the Kelvin scale, which is named after its creator. You can see the Kelvin scale in Figure 8-17.

When photographers talk about "warm light" and "cool light," though, they aren't referring to the position on the Kelvin scale — or at least not in the way most people think of temperatures, with a higher number meaning hotter. Instead, the terms describe the visual appearance of the light. Warm light, produced by candles and incandescent lights, falls in the red-yellow spectrum you see at the bottom of the Kelvin scale in Figure 8-17; cool light, in the blue-green spectrum, appears at the top of the Kelvin scale.

At any rate, most people don't notice these fluctuating colors of light because human eyes automatically compensate for them. Except in very extreme lighting conditions, we perceive

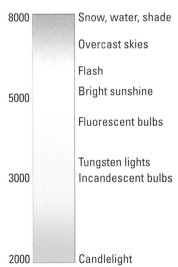

Figure 8-17: Each light source emits a specific color.

a white tablecloth as white no matter whether it's lit by candlelight, fluorescent light, or regular houselights.

Similarly, a digital camera compensates for different colors of light through *white balancing*. Simply put, white balancing neutralizes light so that whites are always white, which in turn ensures that other colors are rendered accurately. If the camera senses warm light, it shifts colors slightly to the cool side of the color spectrum; in cool light, the camera shifts colors the opposite direction.

The good news is that, as with your eyes, your camera's Auto White Balance setting tackles this process remarkably well in most situations, which means that you can usually ignore it and concentrate on other aspects of your picture. But if your scene is lit by two or more light sources that cast different colors, the white balance sensor can get confused, producing an unwanted color cast like the one you see in the left image in Figure 8-18.

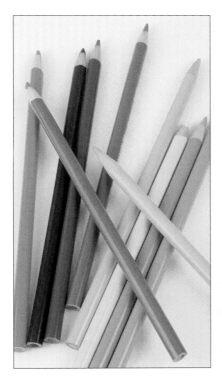 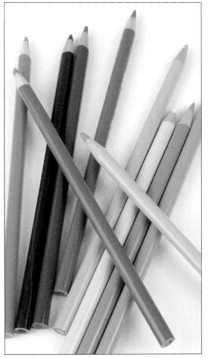

Figure 8-18: Multiple light sources resulted in a yellow color cast in Auto White Balance mode (left); switching to the Incandescent setting solved the problem (right).

I shot this product image in my home studio using tungsten photo lights, which produce light with a color temperature similar to regular household incandescent bulbs. The problem is that the windows in that room also permit some pretty strong daylight to filter through. In Auto White Balance mode, the camera reacted to that daylight — which has a cool color cast — and applied too much warming, giving my original image a yellow tint. No problem: I just switched the White Balance mode from Auto to the Incandescent setting. The right image in Figure 8-18 shows the corrected colors.

There's one little problem with white balancing as it's implemented on your D3100, though. You can't make this kind of manual white balance selection if you shoot in the fully automatic exposure modes. So if you spy color problems in your camera monitor, switch to P, S, A, or M exposure mode. (Chapter 7 details all four modes.) Guide mode does enable you to adjust white balance, but only if you choose the Advanced Operation option and only after you exit the guided menus and return to the Shooting Info screen.

Note, too, that unlike the autofocusing features discussed in the first part of this chapter, the White Balance setting is available during Live View photography as well as viewfinder photography. Your setting also affects colors in any movies you record. See Chapter 4 for complete details about Live View and movie shooting.

The next section explains precisely how to make a simple white balance correction; following that, you can explore some advanced white balance options.

Changing the White Balance setting

The current White Balance setting appears in the Shooting Info screen, as shown in Figure 8-19. The manual settings (settings other than Auto) are represented by the icons you see in Table 8-1. During Live View and movie shooting, an icon representing the setting appears in the top-right corner of the monitor; again, details about those shooting modes and where to locate the various settings awaits in Chapter 4.

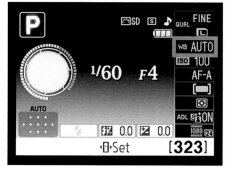

Figure 8-19: This icon represents the current White Balance setting.

Table 8-1	Manual White Balance Settings
Symbol	**Light Source**
☀	Incandescent
☀	Fluorescent
☀	Direct sunlight
⚡	Flash
☁	Cloudy
🏠	Shade
PRE	Preset

As with most of the critical photography settings, you can adjust the White Balance setting in a few ways:

✔ **Quick Settings screen:** Remember, you can get to this screen by pressing the Info Edit button (shown in the margin here). Press once if the Shooting Info screen is already visible; otherwise, press twice. After highlighting the White Balance option, as shown on the left in Figure 8-20, press OK to display the menu shown on the right. Highlight the desired setting, and press OK.

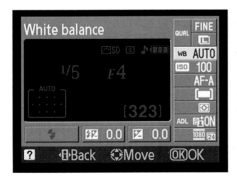
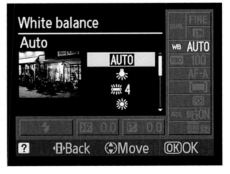

Figure 8-20: You can modify white balance through the Quick Settings display.

✓ **Shooting menu:** You also can adjust the White Balance setting through the Shooting menu, as shown in Figure 8-21. Going this route gives you access to some additional White Balance settings; details on that topic momentarily.

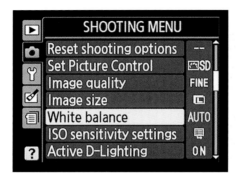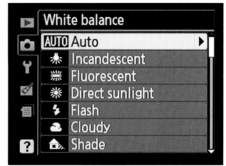

Figure 8-21: To uncover additional White Balance options, hit the Shooting menu.

✓ **Fn (Function) button plus Command dial:** Through a menu option covered in Chapter 11, you can set the Fn button on the side of the camera to directly bring up the White Balance setting. If you do so, however, the button no longer serves its default purpose, which is to call up the ISO Sensitivity setting.

Okay, now for the aforementioned details about using the Shooting menu to adjust the White Balance setting. Via the menus, you can accomplish the following additional white balance goals:

✓ **Fine-tune the settings:** If you choose any setting but Fluorescent, pressing OK takes you to a screen where you can fine-tune the setting, a process I explain in the next section. If you don't want to make any further adjustment, just press OK to exit the fine-tuning screen and return to the Shooting menu.

✓ **Select a specific type of Fluorescent bulb:** When you choose Fluorescent from the menu, as shown on the left in Figure 8-22, pressing OK displays the second screen in the figure, where you can select a specific type of bulb. Select the option that most closely matches your bulbs and then press OK. You then go to the fine-tuning screen. Again, just press OK if you don't want to tweak the setting.

After you select a fluorescent bulb type, that option is always used when you change white balance through the Shooting Info display (as outlined previously) and choose the Fluorescent White Balance setting. Again, you can change the bulb type only through the Shooting menu.

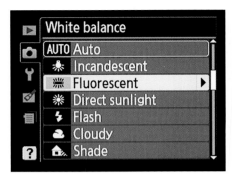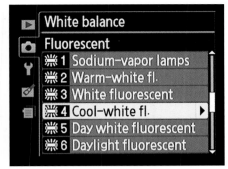

Figure 8-22: If you adjust white balance through the Shooting menu, you can select a specific type of fluorescent bulb.

✓ **Create a custom white balance preset:** Selecting the PRE option from the menu enables you to create and store a precise, customized White Balance setting, as explained in the upcoming "Creating white balance presets" section, in this chapter. This setting is the fastest way to achieve accurate colors when your scene is lit by multiple light sources that have differing color temperatures.

Your selected White Balance setting remains in force for the P, S, A, and M exposure modes until you change it. So you may want to get in the habit of resetting the option to the Auto setting after you finish shooting whatever subject it was that caused you to switch to manual white balance mode.

Fine-tuning White Balance settings

You can fine-tune any White Balance setting except a custom preset that you create through the PRE option. Make the adjustment as spelled out in these steps:

1. **Display the Shooting menu, highlight White Balance, and press OK.**

2. **Highlight the White Balance setting you want to adjust, as shown on the left in Figure 8-23, and press OK.**

   You're taken to a screen where you can do your fine-tuning, as shown on the right in Figure 8-23.

   If you select Fluorescent, you first go to a screen where you select a specific type of bulb, as covered in the preceding section. After you highlight your choice, press OK to get to the fine-tuning screen.

Adjustment marker

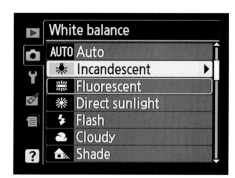
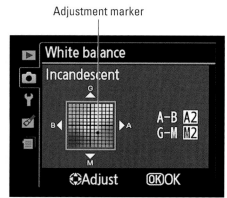

Figure 8-23: You can fine-tune the White Balance settings via the Shooting menu.

3. **Fine-tune the setting by using the Multi Selector to move the white balance shift marker in the color grid.**

   The grid is set up around two color pairs: Green and Magenta, represented by G and M; and Blue and Amber, represented by B and A. By pressing the Multi Selector, you can move the adjustment marker — that little black box labeled in Figure 8-23 — around the grid.

   As you move the marker, the A–B and G–M boxes on the right side of the screen show you the current amount of color shift. A value of 0 indicates the default amount of color compensation applied by the selected White Balance setting. In Figure 8-23, for example, I moved the marker two levels toward amber and two levels toward magenta to specify that I wanted colors to be a tad warmer.

   If you're familiar with traditional colored lens filters, you may know that the density of a filter, which determines the degree of color correction it provides, is measured in *mireds* (pronounced *my-redds*). The white balance grid is designed around this system: Moving the marker one level is the equivalent of adding a filter with a density of 5 mireds.

4. **Press OK to complete the adjustment.**

   After you adjust a White Balance setting, an asterisk appears next to the icon representing the setting on the Shooting menu, as shown in Figure 8-24. You see an asterisk next to the White Balance setting in the Shooting Info display as well.

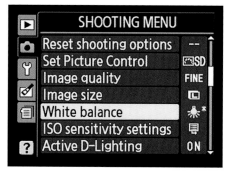

Figure 8-24: The asterisk indicates that you applied a fine-tuning adjustment to the White Balance setting.

Creating white balance presets

If none of the standard White Balance settings do the trick and you don't want to fool with fine-tuning them, take advantage of the PRE (Preset Manual) feature. This option enables you to do two things:

- Base white balance on a direct measurement of the actual lighting conditions.
- Match white balance to an existing photo.

The next two sections provide you with the step-by-step instructions.

Setting white balance with direct measurement

To use this technique, you need a piece of card stock that's either neutral gray or absolute white — not eggshell white, sand white, or any other close-but-not-perfect white. (You can buy reference cards made just for this purpose in many camera stores for less than $20.)

Position the reference card so that it receives the same lighting you'll use for your photo. Then take these steps:

1. **Set the camera to the P, S, A, or M exposure mode.**

   If the exposure meter reports that your image will be under- or over-exposed at the current exposure settings, make the necessary adjustments now. (Chapter 7 tells you how.) Otherwise, the camera can't create your custom white balance preset.

2. **Frame your shot so that the reference card completely fills the viewfinder.**

3. **From the Shooting menu, select White Balance, press OK, and select the PRE (Preset Manual) White Balance setting, as shown on the left in Figure 8-25.**

4. **Press the Multi Selector right, select Measure, as shown on the right in the figure, and press OK.**

   A warning appears, asking you whether you want to overwrite existing data.

5. **Select Yes and press OK.**

   You see another message, this time telling you to take your picture. You have about six seconds to do so. (The letters PRE flash in the viewfinder and Shooting Info display to let you know the camera's ready to record your white balance reference image.)

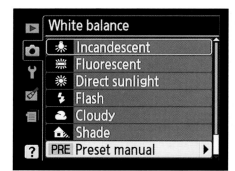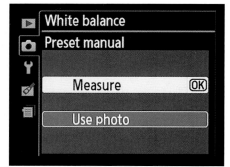

Figure 8-25: Select these options to set white balance by measuring a white or gray card.

6. Take the reference shot.

If the camera is successful at recording the white balance data, the letters *Gd* flash in the viewfinder and the message "Data Acquired" appears in the Shooting Information display. If the camera couldn't set the custom white balance, you instead see the message *No Gd* in the viewfinder, and a message in the Shooting Information display urges you to try again. Try adjusting your lighting before doing so.

After you complete the process, the camera automatically sets the White Balance option to PRE so you can begin using your preset. You see the letters PRE in the White Balance area of the Shooting Info display, as shown in Figure 8-26.

Any time you want to select and use the preset, switch to the PRE White Balance setting, either via the Shooting menu or Quick Settings screen Your custom setting is stored in the camera until you override it with a new preset.

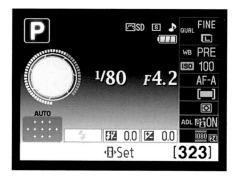

Figure 8-26: Select the PRE (Preset Manual) option to use your custom White Balance setting.

By the way, if you do set the Fn button to invoke the White Balance setting, it offers a related timesaving feature: If you press and hold the button for a few seconds while the PRE setting is in force, the camera automatically sets itself up to record a new preset reference shot. After the letters PRE start flashing in the viewfinder or Shooting Info screen, just snap your reference picture.

Matching white balance to an existing photo

Suppose that you're the marketing manager for a small business, and one of your jobs is to shoot portraits of the company big-wigs for the annual report. You build a small studio just for that purpose, complete with a couple photography lights and a nice, conservative beige backdrop.

Of course, the big-wigs can't all come to get their pictures taken in the same month, let alone on the same day. But you have to make sure that the colors in that beige backdrop remain consistent for each shot, no matter how much time passes between photo sessions. This scenario is one possible use for an advanced White Balance feature that enables you to base white balance on an existing photo.

Basing white balance on an existing photo works well only in strictly controlled lighting situations, where the color temperature of your lights is consistent from day to day. Otherwise, the White Balance setting that produces color accuracy when you shoot Big Boss Number One may add an ugly color cast to the one you snap of Big Boss Number Two.

To give this option a try, follow these steps:

1. **Copy the picture that you want to use as the reference photo to your camera memory card, if it isn't already stored there.**

   You can copy the picture to the card using a card reader and whatever method you usually use to transfer files from one drive to another. Assuming that you're using the default folder names, copy the file to the 100D3100 folder, inside the main DCIM folder. (See Chapter 5 for help with working with files and folders.)

2. **Open the Shooting menu, highlight White Balance, and press OK.**

3. **Select PRE (Preset Manual) and press the Multi Selector right.**

   The screen shown on the left in Figure 8-27 appears.

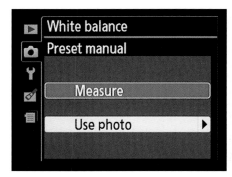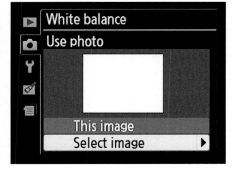

Figure 8-27: You can create a White Balance preset based on an existing photo.

4. **Highlight Use Photo and press OK.**

   The options shown on the right in Figure 8-27 appear. If you haven't yet used the photo option to store a preset, you see an empty white box in the middle of the screen, as shown in the figure. If you previously selected a photo to use as a preset reference, the thumbnail for that image appears instead.

5. **Select the photo you want to use as your reference image.**

   If the photo you want to use is already displayed on the screen, highlight This Image and press OK. Otherwise, highlight Select Image and then press the Multi Selector right to access screens that let you navigate to the photo you want to use as a basis for white balance. Press OK to return to the screen shown on the right in Figure 8-27. Your selected photo appears on the screen.

6. **Highlight This Image and press OK to set the preset white balance based on the selected photo.**

Whenever you want to base white balance on your selected photo, just set the White Balance setting to the PRE option.

Choosing a Color Space: sRGB versus Adobe RGB

By default, your camera captures images using the *sRGB color mode,* which simply refers to an industry-standard spectrum of colors. (The *s* is for *standard,* and the *RGB* is for *red, green, blue,* which are the primary colors in the digital color world.) The sRGB color mode was created to help ensure color consistency as an image moves from camera (or scanner) to monitor and printer; the idea was to create a spectrum of colors that all these devices can reproduce.

However, the sRGB color spectrum leaves out some colors that *can* be reproduced in print and onscreen, at least by some devices. So as an alternative, your camera also enables you to shoot in the Adobe RGB color mode, which includes a larger spectrum (or *gamut*) of colors. Figure 8-28 offers an illustration of the two spectrums.

Some colors in the Adobe RGB spectrum can't be reproduced in print. (The printer just substitutes the closest printable color, if necessary.) Still, I usually shoot in Adobe RGB mode because I see no reason to limit myself to a smaller spectrum from the get-go.

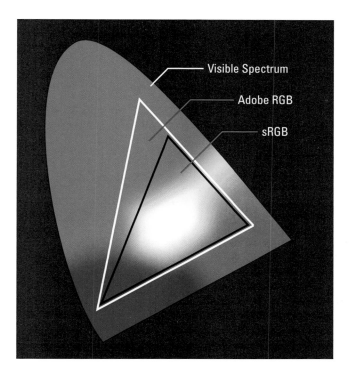

Figure 8-28: Adobe RGB includes some colors not found in the sRGB spectrum.

However, just because I use Adobe RGB doesn't mean that it's right for you. First, if you plan to print and share your photos without making any adjustments in your photo editor, you're usually better off sticking with sRGB because most printers and Web browsers are designed around that color space. Second, know that to retain all your original Adobe RGB colors when you work with your photos, your editing software must support that color space — not all programs do. You also must be willing to study the whole topic of digital color a little bit because you need to use some specific settings to avoid really mucking up the color works.

If you want to go with Adobe RGB instead of sRGB, visit the Shooting menu and highlight the Color Space option, as shown on the left in Figure 8-29. Press OK to display the screen shown on the right in the figure. Select Adobe RGB and press OK again.

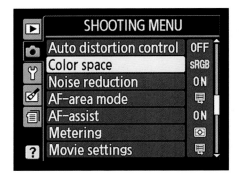 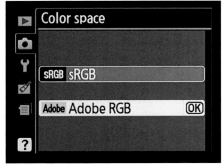

Figure 8-29: Choose Adobe RGB for a broader color spectrum.

 You can tell whether you captured an image in the Adobe RGB format by looking at its filename: Adobe RGB images start with an underscore, as in _DSC0627.jpg. For pictures captured in the sRGB color space, the underscore appears in the middle of the filename, as in DSC_0627.jpg. See Chapter 5 for more tips on decoding picture filenames.

Taking a Quick Look at Picture Controls

A feature that Nikon calls *Picture Controls* offers one more way to tweak image sharpening, color, and contrast when you shoot in the P, S, A, and M exposure modes and choose one of the JPEG options for the Image Quality setting. (Chapter 2 explains the Image Quality setting.)

 Sharpening, in case you're new to the digital meaning of the term, refers to a software process that adjusts contrast in a way that creates the illusion of slightly sharper focus. I emphasize, "slightly sharper focus." Sharpening produces a subtle *tweak,* and it's not a fix for poor focus.

An icon representing the current Picture Control appears in the Shooting Info screen, as shown in Figure 8-30. But you can't adjust the setting through the Quick Settings display; instead, use the Shooting menu, as shown in Figure 8-31.

Picture Control

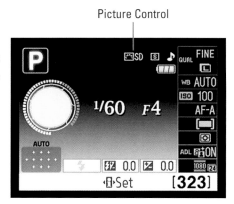

Figure 8-30: Picture Controls apply preset adjustments to color, sharpening, and other photo characteristics to images you shoot in the JPEG file format.

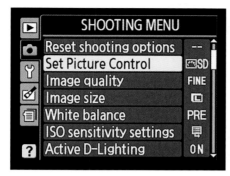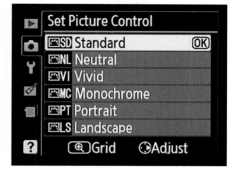

Figure 8-31: You can access the Picture Control options only through the Shooting menu.

Whichever route you go, you can choose from six Picture Controls, which are represented in the Shooting Info screen by two-letter codes and produce the following results:

- **Standard (SD):** The default setting for the P, S, A, and M exposure modes, this option captures the image normally — that is, using the characteristics that Nikon offers up as suitable for the majority of subjects. You also are assigned this mode if you shoot in the Auto, Auto No Flash, Sports, Child, and Close Up exposure modes.

- **Neutral (NL):** At this setting, the camera doesn't enhance color, contrast, and sharpening as much as in the other modes. The setting is designed for people who want to precisely manipulate these picture characteristics in a photo editor. By not overworking colors, sharpening, and so on when producing your original file, the camera delivers an original that gives you more latitude in the digital darkroom.

- **Vivid (VI):** In this mode, the camera amps up color saturation, contrast, and sharpening.

- **Monochrome (MC):** This setting produces black-and-white photos. Only in the digital world, they're called *grayscale images* because a true black-and-white image contains only black and white, with no shades of gray.

I'm not keen on creating grayscale images this way. I prefer to shoot in full color and then do my own grayscale conversion in my photo editor. That technique just gives you more control over the look of your black-and-white photos. Assuming that you work with a decent photo editor, you can control what original tones are emphasized in your grayscale version, for example. Additionally, keep in mind that you can always convert a color image to grayscale, but you can't go the other direction. You can create a black-and-white copy of your color image right in the camera, in fact; Chapter 10 shows you how.

- **Portrait (PT):** This mode tweaks colors and sharpening in a way that is designed to produce nice skin texture and pleasing skin tones. (If you shoot in the Portrait or Night Portrait automatic exposure modes, the camera selects this Picture Control for you.)

✓ **Landscape (LS):** This mode emphasizes blues and greens. As you might expect, it's the mode used by the Landscape Scene mode.

The extent to which Picture Controls affect your image depends on the subject as well as the exposure settings you choose and the lighting conditions. But Figure 8-32 gives you a general idea of what to expect. As you can see, the differences between the various Picture Controls are pretty subtle, with the exception of the Monochrome option, of course.

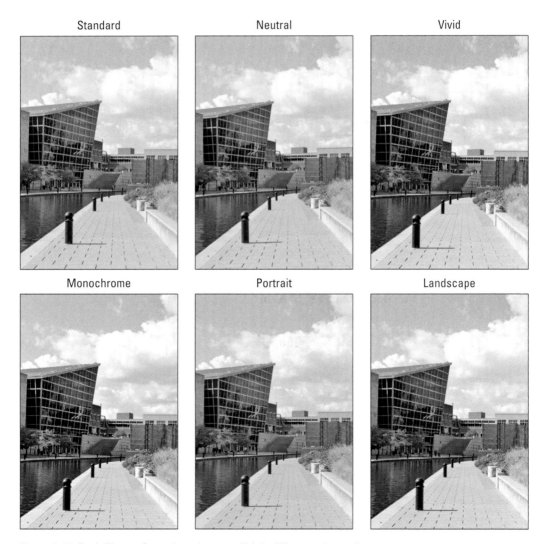

Standard   Neutral   Vivid

Monochrome   Portrait   Landscape

Figure 8-32: Each Picture Control produces a slightly different take on the scene.

I recommend that most people stick with the default Picture Control settings, for two reasons. First, you have way more important camera settings to worry about — aperture, shutter speed, autofocus, and all the rest. Why add one more setting to your list, especially when the impact of changing it is minimal?

Second, if you really want to mess with the characteristics that the Picture Control options affect, you're much better off shooting in the Raw (NEF) format and then making those adjustments on a picture-by-picture basis in your Raw converter. In Nikon ViewNX 2, you can even assign any of the existing Picture Controls to your Raw files and then compare how each one affects the image. The camera does tag your Raw file with whatever Picture Control is active when you take the shot, but the image adjustments are in no way set in stone, or even in sand — you can tweak your photo at will. (The selected Picture Control does affect the JPEG preview that's used to display the Raw image thumbnails in ViewNX and other browsers.)

However, in the interest of full disclosure, I should alert you to a feature that may make Picture Controls a little more useful to some people: You can modify any Picture Control to more closely render a scene the way you envision it. So, for example, if you like the bold colors of Landscape mode but don't think the effect goes far enough, you can adjust the setting to amp up colors even more.

To reserve page space in this book for functions that experience tells me will be the most useful to the most readers, I opted not to provide full details about customizing Picture Controls. But the following steps provide a quick overview of the process so that if you encounter the menu screens that contain the related options, you'll have some idea what you're seeing. So here are the basics:

1. **Set the Mode dial to P, S, A, or M.**

    These are the only modes that let you modify a Picture Control.

2. **Display the Shooting menu, choose Set Picture Control, and press OK.**

3. **Highlight the Picture Control you want to modify.**

    For example, I highlighted the Vivid setting on the left in Figure 8-33.

4. **Press the Multi Selector right.**

    You see the screen shown on the right in Figure 8-33, containing sliders that you use to modify the Picture Control. Which options you can adjust depend on your selected Picture Control.

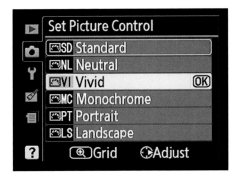 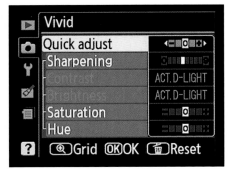

Figure 8-33: After selecting a Picture Control, press right to display options for adjusting its effect on your pictures.

5. **Highlight a picture characteristic and then press the Multi Selector right or left to adjust the setting.**

A couple tips:

- Some Picture Controls offer a Quick Adjust setting, which enables you to easily increase or decrease the overall effect of the Picture Control. A positive value produces a more exaggerated effect; set the slider to 0 to return to the default setting.

- To display a grid that lets you see how your selected Picture Control compares with the others in terms of color saturation and contrast, as shown in Figure 8-34, press and hold the Zoom In button. (I vote this screen most likely to confound new camera users who stumble across it.) You can't actually change any camera settings via this screen — it's for informational purposes only.

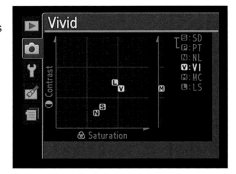

- The little line under the scale for each adjustment option represents the default setting for the selected Picture Control.

- Reset all the options to their defaults by pressing the Delete button.

Figure 8-34: Press the Zoom In button to display a grid that ranks each Picture Style according to its level of saturation and contrast.

6. Press OK to save your changes and exit the adjustment screen.

As when you fine-tune a White Balance setting, an asterisk appears next to the edited Picture Style in the menu and Shooting Info screen to remind you that you have adjusted it.

Again, these steps are intended just as a starting point for those who are interested in playing with Picture Styles. Complete details on each of the Picture Control adjustment options are found in the electronic version of the camera manual, stored on one of the two CDs that shipped with your camera. (The other CD contains the Nikon software.) You can read the manual in Adobe Acrobat or any other program that can open PDF files. The paper manual contains only basic operating instructions, and the Picture Control editing functions didn't make the cut.

Putting It All Together

*E*arlier chapters of this book break down each and every picture-taking feature on your D3100, describing in detail how the various controls affect exposure, picture quality, focus, color, and the like. This chapter pulls all that information together to help you set up your camera for specific types of photography.

The first section offers a quick summary of critical picture-taking settings that should serve you well no matter what your subject. Following that, I offer my advice on which settings to use for portraits, action shots, landscapes, and close-ups. To wrap up things, the end of the chapter includes some miscellaneous tips for dealing with special shooting situations and subjects.

Keep in mind that although I present specific recommendations here, there are no hard and fast rules as to the "right way" to shoot a portrait, a landscape, or whatever. So feel free to wander off on your own, tweaking this exposure setting or adjusting that focus control, to discover your own creative vision. Experimentation is part of the fun of photography, after all — and thanks to your camera monitor and the Delete button, it's an easy, completely free proposition.

Recapping Basic Picture Settings

Your subject, creative goals, and lighting conditions determine which settings you should use for some picture-taking options, such as aperture and shutter speed. I offer my take on those options throughout this chapter. But for many basic options, I recommend the same settings for almost every shooting scenario. Table 9-1 shows you those recommendations and also lists the chapter where you can find details about each setting.

The settings reflect the choices for normal, through-the-viewfinder photography; Chapter 4 guides you through the options available for Live View photography and movie recording. For Live View photography, most settings work the same as discussed here, with the exception of the autofocus options.

Table 9-1	All-Purpose Picture-Taking Settings	
Option	**Recommended Setting**	**Chapter**
Image Quality	JPEG Fine or NEF (Raw)	2
Image Size	Large or medium	2
White Balance*	Auto	8
ISO Sensitivity**	100	7
Focus mode	AF-A (Auto-servo)	8
AF-area mode	Action photos: Dynamic Area; all others, Single Point	8
Release mode	Action photos: Continuous; all others: Single	2
Metering*	Matrix	7
Active D-Lighting*	Off	7

*Adjustable only in P, S, A, and M exposure modes.
**Not adjustable in Auto and Auto Flash Off modes.

Setting Up for Specific Scenes

For the most part, the settings detailed in the preceding section fall into the "set 'em and forget 'em" category. That leaves you free to concentrate on a handful of other camera options, such as aperture and shutter speed, that you can manipulate to achieve a specific photographic goal.

The next four sections explain which of these additional options typically produce the best results when you're shooting portraits, action shots, landscapes, and close-ups. I offer a few compositional and creative tips along the way — but again, remember that beauty is in the eye of the beholder, and for every so-called rule, there are plenty of great images that prove the exception.

Shooting still portraits

By *still portrait,* I mean that your subject isn't moving. For subjects who aren't keen on sitting still long enough to have their picture taken — children, pets, and even some teenagers I know — skip ahead to the next section and use the techniques given for action photography instead.

Assuming that you do have a subject willing to pose, the classic portraiture approach is to keep the subject sharply focused while throwing the background into soft focus. This artistic choice emphasizes the subject and helps diminish the impact of any distracting background objects in cases where you can't control the setting. The following steps show you how to achieve this look:

1. **Set the Mode dial to A (aperture-priority autoexposure) and select the lowest f-stop value possible.**

   As Chapter 7 explains, a low f-stop setting opens the aperture, which not only allows more light to enter the camera but also shortens depth of field, or the range of sharp focus. So dialing in a low f-stop value is the first step in softening your portrait background. (The f-stop range available to you depends on your lens.) Also keep in mind that the farther your subject is from the background, the more blurring you can achieve.

   I recommend aperture-priority mode when depth of field is a primary concern because you can control the f-stop while relying on the camera to select the shutter speed that will properly expose the image. Just rotate the Command dial to select your desired f-stop. (You do need to pay attention to shutter speed also, however, to make sure that it's not so slow that any movement of the subject or camera will blur the image.)

   If you aren't comfortable with this advanced exposure mode, Portrait and Child mode also result in a more open aperture, although the exact f-stop setting is out of your control. You should note, too, that both of those modes make subtle adjustments to color and sharpening that may or may not be what you have in mind. See Chapter 3 for details.

   Whichever mode you choose, you can monitor the current f-stop and shutter speed on the Shooting Info display and in the viewfinder, as shown in Figure 9-1.

Shutter speed   Aperture

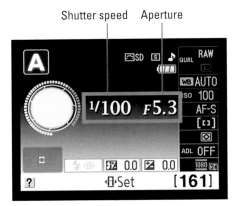
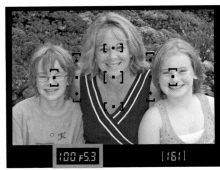

Figure 9-1: You can monitor aperture and shutter speed settings in two places.

2. To further soften the background, zoom in, get closer, or both.

As covered in Chapter 8, zooming in to a longer focal length also reduces depth of field, as does moving physically closer to your subject.

A lens with a focal length of 85–120mm is ideal for a classic head and shoulders portrait. But don't fret if you have only the 18–55mm kit lens; just zoom in all the way to the 55mm setting. You should avoid using a much shorter focal length (a wider-angle lens) for portraits. They can cause features to appear distorted — sort of like how people look when you view them through a security peephole in a door.

3. For indoor portraits, shoot flash-free if possible.

Shooting by available light rather than flash produces softer illumination and avoids the problem of red-eye. To get enough light to go flash-free, turn on room lights or, during daylight, pose your subject next to a sunny window, as I did for the image in Figure 9-2.

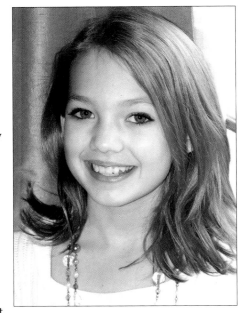

Figure 9-2: For more pleasing indoor portraits, shoot by available light instead of using flash.

In the A exposure mode, simply keeping the built-in flash unit closed disables the flash. In Portrait and Child modes, the camera automatically pops up the flash unit in dim lighting. To disable the flash, in those modes, the easiest option is to press the Flash button as you rotate the Command dial to select the Off setting. (You can view the current setting in the Shooting Info display.)

If flash is unavoidable, see my list of flash tips at the end of the steps to get better results.

4. For outdoor portraits, use a flash if possible.

Even in daylight, a flash adds a beneficial pop of light to subjects' faces, as illustrated in Figure 9-3. A flash is especially important when the background is brighter than the subjects, as in this example.

No flash

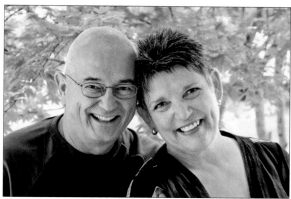

Fill flash

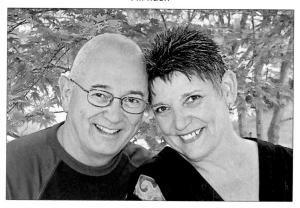

Figure 9-3: To properly illuminate the face in outdoor portraits, use fill flash.

In the A exposure mode, you can just press the Flash button on the side of the camera to enable the flash. For daytime portraits, use the fill flash setting. (That's the regular, basic Flash mode.) For nighttime images, try red-eye reduction or Slow-Sync mode; again, see the flash tips at the end of these steps to use either mode most effectively.

Unfortunately, Portrait and Child mode use Auto flash, and if the ambient light is very bright, the flash may not fire. Switch to an advanced exposure mode (P, S, A, or M) to regain flash control. But do note that whatever exposure mode you use, the top shutter speed available when you use flash with the D3100 is 1/200 second, so in extremely bright light, you may need to stop down the aperture to avoid overexposing the photo. Doing so, of course, brings the background into sharper focus. So try to move the subject into a shaded area instead.

5. **Press and hold the shutter button halfway to initiate exposure metering and autofocusing.**

Make sure that an active autofocus point falls over your subject. Chapter 8 explains more about autofocus, but if you have trouble, simply set your lens to manual focus mode and then twist the focusing ring to set focus. See Chapter 1 for help with manual focusing.

6. **Press the shutter button the rest of the way to capture the image.**

Again, these steps just give you a starting point for taking better portraits. A few other tips can also improve your people pics:

✔ **Pay attention to the background.** Scan the entire frame looking for intrusive objects that may distract the eye from the subject. If necessary, reposition the subject against a more flattering backdrop. Inside, a softly textured wall works well; outdoors, trees and shrubs can provide nice backdrops as long as they aren't so ornate or colorful that they diminish the subject (for example, a magnolia tree laden with blooms).

✔ **Pay attention to white balance if your subject is lit by both flash and ambient light.** If you set the White Balance setting to Auto, as I recommend in Table 9-1, enabling flash tells the camera to warm colors to compensate for the cool light of a flash. If your subject is also lit by room lights or sunlight, the result may be colors that are slightly warmer than neutral. This warming effect typically looks nice in portraits, giving the skin a subtle glow. But if you aren't happy with the result or want even more warming, see Chapter 8 to find out how to fine-tune white balance. Again, you can make this adjustment only in P, S, A, or M exposure modes.

✔ **When flash is unavoidable, try these tricks to produce better results.** The following techniques can help solve flash-related issues:

- *Indoors, turn on as many room lights as possible.* With more ambient light, you reduce the flash power that's needed to expose the picture. This step also causes the pupils to constrict, further reducing the chances of red-eye. (Pay heed to my white balance warning, however.) As an added benefit, the smaller pupil allows more of the subject's iris to be visible in the portrait, so you see more eye color.

- *Try setting the flash to red-eye reduction or Slow-Sync mode.* If you choose the first option, warn your subject to expect both a preliminary pop of light from the AF-assist lamp, which constricts pupils, and the actual flash. And remember that slow-sync flash uses a slower-than-normal shutter speed, which produces softer lighting and brighter backgrounds than normal flash. You can set the Flash mode to Slow-Sync in A and P modes, and it's the default flash setting for the Night Portrait mode as well.

Take a look at Figure 9-4 for an example of how slow-sync flash can really improve an indoor portrait. When I used regular flash, the shutter speed was 1/60 second. At that speed, the camera has little time to soak up any ambient light. As a result, the scene is lit primarily by the flash. That caused two problems: The strong flash created some "hot spots" on the subject's skin, and the window frame is much more prominent because of the contrast between it and the darker bushes outside the window. Although it was daylight when I took the picture, the skies were overcast, so at 1/60 second, the exterior appears dark.

In the slow-sync example, shot at 1/4 second, the exposure time was long enough to permit the ambient light to brighten the exteriors to the point that the window frame almost blends into the background. And because much less flash power was needed to expose the subject, the lighting is much more flattering. In this case, the bright background also helps to set the subject apart because of her dark hair and shirt. If the subject had been a pale blonde, this setup wouldn't have worked as well, of course. Again, too, note the warming effect that occurs when you use Auto White Balance and shoot in a combination of flash and daylight.

Any time you use slow-sync flash, don't forget that a slower-than-normal shutter speed means an increased risk of blur due to camera shake. So always use a tripod or otherwise steady the camera. And remind your subjects to stay absolutely still, too, because they will appear blurry if they move during the exposure. I was fortunate to have both a tripod and a cooperative subject for my examples, but I probably wouldn't try slow-sync for portraits of young children or pets.

Regular fill flash, 1/60 second

Slow-sync flash, 1/4 second

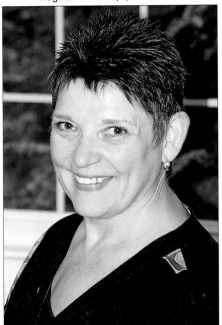 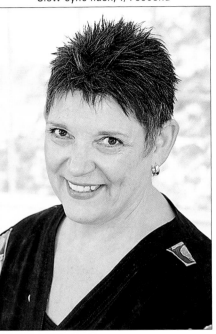

Figure 9-4: Slow-sync flash produces softer, more even lighting and brighter backgrounds.

- *For professional results, use an external flash with a rotating flash head.* Then aim the flash head upward so that the flash light bounces off the ceiling and falls softly down onto the subject. An external flash isn't cheap, but the results make the purchase worthwhile if you shoot lots of portraits. Compare the two portraits in Figure 9-5 for an illustration. In the first example, the built-in flash resulted in strong shadowing behind the subject and harsh, concentrated light. To produce the better result on the right, I used the Nikon Speedlight SB-600 and bounced the light off the ceiling.

One word of warning about bounce flash, though: Make sure that the ceiling or other surface you use to bounce the light is white. Otherwise, the flash light will pick up the color of the surface and influence the color of your subject.

- *To reduce shadowing from the flash, move your subject farther from the background.* I took this extra step for the right image in Figure 9-5. The increased distance not only reduced shadowing but also softened the focus of the wall a bit (because of the short depth of field resulting from my f-stop and focal length).

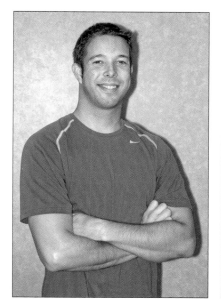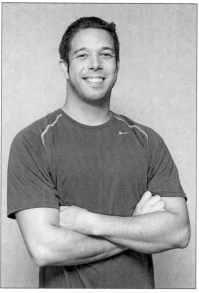

Figure 9-5: To eliminate harsh lighting and strong shadows (left), I used bounce flash and moved the subject farther from the background (right).

A good general rule is to position your subjects far enough from the background that they can't touch it. If that isn't possible, though, try going the other direction: If the person's head is smack up against the background, any shadow will be smaller and less noticeable. For example, you get less shadowing when a subject's head is resting against a sofa cushion than if that person is sitting upright, with the head a foot or so away from the cushion.

• *Invest in a flash diffuser to further soften the light.* Whether you use the built-in flash or an external flash, attaching a diffuser is also a good idea. A *diffuser* is simply a piece of transluscent plastic or fabric that you place over the flash to soften and spread the light — much like sheer curtains diffuse window light. Diffusers come in lots of different designs, including small, fold-flat models that fit over the built-in flash.

✓ **Frame the subject loosely to allow for later cropping to a variety of frame sizes.** Your D3100 produces images that have an aspect ratio of 3:2. That means that your portrait perfectly fits a 4-x-6-inch print size but will require cropping to print at any other proportions, such as 5 x 7 or 8 x 10. Chapter 6 talks more about this issue.

Capturing action

A fast shutter speed is the key to capturing a blur-free shot of any moving subject, whether it's a flower in the breeze, a spinning Ferris wheel, or, as in the case of Figure 9-6, a racing cyclist.

Along with the basic capture settings outlined in Table 9-1, try the techniques in the following steps to photograph a subject in motion:

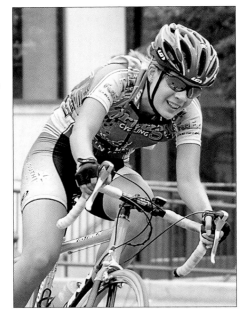

Figure 9-6: Use a high shutter speed to freeze motion.

1. **Set the Mode dial to S (shutter-priority autoexposure).**

   In this mode, you control the shutter speed, and the camera takes care of choosing an aperture setting that will produce a good exposure.

   If you aren't ready to step up to this advanced exposure mode, explained in Chapter 7, try using Sports mode, detailed in Chapter 3. But be aware that you have no control over many other aspects of your picture (such as white balance, flash, and so on) in that mode.

2. **Rotate the Command dial to select the shutter speed.**

   (Refer to Figure 9-1 to locate shutter speed in the viewfinder and Shooting Info display.) After you select the shutter speed, the camera selects an aperture (f-stop) to match.

   What shutter speed do you need exactly? Well, it depends on the speed at which your subject is moving, so you need to experiment. But generally speaking, 1/320 second should be plenty for all but the fastest subjects (race cars, boats, and so on). For very slow subjects, you can even go as low as 1/250 or 1/125 second. My subject in Figure 9-6 was zipping along at a pretty fast pace, so I set the shutter speed to 1/500 second just to be on the safe side.

3. **Raise the ISO setting or add flash to produce a brighter exposure, if needed.**

   In dim lighting, you may not be able to get a good exposure at a low ISO; the camera simply may not be able to open the aperture wide enough to accommodate a fast shutter speed. Raising the ISO does increase the possibility of noise, but a noisy shot is better than a blurry shot.

Adding flash is a bit tricky for action shots, unfortunately. First, the flash needs time to recycle between shots, so try to go without if you want to capture images at a fast pace. Second, the built-in flash has limited range — so don't waste your time if your subject isn't close by. And third, remember that the fastest shutter speed you can use with flash is 1/200 second, which may not be high enough to capture a quickly moving subject without blur.

If you do decide to use flash, you must bail out of Sports mode; it doesn't permit you to use flash.

4. For rapid-fire shooting, set the Release mode to the Continuous setting.

In this mode, you can capture multiple images with a single press of the shutter button. As long as you hold down the button, the camera continues to record images. Here again, though, you need to go flash-free; you can't use the Continuous capture mode with flash because it isn't compatible with flash photography.

5. For fastest shooting, switch to manual focusing.

Manual focusing eliminates the time the camera needs to lock focus in autofocus mode. Chapter 8 provides details on manual focusing, if you need help.

If you do use autofocus, try these two autofocus settings for best performance:

- Set the AF-area mode to Dynamic Area.

- Set the Focus mode to AF-C (continuous-servo autofocus).

Chapter 8 details these autofocus options. Note that in the fully automatic exposure modes, however, you can choose from only two Focus modes, AF-A and MF (manual focus). Fortunately, in AF-A mode, the camera automatically switches to AF-C when it senses movement in front of the lens.

6. Turn off Image Review.

You turn off Image Review via the Playback menu. Turning off this option can help speed up the time your camera needs to recover between shots.

7. Compose the subject to allow for movement across the frame.

Frame your shot a little wider than you normally might so that you lessen the risk that your subject will move out of the frame before you record the image. You can always crop to a tighter composition later. (I used this approach for my cyclist image — the original shot includes a lot of background that I later cropped away.) It's also a good idea to leave more room in front of the subject than behind it. This makes it obvious that your subject is going somewhere.

Using these techniques should give you a better chance of capturing any fast-moving subject. But action-shooting strategies also are helpful for shooting candid portraits of kids and pets. Even if they aren't currently running, leaping, or otherwise cavorting, snapping a shot before they do move or change positions is often tough. So if an interaction or scene catches your eye, set your camera into action mode and then just fire off a series of shots as fast as you can.

For example, one recent afternoon, I spotted my furball and his equally fluffy new neighbor introducing themselves to each other through the fence that separates their yards. I ran and grabbed my camera, flipped it into shutter-priority mode, set the shutter speed to 1/320, and just started shooting. Most of the images were throwaways; you can see some of them in Figure 9-7. But somewhere around the tenth frame, I captured the moment you see in Figure 9-8, which puts a whole new twist on the phrase "gossiping over the backyard fence." Two seconds later, the dogs got bored with each other and scampered away into their respective yards, but thanks to a fast shutter, I got the shot that I wanted.

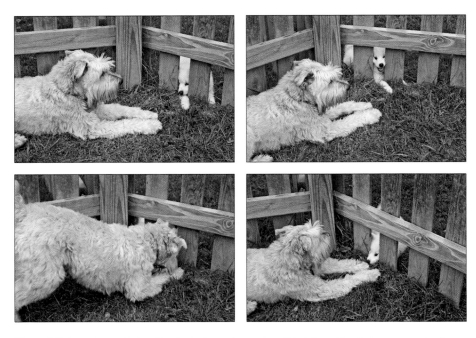

Figure 9-7: I used speed-shooting techniques to capture this interaction between a pair of pups.

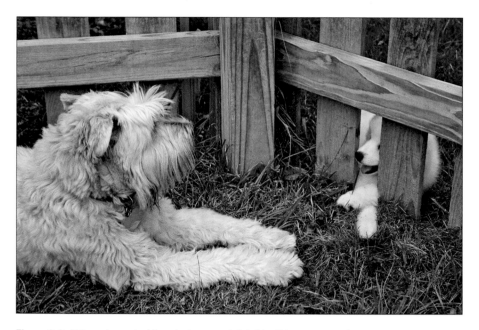

Figure 9-8: Although most of the shots were deletable, this one was a keeper.

Capturing scenic vistas

Providing specific capture settings for landscape photography is tricky because there's no single best approach to capturing a beautiful stretch of countryside, a city skyline, or other vast subject. Take depth of field, for example: One person's idea of a super cityscape might be to keep all buildings in the scene sharply focused. But another photographer might prefer to shoot the same scene so that a foreground building is sharply focused while the others are less so, thus drawing the eye to that first building.

That said, I can offer a few tips to help you photograph a landscape the way *you* see it:

✔ **Shoot in aperture-priority autoexposure mode (A) so that you can control depth of field.** If you want extreme depth of field so that both near and distant objects are sharply focused, as in Figure 9-9, select a high f-stop value. I used an aperture of f/18 for this shot. For short depth of field, use a low value.

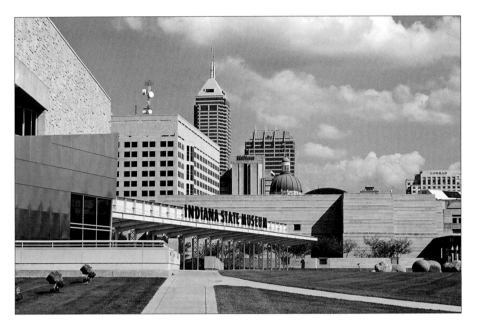

Figure 9-9: Use a high f-stop value (or Landscape mode) to keep foreground and background sharply focused.

You can also use Landscape mode to achieve the first objective. In this mode, the camera automatically selects a high f-stop number, but you have no control over the exact value (or certain other picture-taking settings). And in dim lighting, the camera may be forced to select a low f-stop setting.

✔ **If the exposure requires a slow shutter, use a tripod to avoid blurring.** The downside to a high f-stop is that you need a slower shutter speed to produce a good exposure. If the shutter speed drops below what you can comfortably hand-hold, use a tripod to avoid picture-blurring camera shake. Remember that when you use a tripod, Nikon recommends that you turn off Vibration Reduction if you're using a kit lens.

No tripod handy? Look for any solid surface on which you can steady the camera. In all exposure modes except Auto and Auto Flash Off, you can increase the ISO Sensitivity setting to allow a faster shutter, too, but that option brings with it the chances of increased image noise. See Chapter 7 for details.

✔ **For dramatic waterfall shots, consider using a slow shutter to create that "misty" look.** The slow shutter blurs the water, giving it a soft, romantic appearance, as shown in Figure 9-10. Again, use a tripod to ensure that the rest of the scene doesn't also blur due to camera shake. You can also use a slow shutter speed to create a heightened sense of motion and, in scenes that feature very colorful subjects, cool abstract images like the one in Figure 9-11. This image is another version of the carnival-ride picture featured in the Guide mode section of Chapter 3. For that photo, I used a shutter speed of 1/30 second; for the one shown here, I slowed things down to 1/5 second. In both cases, I used a tripod, but because nearly everything in the frame was moving, the entirety of both photos is blurry — the 1/5 second version is simply more blurry because of the slower shutter.

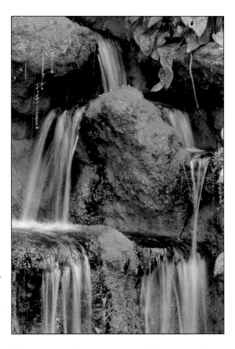

 In very bright light, you may overexpose the image at a very slow shutter, even if you stop the aperture all the way down and select the camera's lowest ISO setting. As a solution, consider investing in a *neutral density filter* for your lens. This type of filter works

Figure 9-10: For misty waterfalls, use a slow shutter speed and a tripod.

something like sunglasses for your camera: It simply reduces the amount of light that passes through the lens, without affecting image colors, so that you can use a slower shutter than would otherwise be possible.

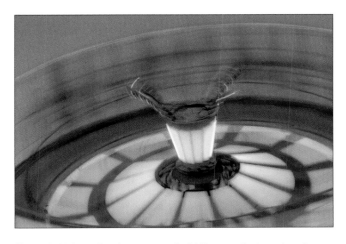

Figure 9-11: I used a shutter speed of 1/5 second when shooting a whirling carnival ride to create this abstract image.

✔ **At sunrise or sunset, base exposure on the sky.** The foreground will be dark, but you can usually brighten it in a photo editor if needed. If you base exposure on the foreground, on the other hand, the sky will become so bright that all the color will be washed out — a problem you usually can't fix after the fact.

Also experiment with turning Active D-Lighting on and off. Chapter 7 explains this feature, which brightens dark areas in a way that doesn't blow out highlights, leaving your sky colors intact. You need to use P, S, A, or M as your exposure mode, though, because the other modes don't let you control Active D-Lighting.

✔ **For cool nighttime city pics, experiment with slow shutter.** Assuming that cars or other vehicles are moving through the scene, the result is neon trails of light like those you see in the foreground of the image in Figure 9-12. Shutter speed for this image was about 10 seconds.

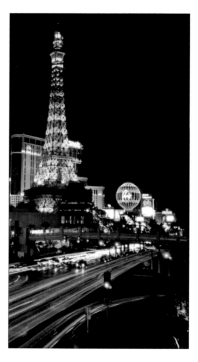

Figure 9-12: A slow shutter also creates neon light trails in city-street scenes.

Instead of changing the shutter speed manually between each shot, try *bulb* mode. Available only in M (manual) exposure mode, this option records an image for as long as you hold down the shutter button. So just take a series of images, holding the button down for different lengths of time for each shot. In bulb mode, you also can exceed the standard maximum exposure time of 30 seconds.

✔ **For the best lighting, shoot during the "magic hours."** That's the term photographers use for early morning and late afternoon, when the light cast by the sun is soft and warm, giving everything that beautiful, gently warmed look.

Can't wait for the perfect light? Tweak your camera's White Balance setting, using the instructions laid out in Chapter 8, to simulate magic-hour light.

✔ **In tricky light, bracket exposures.** *Bracketing* simply means to take the same picture at several different exposure settings to increase the odds that at least one of them will capture the scene the way you envision. Bracketing is especially a good idea in difficult lighting situations, such as sunrise and sunset. You need to use one of the advanced exposure modes to bracket with the D3100, though. In P, A, and S modes, use the

Exposure Compensation feature, introduced in Chapter 7, to produce your series of brighter and darker images. In M mode, you can simply adjust the shutter speed or aperture setting between shots.

Capturing dynamic close-ups

For great close-up shots, try these techniques:

- ✔ **Check your owner's manual to find out the minimum close-focusing distance of your lens.** How "up close and personal" you can get to your subject depends on your lens, not the camera body.

- ✔ **Take control over depth of field by setting the camera mode to A (aperture-priority autoexposure) mode.** Whether you want a shallow, medium, or extreme depth of field depends on the point of your photo. In classic nature photography, for example, the artistic tradition is a very shallow depth of field, as shown in Figure 9-13, and requires an open aperture (low f-stop value). But if you want the viewer to be able to clearly see all details throughout the frame — for example, if you're shooting a product shot for your company's sales catalog — you need to go the other direction, stopping down the aperture as far as possible.

  Not ready for the advanced exposure modes yet? Try Close Up mode instead. (It's the one marked with the little flower on your Mode dial.) In this mode, the camera automatically opens the aperture to achieve a short depth of field and bases focus on the center of the frame. The range of apertures available to the camera depends on your lens and the lighting conditions.

- ✔ **Remember that zooming in and getting close to your subject both decrease depth of field.** So back to that product shot: If you need depth of field beyond what you can achieve with the aperture setting, you may need to back away, zoom out, or both. (You can always crop your image to show just the parts of the subject that you want to feature.)

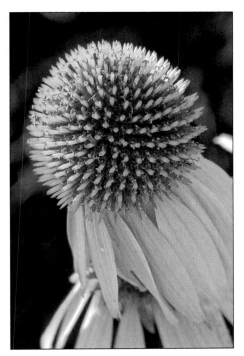

Figure 9-13: Shallow depth of field is a classic technique for close-up floral images.

- ✔ **When shooting flowers and other nature scenes outdoors, pay attention to shutter speed, too.** Even a slight breeze may cause your subject to move, causing blurring at slow shutter speeds.

- ✔ **Use flash for better outdoor lighting.** Just as with portraits, a tiny bit of flash typically improves close-ups when the sun is your primary light source. Again, though, keep in mind that the maximum shutter speed possible when you use the built-in flash is 1/200 second. So in very bright light, you may need to use a high f-stop setting to avoid overexposing the picture. If you shoot in an advanced exposure mode (P, S, A, or M), you can also adjust the flash output via the Flash Compensation control. Chapter 7 offers details.

- ✔ **When shooting indoors, try not to use flash as your primary light source.** Because you're shooting at close range, the light from your flash may be too harsh even at a low Flash Compensation setting. If flash is inevitable, turn on as many room lights as possible to reduce the flash power that's needed — even a hardware-store shop light can do in a pinch as a lighting source. (Remember that if you have multiple light sources, though, you may need to tweak the White Balance setting.)

- ✔ **To really get close to your subject, invest in a macro lens or a set of diopters.** A true macro lens, which enables you to get really, really close to your subjects, is an expensive proposition; expect to pay around $200 or more. But if you enjoy capturing the tiny details in life, it's worth the investment.

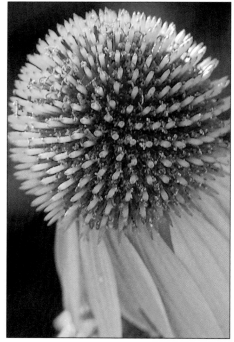

For a less expensive way to go, you can spend about $40 for a set of *diopters,* which are sort of like reading glasses that you screw onto your existing lens. Diopters come in several strengths — +1, +2, + 4, and so on — with a higher number indicating a greater magnifying power. I took this approach to capture the extreme close-up in Figure 9-14, attaching a +2 diopter to my lens. The downfall of diopters, sadly, is that they typically produce images that are very soft around the edges, a problem that doesn't occur with a good macro lens.

Figure 9-14: To extend your lens' close-focus ability, you can add magnifying diopters.

Coping with Special Situations

A few subjects and shooting situations pose some additional challenges not already covered in earlier sections. So to wrap up this chapter, here's a quick list of ideas for tackling a variety of common tough-shot photos:

- **Shooting through glass:** To capture subjects that are behind glass, such as animals at a zoo, you can try a couple tricks. First, set your camera to manual focusing — the glass barrier can give the autofocus mechanism fits. Disable your flash to avoid creating any unwanted reflections, too. Then, if you can get close enough, your best odds are to put the lens right up to the glass (be careful not to scratch your lens). If you must stand farther away, try to position your lens at a 90-degree angle to the glass. I used this approach in Figure 9-15 to photograph the snake, who was, thankfully, behind glass.

- **Shooting out a car window:** Set the camera to shutter-priority autoexposure or manual mode and dial in a fast shutter speed to compensate for the movement of the car. Also turn on Vibration Reduction, if your lens offers it. Oh, and keep a tight grip on your camera.

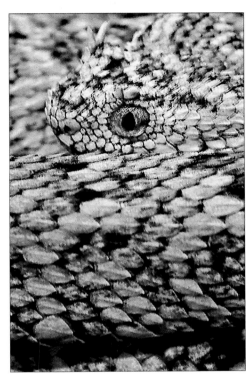

Figure 9-15: He's watching you . . .

- **Shooting fireworks:** First off, use a tripod; fireworks require a long exposure, and trying to handhold your camera simply isn't going to work. If using a zoom lens, zoom out to the shortest focal length (widest angle). Switch to manual focusing and set focus at infinity (the farthest focus point possible on your lens). Set the exposure mode to manual, choose a relatively high f-stop setting — say, f/16 or so — and start at a shutter speed of 1 to 5 seconds. From there, it's simply a matter of experimenting with different shutter speeds. Also play with the timing of the shutter release, starting some exposures at the moment the fireworks are shot up, some at the moment they burst open, and so on. For the example featured in Figure 9-16, shutter speed was about 5 seconds and began the exposure as the rocket was going up — that's what creates the "corkscrew" of light that rises up through the frame.

Be especially gentle when you press the shutter button — with a very slow shutter, you can easily create enough camera movement to blur the image. If you purchased the accessory remote control for your camera, this is a good situation in which to use it. You can also set the self-timer to 2 seconds, which gives the camera time to stabilize after you press the shutter button. (See Chapter 2 for help with the self-timer setting.)

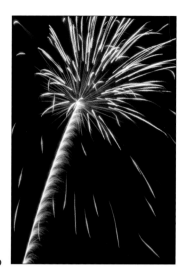

Figure 9-16: I used a shutter speed of 5 seconds to capture this fireworks shot.

✔ **Shooting reflective surfaces:** In outdoor shots taken in bright sun, you can reduce glare from reflective surfaces, such as glass and metal, by using a *circular polarizing filter,* which you can buy for about $40. A polarizing filter can also help out when you're shooting through glass.

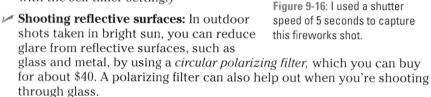

But know that for the filter to work, the sun, your subject, and your camera lens must be precisely positioned. Your lens must be at a 90-degree angle from the sun, for example, and the light source must also be reflecting off the surface at a certain angle and direction. In addition, a polarizing filter also intensifies blue skies in some scenarios, which may or may not be to your liking. In other words, a polarizing filter isn't a surefire cure-all.

A more reliable option for shooting small reflective objects is to invest in a light cube or light tent such as the ones shown in Figure 9-17, from Cloud Dome (www.clouddome.com) and Lastolite (www.lastolite.com), respectively. You place the reflective object inside the tent or cube and then position your lights around the outside. The cube or tent acts as a light diffuser, reducing reflections. Prices range from about $50 to $200, depending on size and features.

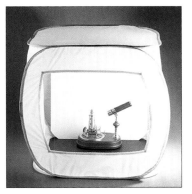 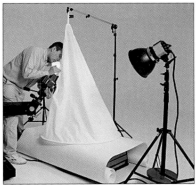

Cloud Dome, Inc. *Lastolite Limited*

Figure 9-17: Investing in a light cube or tent makes photographing reflective objects much easier.

✏ **Shooting in strong backlighting:** When the light behind your subject is very strong, the result is often an underexposed subject. You can try using flash to better expose the subject, assuming that you're shooting in an exposure mode that permits flash. The Active D-Lighting feature, which captures the image in a way that retains better detail in the shadows without blowing out highlights, may also help. (Chapter 7 offers an example.)

But for another creative choice, you can purposely underexpose the subject to create a silhouette effect, as shown in Figure 9-18. Set your camera to an advanced exposure mode, disable flash and Active D-Lighting, and then base your exposure on the sky so that the darker areas of the frame remain dark.

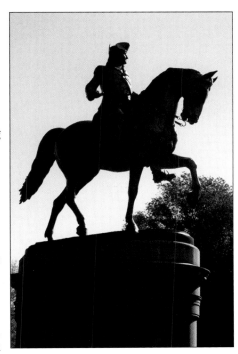

Figure 9-18: Experiment with shooting backlit subjects in silhouette.

Part IV
The Part of Tens

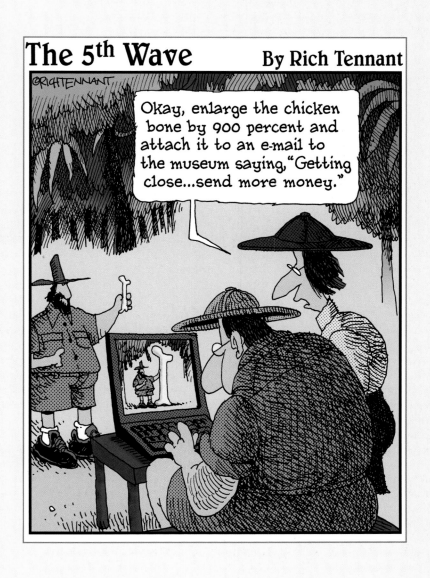

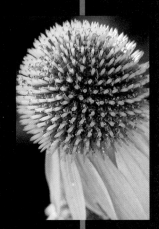

In this part . . .

In time-honored *For Dummies* tradition, this part of the book contains additional tidbits of information presented in the always popular "Top Ten" list format. Chapter 10 shows you how to do some minor picture touchups, such as cropping and adjusting exposure, by using tools on your camera's Retouch menu. Following that, Chapter 11 introduces you to ten camera functions that I consider specialty tools — bonus options that, while not at the top of the list of the features I suggest you study, are nonetheless interesting to explore when you have a free moment or two.

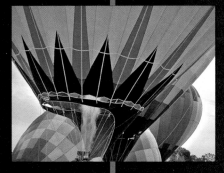

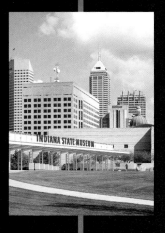

10

Ten Fun and Practical Retouch Menu Features

*E*very photographer produces a clunker image now and then. When it happens to you, don't be too quick to reach for the Delete button because many common problems are surprisingly easy to fix. In fact, you often can repair your photos right in the camera, thanks to tools found on the Retouch menu. You can even create some special effects with certain menu options.

This chapter offers step-by-step recipes for using ten of these photo-repair and enhancement features. Additionally, I received special dispensation from the *For Dummies* folks to start off things with an additional section that summarizes tips that relate to all the Retouch menu options. In the words of Nigel Tufnel from the legendary rock band Spinal Tap, "This one goes to 11!"

Applying the Retouch Menu Filters

You can get to the Retouch menu features in two ways:

✔ Display the menu, select the tool you want to use, and press OK. You're then presented with thumbnails of your photos. Use the Multi Selector to move the yellow highlight box over the photo you want to adjust and press OK. You next see options related to the selected tool.

✔ Switch the camera to playback mode, display your photo in single-frame view, and press OK. (Remember, you can shift from thumbnail display to single-frame view simply by pressing OK.) The Retouch menu then appears superimposed over your photo, as shown on the left in Figure 10-1. Select the tool you want to use and press OK again to apply the tool to your picture, as shown on the right. I prefer the second method so that's how I approach things in this chapter, but it's entirely a personal choice.

However, you can't use this method for one Retouch menu option: Image Overlay, which combines two photos to create a third, blended image, requires you to use the first method of accessing the menu.

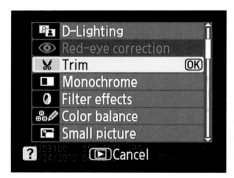
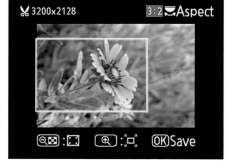

Figure 10-1: In single-frame playback view, press OK, select a retouching tool, and press OK again to apply the tool to your picture.

A few other critical factoids to note before you experiment with the Retouch menu tools:

✔ **Your originals remain intact.** When you apply a correction or enhancement from the Retouch menu, the camera creates a copy of your original photo and then makes the changes to the copy only. Your original is preserved untouched.

✔ **All menu options work with either JPEG or Raw (NEF) originals except Image Overlay.** The Image Overlay feature, which combines two pictures and is detailed in Chapter 11, works only with Raw files. See Chapter 2 for an explanation of JPEG and Raw file types.

✔ **Retouched copies for all alterations except Image Overlay are saved in the JPEG file format.** The retouched copy uses the same JPEG quality setting as the original (Fine, Normal, or Basic). For the Image Overlay option, you can choose to store the combined photo in the JPEG or Raw format.

✔ **You can apply each correction to the same picture only once.** The exception is the Image Overlay feature — you can use the technique outlined in Chapter 11 to overlay more than two pictures.

✔ **File numbers of retouched copies don't match those of the originals.** Make note of the filename the retouched version is assigned so that you can easily track it down later. What numbering the camera chooses depends on the numbers of the files already on your memory card.

✔ **Except for Image Overlay pictures, edited files are assigned a filename that begins with a special three-letter code.** The codes are as follows:

  • *SSC:* Used for photos that you resize using the Small Picture function. Chapter 6 covers the Small Picture feature, which is useful for creating low-resolution copies of your photos for e-mail sharing.

  • *CSC:* Indicates that you applied one of the other Retouch menu corrections.

Image Overlay pictures retain the original DSC or _DSC file prefix, which can make it difficult to distinguish them from a Raw original. (DSC means that the image was captured using the sRGB color profile; _DSC indicates the Adobe RGB color profile.) The key is to look for the Retouch information during picture playback; see Chapter 5 to find out more about where to find this bit of data. Chapter 8 discusses color profiles.

✔ **You can compare the original and the retouched version through the Before and After menu option.** To use this feature, start by displaying either the original or the retouched version in full-frame playback. Then press OK, select Before and After, as shown on the left in Figure 10-2, and press OK again. Now you see the original image on one side and the retouched version on the other, as shown in the second screen in the figure. At the top of the screen, labels indicate the Retouch tool that you applied to the photo. (I applied the cropping tool, Trim, in Figure 10-2.)

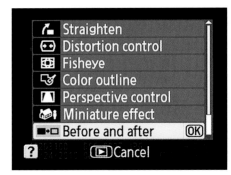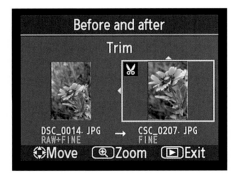

Figure 10-2: Use the Before and After Comparison option to see whether you prefer the retouched version of a photo to the original.

These additional tricks work in Before and After display:

- If you applied more than one Retouch tool to the picture, press the Multi Selector right and left to display individual thumbnails that show how each tool affected the picture.

- If you create multiple retouched versions of the same original — for example, if you create a monochrome version, save that, and then crop the original image and save that — you use a different technique to compare all the versions. First, press the Multi Selector right or left to surround the After image with the yellow highlight box. Now press the Multi Selector up and down to scroll through all the retouched versions.

- To temporarily view the original or retouched image at full-frame view, use the Multi Selector to highlight its thumbnail and then press and hold the Zoom In button. Release the button to return to Before and After view.

To exit Before and After view and return to single-image playback, press the Playback button.

Removing Red-Eye

From my experience, red-eye isn't a major problem with the D3100. Typically, the problem occurs only in very dark lighting, which makes sense: When little ambient light is available, the pupils of the subjects' eyes widen, creating more potential for the flash light to cause red-eye reflection.

If you spot a red-eye problem, however, give the Red-Eye Correction filter a try:

1. **Display your photo in single-image view and press OK.**

   The Retouch menu appears over your photo. (Note that the Red-Eye Correction option appears dimmed in the menu for photos taken without flash.)

2. **Highlight Red-Eye Correction, as shown on the left in Figure 10-3, and press OK.**

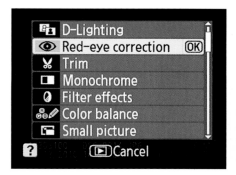 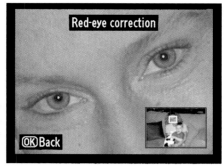

Figure 10-3: An automated red-eye remover is built right into your camera.

If the camera detects red-eye, it applies the removal filter and displays the results in the monitor. If the camera can't find any red-eye, it displays a message telling you so.

3. **Carefully inspect the repair.**

   Press the Zoom In button to magnify the display so that you can check the camera's work, as shown on the right in Figure 10-3. To scroll the display, press the Multi Selector up, down, right, or left. The yellow box in the tiny navigation window in the lower-right corner of the screen indicates the area of the picture that you're currently viewing.

4. **If you approve of the correction, press OK twice.**

   The first OK returns the display to normal magnification; the second creates the retouched copy.

5. **If you're not happy with the results, press OK to return to normal magnification. Then press the Playback button to cancel the repair.**

If the in-camera red-eye repair fails you, most photo-editing programs have red-eye removal tools that let you get the job done. Unfortunately, no red-eye remover works on animal eyes. Red-eye removal tools know how to detect and replace only red-eye pixels, and animal eyes typically turn yellow, white, or green in response to a flash. The easiest solution is to use the brush tool found in most photo editors to paint the proper eye colors.

Shadow Recovery with D-Lighting

Chapter 7 introduces you to Active D-Lighting. If you turn on this option when you shoot a picture, the camera captures the image in a way that brightens the darkest parts of the image, bringing shadow detail into the light but leaving highlight details intact. It's a great trick for dealing with high-contrast scenes or subjects that are backlit.

You also can apply a similar adjustment after you take a picture by choosing the D-Lighting option on the Retouch menu. I did just that for the photo in Figure 10-4, where strong backlighting left the balloon underexposed in the original image.

Original image   D-Lighting, High

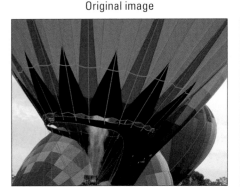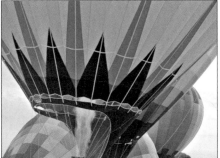

Figure 10-4: An underexposed photo (left) gets help from the D-Lighting filter (right).

Here's how to apply the filter:

1. **Display your photo in single-image mode and then press OK to display the Retouch menu.**

2. **Highlight D-Lighting, as shown on the left in Figure 10-5, and press OK.**

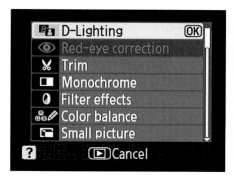
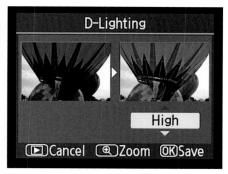

Figure 10-5: Apply the D-Lighting filter via the Retouch menu.

You see a thumbnail of your original image along with a second thumbnail previewing the D-Lighting effect, as shown in the right image in Figure 10-5.

3. **Select the level of adjustment by pressing the Multi Selector up or down.**

   You get three levels: Low, Normal, and High. I used High for the repair to my balloon image.

   To get a closer view of the adjusted photo, press and hold the Zoom In button. Release the button to return to the two-thumbnail display.

4. **To go forward with the correction, press OK.**

   The camera creates your retouched copy.

 You can't apply D-Lighting to a picture taken using the Monochrome Picture Control. (See Chapter 8 for details on Picture Controls.) Nor does D-Lighting work on any pictures to which you've applied the Quick Retouch filter, covered next, or the Monochrome filter, detailed a little later in this chapter.

Boosting Shadows, Contrast, and Saturation Together

The Quick Retouch filter increases contrast and saturation and, if your subject is backlit, also applies a D-Lighting adjustment to restore some shadow detail that otherwise might be lost. In other words, Quick Retouch is sort of like D-Lighting on steroids.

Figure 10-6 illustrates the difference between the two filters. The first example shows my original, a close-up shot of a tree bud about to emerge. I applied the D-Lighting filter to the second example, which brightened the darkest areas of the image. In the final example, I applied the Quick Retouch filter. Again, shadows got a slight bump up the brightness scale. But the filter also increased color saturation and adjusted the overall image to expand the tonal range across the entire brightness spectrum, from very dark to very bright. In this photo, the saturation change is most noticeable in the yellows and reds of the tree bud. (The sky color may initially appear to be less saturated, but in fact, it's just a lighter hue than the original, thanks to the contrast adjustment.)

To try the filter, display your photo in single-image playback mode and press OK to bring up the Retouch menu. Highlight Quick Retouch, as shown on the left in Figure 10-7, and press OK to display the right screen in the figure.

As with the D-Lighting filter, you can set the level of adjustment to Low, Normal, or High. Just press the Multi Selector up or down to change the setting. (For my example photos, I applied both the D-Lighting and Quick Retouch filters at the Normal level.) Press OK to finalize the job and create your retouched copy.

Note that the same issues related to D-Lighting, spelled out in the preceding section, apply here as well: You can't apply the Quick Retouch filter to monochrome images. Additionally,

Original

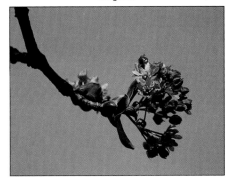

D-Lighting

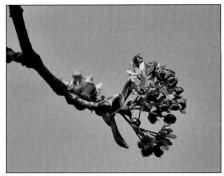

Quick Retouch

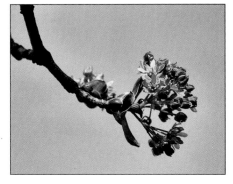

Figure 10-6: Quick Retouch brightens shadows and also increases saturation and contrast, producing a slightly different result than D-Lighting.

you can't apply the Quick Retouch filter to a retouched copy that you created by applying the D-Lighting filter, and vice versa. However, you can create two retouched copies of your original image, applying D-Lighting to one and Quick Retouch to the other. You then can use the Before and After feature, explained at the beginning of this chapter, to compare the retouched versions to see which one you prefer.

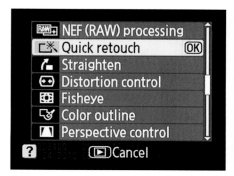 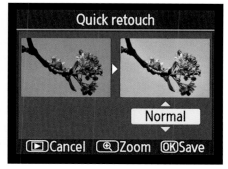

Figure 10-7: Press the Multi Selector up or down to adjust the amount of the correction.

Tweaking Color in Two Ways

Chapter 8 explains how to use your camera's White Balance and Picture Control features to manipulate photo colors. But even if you play with those settings all day, you may wind up with colors that you want to tweak just a tad.

You can boost color saturation with the Quick Retouch filter, explained in the preceding section. But that tool also adjusts contrast and, depending on the photo, also applies a D-Lighting correction. With the Filter Effects and Color Balance tools, however, you can manipulate color only. The next two sections tell all.

Applying digital lens filters

As shown in Figure 10-8, the Filter Effects option offers five color-manipulation filters that are designed to mimic the results produced by traditional lens filters. The other two filters on the menu, Cross Screen and Soft, are special-effects filters; you can read about both in Chapter 11.

The five color-shifting filters work like so:

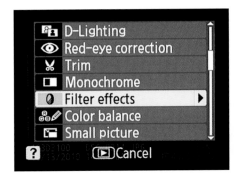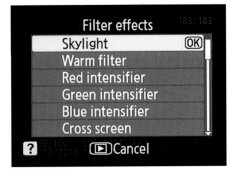

Figure 10-8: You can choose from seven effects that mimic traditional lens filters.

- **Skylight filter:** This filter reduces the amount of blue in an image. The result is a very subtle warming effect. That is, colors take on a bit of a reddish cast.

- **Warm filter:** This one produces a warming effect that's just a bit stronger than the Skylight filter.

- **Color intensifiers:** You can boost the intensity of reds, greens, or blues individually by applying these filters.

As an example, Figure 10-9 shows you an original image and three adjusted versions. As you can see, the Skylight and Warm filters are both very subtle; in this image, the effects are most noticeable in the sky. The fourth example shows a variation created by using the Color Balance filter, explained in the next section, and shifting colors toward the cool (bluish) side of the color spectrum.

Follow these steps to apply the Filter Effects color tools:

1. **Display your photo in single-frame playback mode and press OK to display the Retouch menu.**

2. **Highlight Filter Effects and press OK.**

   You see the list of available filters. (Refer to Figure 10-8.)

3. **Highlight the filter you want to use and press OK.**

   The camera displays a preview of how your photo will look if you apply the filter.

4. **To apply the Skylight or Warm filter, press OK.**

   Or press the Playback button if you want to cancel the filter application. You can't adjust the intensity of these two filters.

5. For the color-intensifier filters, press the Multi Selector up or down to specify the amount of color shift. Then press OK.

Original image

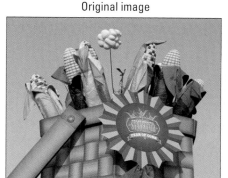

Skylight filter

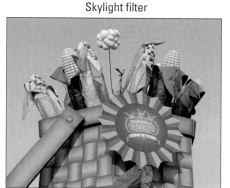

Warm filter

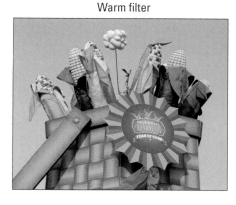

Color Balance filter, shifted to blue

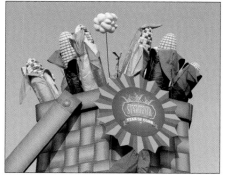

Figure 10-9: Here you see the results of applying two Filter Effects adjustments and a Color Balance shift.

Manipulating color balance

The Color Balance tool enables you to adjust colors with more finesse than the Filter Effects options. With this filter, you can shift colors toward any part of the color spectrum. For example, shifting colors toward the cooler — bluer — spectrum produced the fourth example in Figure 10-9.

Take these steps to give it a whirl:

1. Display your photo in single-image playback mode and press OK.

Up pops the Retouch menu.

2. **Highlight Color Balance, as shown on the left in Figure 10-10.**

Color shift marker

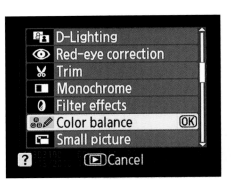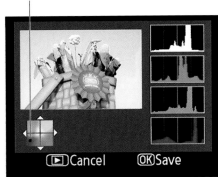

Figure 10-10: Press the Multi Selector to move the color-shift marker and adjust color balance.

3. **Press OK to display the screen shown on the right in the figure.**

   The important control here is the color grid in the lower-left corner. Notice the tiny black square inside the grid, labeled color shift marker in the figure.

4. **Use the Multi Selector to move the color shift marker in the direction of the color adjustment you want to make.**

   Press up to make the image more green, press right to make it more red, and so on. In the figure, I positioned the marker to emphasize blue tones, for example.

   The histograms on the right side of the display show you the resulting impact on overall image brightness, as well as on the individual red, green, and blue brightness values — a bit of information that's helpful if you're an experienced student in the science of reading histograms. (Chapter 5 gives you an introduction.) If not, just check the image preview to monitor your results.

5. **Press OK to create the color-adjusted copy of your photo.**

Creating Monochrome Photos

With the Monochrome Picture Control feature covered in Chapter 8, you can shoot black-and-white photos. Technically, the camera takes a full-color picture and then strips it of color as it's recording the image to the memory card, but the end result is the same.

As an alternative, you can create a black-and-white copy of an existing color photo by applying the Monochrome option on the Retouch menu. You can also create sepia and *cyanotype* (blue and white) images via the Monochrome option. Figure 10-11 shows you examples of all three effects.

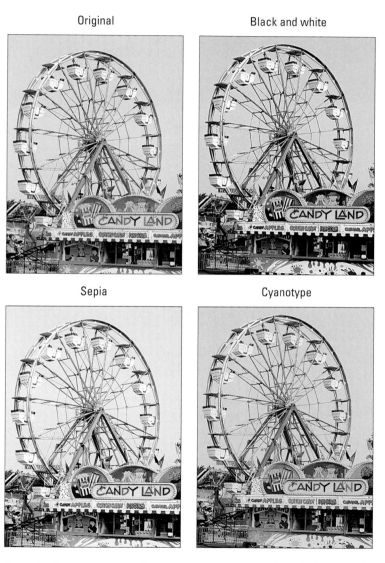

Figure 10-11: You can create three monochrome effects through the Retouch menu.

I prefer to convert my color photos to monochrome images in my photo editor; going that route simply offers more control, not to mention the fact that it's easier to preview your results on a large computer monitor than on the camera monitor. Still, I know that not everyone's as much of a photo-editing geek as I am, so I present to you here the steps involved in applying the Monochrome effects to a color original in your camera:

1. **Display your photo in single-image view and press OK to bring the Retouch menu to life, as shown on the left in Figure 10-12.**

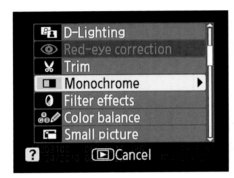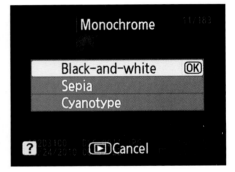

Figure 10-12: Select a filter and press OK to start the process.

2. **Highlight Monochrome and press OK to display the three effect options, as shown on the right in the figure.**

3. **Highlight the effect that you want to apply and press OK.**

   You then see a preview of the image with your selected photo filter applied.

4. **To adjust the intensity of the sepia or cyanotype effect, press the Multi Selector up or down.**

   No adjustment is available for the black-and-white filter.

5. **Press OK to create the monochrome copy.**

Straightening Tilting Horizon Lines

I seem to have a knack for shooting with the camera slightly misaligned with respect to the horizon line, which means that photos like the one on the left in Figure 10-13 often wind up crooked — in this case, everything tilts down toward the right corner of the frame. Perhaps those who say I have a skewed view of life are right? At any rate, my inability to "shoot straight" makes me especially fond of the Straighten tool on the Retouch menu. With this filter, you can rotate tilting horizons back to the proper angle, as shown in the right image in the figure.

Original   Straightened

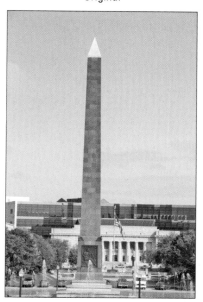 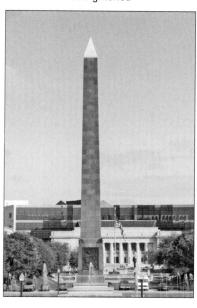

Figure 10-13: You can rotate crooked photos back to a level orientation with the Straighten tool.

To achieve this rotation magic, the camera must crop your image and then enlarge the remaining area — that's why the after photo in Figure 10-13 contains slightly less subject matter than the original. (The same cropping occurs if you make this kind of change in a photo editor.) The camera updates the display as you rotate the photo so that you can get an idea of how much of the original scene may be lost.

Here's how to put the tool to work:

1. **Display the photo in single-image playback mode and then press OK to get to the Retouch menu.**

2. **Highlight Straighten, as shown on the left in Figure 10-14, and press OK.**

   You see a screen similar to the one on the right in the figure, with a grid superimposed on your photo to serve as an alignment aid.

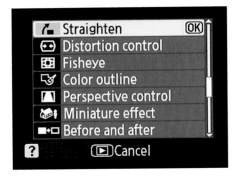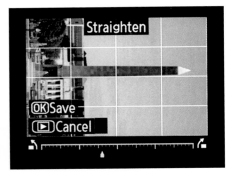

Figure 10-14: Press the Multi Selector right or left to rotate the image in increments of .25 degrees.

3. **To rotate the picture clockwise, press the Multi Selector right.**

   Each press spins the picture by about .25 degrees. You can achieve a maximum rotation of five degrees. The yellow pointer on the little scale under the photo shows you the current amount of rotation.

4. **To rotate in a counter-clockwise direction, press the Multi Selector left.**

5. **When things are no longer off-kilter, press OK to create your retouched copy.**

Removing (Or Creating) Lens Distortion

Certain types of lenses can produce a type of distortion that causes straight lines in a scene to appear curved. Wide-angle lenses, for example, often create *barrel distortion,* in which objects at the center appear to be magnified and pushed forward — as if you wrapped the photo around the outside of a sphere. The effect is perhaps easiest to spot in a rectangular subject like the oil painting in Figure 10-15. Notice that in the original image, on the left, the edges of the painting appear to bow slightly outward. *Pincushion distortion* affects the photo in the opposite way, making center objects appear smaller and farther away, as if you wrapped the photo around the inside of a sphere.

 You can minimize the chances of distortion by researching your lens purchases carefully. Photography magazines and online photography sites regularly measure and report distortion performance in their lens reviews.

Slight barrel distortion

After Distortion Correction filter

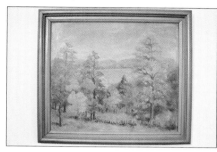 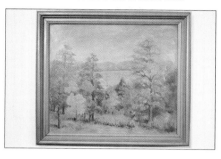

Figure 10-15: Barrel distortion makes straight lines appear to bow outward.

If you do notice a small amount of distortion, try enabling the Auto Distortion Control option on the Shooting menu. This feature attempts to correct distortion as you take the picture. (Chapter 8 has details.) Or you may prefer to wait until after reviewing your photos and then use the Distortion control on the Retouch menu to try to fix things. I applied the filter to create the second version of the subject in Figure 10-15, for example. Less helpful, in my opinion, is a related filter, the Fisheye filter, that actually creates distortion in an attempt to replicate the look of a photo taken with a fisheye lens.

The extent of the in-camera adjustment you can apply is fairly minimal. Additionally, I find it a little difficult to gauge my results on the camera monitor because you can't display any sort of alignment grid over the image to help you find the right degree of correction. For those reasons, I prefer to do this kind of work in my photo editor. Wherever you make the correction, understand that you lose part of your original image area as a result of the distortion correction, just as you do when you apply the like the Straighten tool, covered earlier in this chapter.

All that said, the first step in applying either filter is to display your photo in single-image playback mode and then press OK to display the Retouch menu. Highlight the filter you want to use (Distortion Control or Fisheye) and press OK again. From that point, the process depends on which of the two filters you're using:

- **Distortion Control:** After you press OK to select the Distortion Control filter, you see the screen shown on the left in Figure 10-16. For some lenses, an Auto option is available; as its name implies, this option attempts to automatically apply the right degree of correction. If the Auto option is dimmed or you prefer to do the correction on your own, choose Manual and press OK to display the right screen in the figure.

The little scale under the image represents the degree and direction of shift that you're applying. Press the Multi Selector right to reduce barrel distortion; press left to reduce pincushioning. Press OK when you're ready to make your corrected copy of the photo.

✔ **Fisheye:** After you highlight the filter name and press OK, you see a screen similar to the right one in Figure 10-16. This time, you see the word Fisheye at the top of the screen, however, and the scale at the bottom of the image indicates the strength of the distortion effect. Press the Multi Selector right or left to adjust the amount. Then press OK to create the fisheye copy.

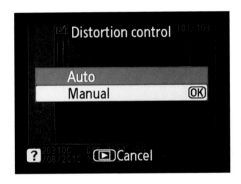 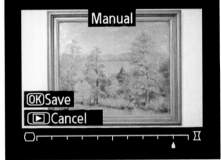

Figure 10-16: Use the Distortion Control filter to reduce barrel or pincushion distortion.

Correcting Perspective

When you photograph a tall building and tilt the camera to get it all in the frame, an effect called *convergence* or *keystoning* occurs. This effect causes vertical structures to appear to be leaning toward the center of the frame. Buildings sometimes even appear to be falling away from you, as shown in the left image in Figure 10-17. (If the lens is tilting down, verticals instead appear to lean outward, and the building appears to be falling toward you.) Through the Retouch menu's Perspective Control feature, you can right those leaning verticals, as shown in the "after" photo on the right in Figure 10-17.

Note, though, that just like the Straighten tool, described earlier in this chapter, you lose some area around the perimeter of your photo as part of the correction process. So when you're shooting this type of subject, frame loosely — that way, you ensure that you don't sacrifice an important part of the scene due to the correction.

Original

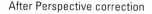

After Perspective correction

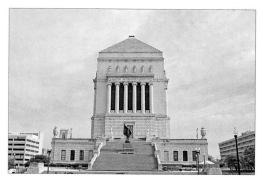
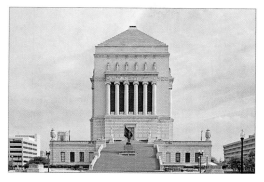

Figure 10-17: The original photo exhibited convergence (left); applying the Perspective Control filter corrected the problem (right).

To try out the feature, follow these steps:

1. **Display your photo in single-image view and press OK to bring the Retouch menu to life.**

2. **Highlight Perspective Control, as shown in the left in Figure 10-18, and press OK.**

   After enabling this filter, you see a grid and a horizontal and vertical scale, as shown on the right in Figure 10-18.

3. **Press the Multi Selector left and right to move the out-of-whack object horizontally.**

4. **Press the Multi Selector up and down to rotate the object toward or away from you.**

5. **Use the guides to get the perspective as close to normal as possible and then press OK to make a copy of the original image with your changes.**

   Depending on the scene, you may not be able to get all structures fully corrected, so just pay attention to the most prominent ones in the scene. For severe distortion problems, you may be able to get better results in your photo editor; in some programs, you can pull and push each side of the image around independently of the others, which enables you to more freely shift perspective than is possible with the type of tool provided in the camera.

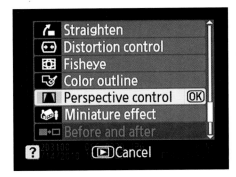
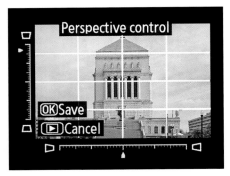

Figure 10-18: Press the Multi Selector to adjust the correction type and amount.

Cropping (Trimming) Your Photo

To *crop* a photo simply means to trim away some of its perimeter. Cropping away excess background can often improve an image, as illustrated by Figures 10-19 and 10-20. When shooting this scene, I couldn't get close enough to the ducks to fill the frame with them, so I simply cropped it after the fact to achieve the desired composition.

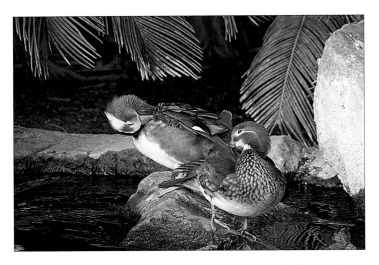

Figure 10-19: The original contains too much extraneous background.

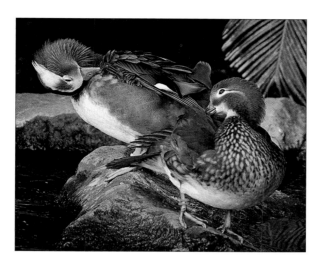

Figure 10-20: Cropping creates a better composition and eliminates background clutter.

With the Trim function on the Retouch menu, you can crop a photo right in the camera. Note a few things about this feature:

✔ You can crop your photo to five different aspect ratios: 3:2, which maintains the original proportions and matches that of a 4 x 6-inch print; 4:3, the proportions of a standard computer monitor or television (that is, not a wide-screen model); 5:4, which gives you the same proportions as an 8 x 10-inch print; 1:1, which results in a square photo; and 16:9, which is the same aspect ratio as a wide-screen monitor or television. If your purpose for cropping is to prepare your image for a frame size that doesn't match any of these aspect ratios, crop in your photo software instead.

✔ For each aspect ratio, you can choose from seven crop sizes. The sizes are stated in pixel terms — for example, if you select the 3:2 aspect ratio, you can crop the photo to measurements of 3840 x 2560, 3200 x 2128, and so on, all the way down to 640 x 424 pixels.

✔ If you captured the original photo using the Raw+JPEG Fine Image Quality setting, the cropped version is saved as a JPEG Fine image. For other JPEG images, the crop version has the same Image Quality level as the original.

✔ After you apply the Trim function, you can't apply any other fixes from the Retouch menu. So make cropping the last of your retouching steps.

Keeping those caveats in mind, trim your image as follows:

1. **Display your photo in single-image view and press OK to launch the Retouch menu.**

2. **Highlight Trim, as shown on the left in Figure 10-21, and press OK.**

   You see a screen similar to the right side of the figure. The yellow highlight box indicates the current cropping frame. Anything outside the frame is set to be trimmed away.

3. **Rotate the Command dial to change the crop aspect ratio.**

   The selected aspect ratio appears in the upper-right corner of the screen, as shown on the right in Figure 10-21.

4. **Adjust the cropping frame size and placement as needed.**

   The current crop size appears in the upper-left corner of the screen. (Refer to Figure 10-21.) You can adjust the size and placement of the cropping frame like so:

   - *Reduce the size of the cropping frame.* Press and release the Zoom Out button. Each press of the button further reduces the crop size.

   - *Enlarge the cropping frame.* Press the Zoom In button to expand the crop boundary and leave more of your image intact.

   - *Reposition the cropping frame.* Press the Multi Selector up, down, right, and left to shift the frame position.

5. **Press OK to create your cropped copy of the original image.**

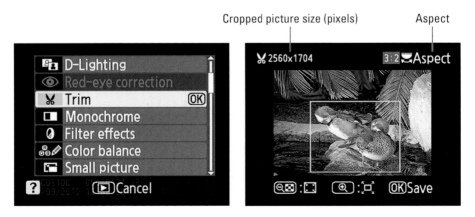

Figure 10-21: Rotate the Command dial to change the proportions of the crop box.

11

Ten Special-Purpose Features to Explore on a Rainy Day

In This Chapter

▶ Adding text comments to images

▶ Creating custom image-storage folders

▶ Changing the function of some controls

▶ Playing with a few more special effects

▶ Combining two photos into one

*C*onsider this chapter the literary equivalent of the end of one of those late-night infomercial offers — the part where the host exclaims, "But wait! There's more!"

The ten features covered in these pages fit the category of "interesting bonus." They aren't the sort of features that drive people to choose one camera over another, and they may come in handy only for certain users, on certain occasions. Still, they're included at no extra charge with your camera purchase, so check 'em out when you have a few spare moments. Who knows; you may discover that one of these bonus features is actually a hidden gem that provides just the solution you need for one of your photography problems.

Annotating Your Images

Through the Image Comment feature on the Setup menu, you can add text comments to your picture files. Suppose, for example, that you're traveling on vacation and visiting a different destination every day. You can annotate all the pictures you take on a particular outing with the name of the location or attraction. You can then view the comments either in Nikon ViewNX 2, which ships free with your camera, or Capture NX 2, which you must buy separately. The comments also appear in some other photo programs that enable you to view metadata.

Here's how the Image Comment feature works:

1. **Display the Setup menu and highlight Image Comment, as shown on the left in Figure 11-1.**

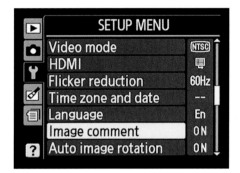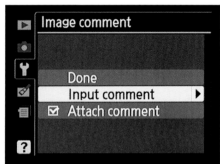

Figure 11-1: You can tag pictures with text comments that you can view in Nikon ViewNX 2.

2. **Press OK to display the right screen in the figure.**

3. **Highlight Input Comment and press the Multi Selector right.**

   You see a keyboard-type screen like the one shown in Figure 11-2.

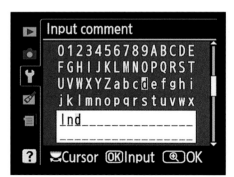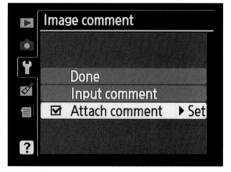

Figure 11-2: Highlight a letter and press the Zoom In button to enter it into the comment box.

4. **Use the Multi Selector to highlight the first letter of the text you want to add.**

   If you scroll the display, you can access additional characters not visible on the initial screen.

5. **Press OK to enter that letter into the display box at the bottom of the screen.**

6. **Keep highlighting letters and pressing OK to continue entering your comment.**

   Your comment can be up to 36 characters long.

   To move the text cursor, rotate the Command dial in the direction you want to shift the cursor.

   To delete a letter, move the cursor under the offending letter and then press the Delete button.

7. **To save the comment, press the Zoom In button.**

8. **Highlight Attach Comment and press the Multi Selector right to put a check mark in the box, as shown on the right in Figure 11-2.**

   The check mark turns on the Image Comment feature.

9. **Highlight Done, as shown in Figure 11-3, and press OK.**

   You return to the Setup menu. The Image Comment menu item is set to On.

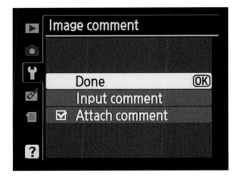

The camera applies your comment to all pictures you take after turning on Image Comment. To disable the feature, revisit the Image Comment menu, highlight Attach Comment, and press the Multi Selector right to toggle the check mark off. Select Done and press OK to make your decision official.

In Nikon ViewNX 2, the comment appears as part of the file metadata, as shown in Figure 11-4. If the Metadata panel is hidden, click the arrow labeled in the figure. (See

Figure 11-3: Be sure to select Done and press OK before exiting the menu.

Chapter 6 for additional information about ViewNX 2.)

Click to hide/display Metadata panel

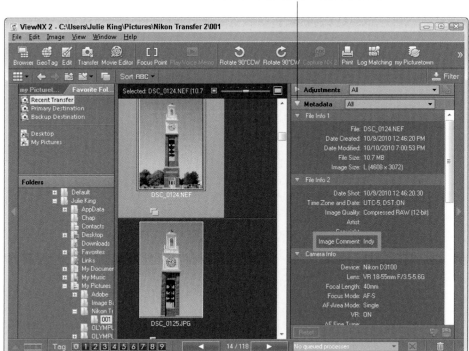

Figure 11-4: Comments appear with other metadata in Nikon ViewNX 2.

Creating Custom Image Folders

By default, your camera initially stores all your images in one folder, which it names 100D3100. Folders have a storage limit of 999 images; when you exceed that number, the camera creates a new folder, assigning a name that indicates the folder number — 101D3100, 102D3100, and so on. You see the full name of the default folders when you view the memory card contents on your computer. While viewing pictures on the camera, you see only a single folder, named D3100, that holds all your pictures, even after you exceed 999 photos and the camera creates a second folder for you.

If you choose, however, you can create your own, custom-named folders. For example, perhaps you sometimes use your camera for business and sometimes for personal use. To keep your images separate, you can set up a DULL folder and a FUN folder — or perhaps something less incriminating, such as WORK and HOME.

Whatever your folder-naming idea, you create custom folders like so:

1. **Display the Setup menu and highlight Storage Folder, as shown on the left in Figure 11-5.**

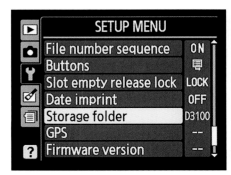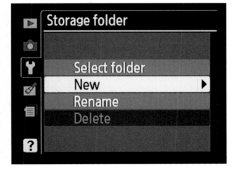

Figure 11-5: You can create custom folders to organize your images right on the camera.

2. **Press OK to display the screen shown on the right in Figure 11-5.**

3. **Highlight New and press the Multi Selector right.**

   You see a keyboard-style screen similar to the one used to create image comments, as described at the start of the chapter. The folder-naming version appears in Figure 11-6.

4. **Enter a folder name up to five characters long.**

   Use these techniques:

   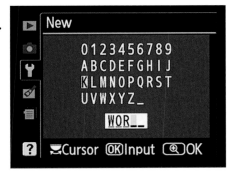

   Figure 11-6: Folder names can contain up to five characters.

   - *To enter a letter,* highlight it by using the Multi Selector. Then press OK.

   - *To move the text cursor,* rotate the Command dial in the direction you want to move the cursor.

   - *To delete a letter,* place the cursor under it and press the Delete button.

5. **After creating your folder name, press the Zoom In button to complete the process and return to the Setup menu.**

   The folder you just created is automatically selected as the active folder.

If you take advantage of this option, remember to specify where you want your pictures stored each time you shoot: Select Storage Folder from the Setup menu and press OK to display the screen shown on the left in Figure 11-7. Highlight Select Folder and press the Multi Selector right to display a list of all your folders, as shown on the right in the figure. Highlight the folder that you want to use and press OK. Your choice also affects which images you can view in playback mode; see Chapter 5 to find out how to select the folder you want to view.

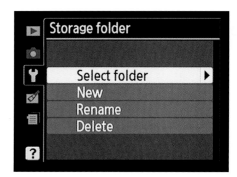
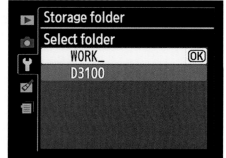

Figure 11-7: Remember to specify where you want to store new images.

If necessary, you can rename a custom folder by using the Rename option on the Storage Folder screen. (Refer to the left screen in Figure 11-7.) The Delete option on the same screen enables you to get rid of all empty folders on the memory card.

Changing the Function Button's Function

Tucked away on the left-front side of the camera, just under the Flash button, the Function (Fn) button is set by default to provide quick access to the ISO Sensitivity setting. By holding down the button and rotating the Command dial, you can adjust the setting without going through the Shooting menu or Quick Settings screen. But if you don't adjust the ISO setting often, you may want to assign one of three other possible functions to the button.

You establish the button's behavior via the Buttons option on the Setup menu, as shown on the left in Figure 11-8. After selecting the option, press OK and choose the Fn Button option, as shown on the right in the figure. You're presented with a list of possible button functions, as shown in Figure 11-9. Here's a quick description of the possible settings:

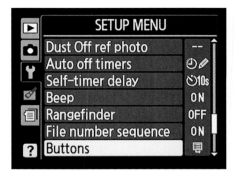 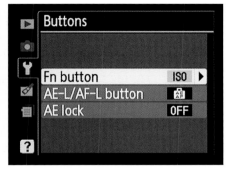

Figure 11-8: You can assign any number of jobs to the Function button.

✓ **Image Quality/Size:** If you select this option, pressing the Fn button while turning the Command dial lets you choose the desired image quality and size. As you rotate the dial, you cycle through the possible combinations of the settings, which you normally select separately, through the Image Quality and Image Size options. Chapter 2 explains these two picture settings.

Figure 11-9: The default option enables you to use the Function button to turn on self-timer shooting for your next picture.

✓ **ISO Sensitivity:** At this default setting, pressing the Fn button while turning the Command dial lets you choose the desired ISO setting. See Chapter 7 for details about the available settings.

✓ **White Balance:** If you select this option, pressing the Fn button while turning the Command dial lets you choose a White Balance setting, but only in P, S, A, and M modes. (You can't adjust white balance in the other exposure modes.) Chapter 8 introduces you to the White Balance feature.

✓ **Active D-Lighting:** If you select this option, pressing the Fn button while turning the Command dial lets you turn Active D-Lighting on and off. Like the White Balance option, this one is adjustable only in the P, S, A, and M exposure modes, however. You can read about Active D-Lighting in Chapter 7.

After selecting the function you want to assign, press OK to lock in your choice.

Customizing the AE-L/AF-L Button

 Set just to the right of the viewfinder, the AE-L/AF-L button enables you to lock focus and exposure settings when you shoot in autoexposure and auto-focus modes, as explored in Chapters 7 and 8.

Normally, autofocus and autoexposure are locked when you press the button, and they remain locked as long as you keep your finger on the button. But you can change the button's behavior via the Buttons option on the Setup menu, as shown on the left in Figure 11-10. After highlighting the AE-L/AF-L Button option, as shown on the right, press OK to display the available settings, as shown in Figure 11-11.

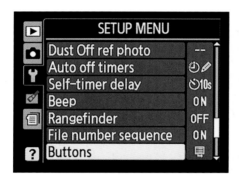
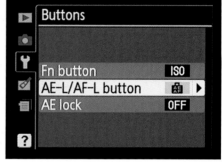

Figure 11-10: You can change the function of the AE-L/AF-L button through the Setup menu.

The options produce these results:

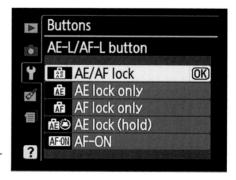

- **AE/AF Lock:** This is the default setting. Focus and exposure remain locked as long as you press the button.

- **AE Lock Only:** Autoexposure is locked as long as you press the button; autofocus isn't affected. (You can still lock focus by pressing the shutter button halfway.)

- **AF Lock Only:** Focus remains locked as long as you press the button. Exposure isn't affected.

Figure 11-11: At the default setting, highlighted here, the button locks exposure and focus together.

- **AE Lock (Hold):** This one locks exposure only with a single press of the button. The exposure lock remains in force until you press the button again or the exposure meters turn off.

✔ **AF-On:** Pressing the button activates the camera's autofocus mechanism. If you choose this option, you can't lock autofocus by pressing the shutter button halfway when using the viewfinder to take pictures. In Live View mode and during movie recording, you still use the shutter button to focus if you set the Focus mode to AF-F. Chapter 4 provides details on Live View and movie shooting.

After highlighting the option you want to use, press OK.

The information that I give in this book with regard to using autofocus and autoexposure assumes that you stick with the default setting. So if you change the button's function, amend my instructions accordingly.

Using the Shutter Button to Lock Exposure and Focus

The Buttons option on the Setup menu offers a third button tweak — AE Lock, as shown in Figure 11-12. This option determines whether pressing the shutter button halfway locks focus only or locks both focus and exposure.

At the default setting, Off, you lock focus only when you press the shutter button halfway. Exposure is adjusted continually up to the time you take the shot. If you change the AE Lock setting to On, your half-press of the shutter button locks both focus and exposure.

As with the AE-L/AF-L button adjustment described in the preceding section, I recommend that you leave this option set to the default while you work with this book. Otherwise, your camera won't behave as described here (or in the camera manual, for that matter). If you encounter a situation that calls for locking exposure and focus together, you can simply use the AE-L/AF-L button, as covered in Chapter 7.

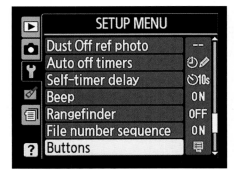
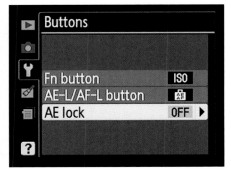

Figure 11-12: If you turn on this option, pressing the shutter button halfway locks exposure and focus.

Adding a Starburst Effect

Want to give your photo a little extra sparkle? Experiment with your D3100's Cross Screen filter. This filter adds a starburst-like effect to the brightest areas of your image, as illustrated in Figure 11-13.

Original Cross Screen filter applied

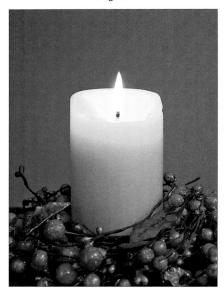 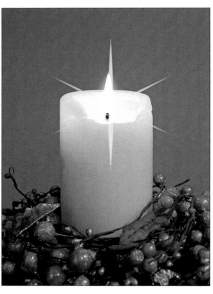

Figure 11-13: The Cross Screen filter adds a starburst effect.

Traditional photographers create this effect by placing a special filter over the camera lens; the filter is sometimes known as a Star filter instead of a Cross Screen filter. With your D3100, you can apply a digital version of the filter via the Retouch menu, as follows:

1. **Display your photo in single-image playback mode and press OK to call up the Retouch menu.**

2. **Highlight Filter Effects, as shown on the left in Figure 11-14, and press OK.**

   You see the Filter Effects submenu, as shown on the right in Figure 11-14.

3. **Highlight Cross Screen and press OK.**

   You see a screen containing a preview that shows you the results of the Cross Screen filter at the current filter settings, as shown in Figure 11-15.

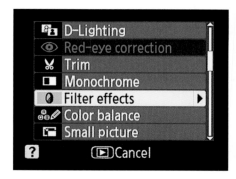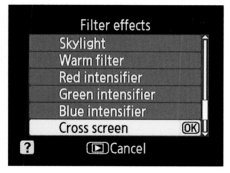

Figure 11-14: Select the filter from the Filter Effects submenu.

4. Adjust the filter settings as needed.

You can adjust the number of points on the star, the intensity of the effect, the length of the star's rays, and the angle of the effect. Just use the Multi Selector to highlight an option and then press the Multi Selector right to display the available settings. Highlight your choice and press OK. I labeled the four options in Figure 11-15.

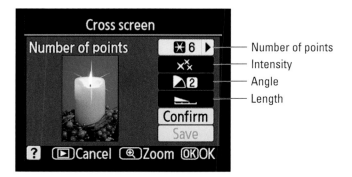

Figure 11-15: You can play with four filter settings to tweak the effect.

5. To update the preview after changing a filter setting, highlight Confirm and press OK.

You can also press and hold the Zoom In button to temporarily view your image in full-screen view. Release the button to return to the normal preview.

6. Highlight Save and press OK to create your star-crossed image.

Keep in mind that the number of starbursts the filter applies depends on your image. You can't change that number; the camera automatically adds the twinkle effect wherever it finds very bright objects. If you want to control the exact placement of the starbursts, you may want to forgo the in-camera filter and find out whether your photo software offers a more flexible star-filter effect. (You can also create the effect manually by painting the cross strokes onto the image in your photo editor.)

It's also important to frame your original image with a little extra "head room" around the object that will get the starburst, as I did in my examples. Otherwise, there isn't room in the picture for the effect.

Creating a Color Outline

As hard as I try, I can't master the skill of drawing. In fact, most three-year-olds can render a scene with more accuracy than I can. But thanks to the Color Outline option on the Retouch menu, I can "fake" a realistic drawing based on any photo, as I did in Figure 11-16. This is a fun project to do with kids, by the way — you can, in essence, create a custom coloring-book page that they can then fill in with watercolors, crayons, or markers.

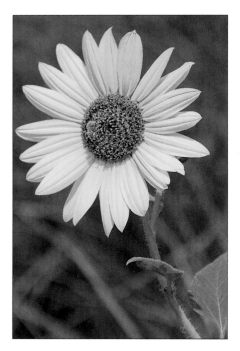
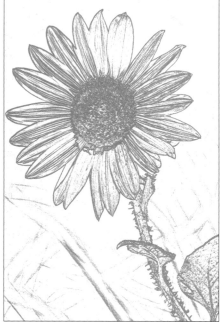

Figure 11-16: You can use a photo as the basis for a color outline.

Try it out:

1. **Display your photo in single-image playback mode and press OK to display the Retouch menu over the image.**

2. **Highlight Color Outline, as shown in Figure 11-17, and press OK.**

   A preview of your art master-piece appears onscreen.

3. **Press OK again.**

   The camera software creates a copy of your image with the effect applied.

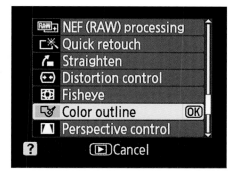

Figure 11-17: Choose Color Outline and then press OK to create the effect.

Softening Focus for a Dreamy Effect

Ever notice that as television and movie stars age, their portraits tend to have a slightly out-of-focus look? The soft focus effect is designed to help mask wrinkles and other signs that one is no longer a dewy-faced teen.

You actually can buy special lenses for your camera that produce this effect, but a cheaper alternative is to apply a focus-softening digital filter like the one found on the D3100's Retouch menu. You can see the results in Figure 11-18. When applied to nature subjects like the one in the figure, the filter creates a look that's similar to the artistic-effects filters you find in many photo-editing programs. Squint hard enough, and you can almost envision a Monet in the making.

Original

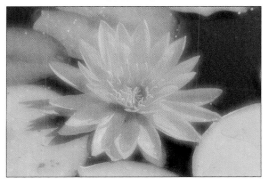

Soften filter

Figure 11-18: I used the Soft filter at the High setting to create a blurry, painterly effect.

Apply the filter like so:

1. **Display your photo in single-image playback mode and press OK to call up the Retouch menu.**

2. **Highlight Filter Effects, press OK, and then highlight Soft, as shown in Figure 11-19.**

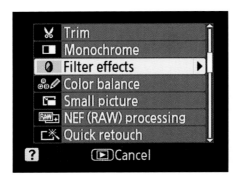 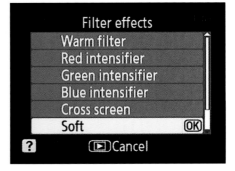

Figure 11-19: The Soft filter is found on the other Filter Effects menu.

3. **Press OK.**

   You see thumbnails of your photo, as shown in Figure 11-20. The left thumbnail is the original; the right thumbnail offers a preview of the filter effect.

4. **Press the Multi Selector up or down to determine how soft you want the image.**

   Your choices are Low (kinda soft), Normal (softer still), and High (pass the foggy goggles). While you're pondering your decision, you can press the Zoom In button to get a better look.

5. **Press OK to apply the filter.**

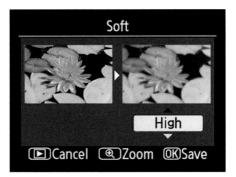

Figure 11-20: Press the Multi Selector up or down to choose the strength of the effect.

Creating a Miniature Effect

Have you ever seen an architect's small-scale models of planned developments? The ones complete with tiny trees and even people? The Miniature Effect on the Retouch menu offers a tool that attempts to create a photographic equivalent by applying a strong blur to all but one portion of a landscape, as shown in Figure 11-21. The left photo is the original; the right shows the result of applying the filter. For this example, I set the focus point on the part of the street occupied by the cars.

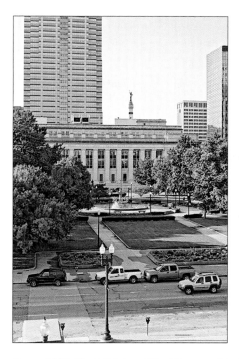 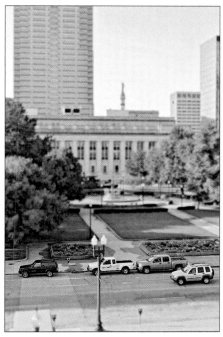

Figure 11-21: The Miniature Effect throws all but a small portion of a scene into very soft focus.

This effect works best if you shoot your subject from a high angle — otherwise, you don't get the miniaturization result. To try it out, take these steps:

1. **Display your photo in full-frame playback and press OK to bring up the Retouch menu.**

2. **Highlight Miniature Effect, as shown on the left in Figure 11-22, and press OK.**

   You see your image in a preview similar to the one shown on the right in the figure.

3. **Use the Multi Selector to position the yellow box over the area you want to keep in sharp focus.**

4. **To preview the effect, press the Zoom In button.**

   When you release the button, you're returned to the screen shown on the right in Figure 11-22. Keep adjusting the placement of the box and previewing the result until you're happy.

5. **To create a copy of your photo with the effect applied, press OK.**

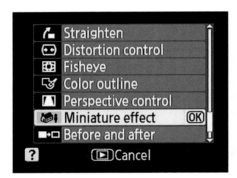
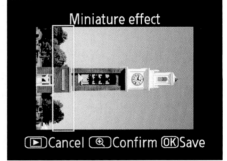

Figure 11-22: Use the Multi Selector to position the yellow rectangle over the area you want to keep in sharp focus.

Combining Two Photos with Image Overlay

Are you into double exposures? Well, you can't officially do a double exposure with the D3100, but the Image Overlay feature found on the Retouch menu enables you to merge two photographs into one. I used this option to combine a photo of a werewolf friend, shown on the top left in Figure 11-23, with a nighttime garden scene, shown on the top right. The result is the ghostly image shown beneath the two originals. Oooh, scary!

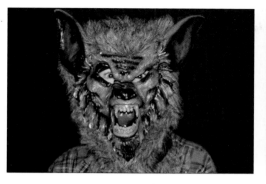
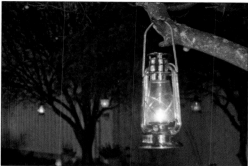
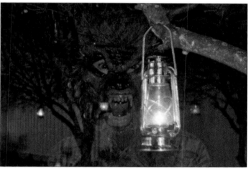

Figure 11-23: Image Overlay merges two Raw (NEF) photos into one.

On the surface, this option sounds kind of cool. The problem is that you can't control the opacity or positioning of the individual images in the combined photo. For example, my overlay picture would've been more successful if I could move the werewolf to the left in the combined image so that he and the lantern aren't blended. And I'd also prefer to keep the background of the second image at full opacity in the overlay image rather than getting a 50:50 mix of that background and the one in the first image, which only creates a fuzzy-looking background in this particular example.

However, there is one effect that you can create successfully with Image Overlay: a "two views" composite like the one in Figure 11-24. But for this trick to work, the background in both images must be the same solid color (black seems to be best), and you must compose your photos so that the subjects don't overlap in the combined photo, as shown here. Otherwise, you get the ghostly effect like you see in Figure 11-23.

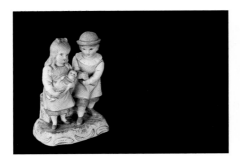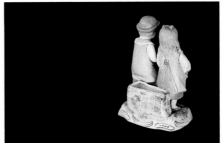

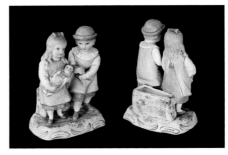

Figure 11-24: If you want each subject to appear solid, use a black background and position the subjects so that they don't overlap.

Additionally, the Image Overlay feature works only with pictures that you shoot in the Camera Raw (NEF) format. For details on Raw, see Chapter 2.

To be honest, I don't use Image Overlay for the purpose of serious photo compositing. I prefer to do this kind of work in my photo-editing software, where I have more control over the blend. In addition, previewing the results of the overlay settings you use is difficult, given the size of the camera monitor.

That said, it's a fun project to try, so give it a go when you have a spare minute. Take these steps:

1. **Using the Image Size and Image Quality options, set the size (pixel count) and file type (Raw or JPEG) for the combined image.**

   The camera saves the final overlay file using the settings you select. Chapter 2 explains these two settings.

2. **Display the Retouch menu and highlight Image Overlay, as shown on the left in Figure 11-25.**

You can't get to this option if you use the other method of applying Retouch commands — displaying your photo first and then pressing OK. You must start at the Retouch menu. (See Chapter 10 for help with using the Retouch menu features.)

3. **Press OK.**

   You see the screen shown on the right in Figure 11-25, with the preview area for Image 1 highlighted. (The yellow border indicates the active preview area.)

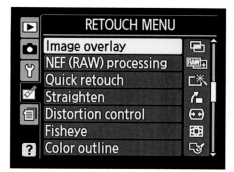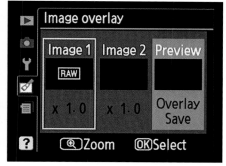

Figure 11-25: The thumbnail marked with the yellow border represents the active image.

4. **Press OK to display thumbnails of your images.**

5. **Select the first of the two images that you want to combine.**

   A yellow border surrounds the currently selected thumbnail. Press the Multi Selector right and left to scroll the display until the border appears around your chosen image. Then press OK.

   The Image Overlay screen now displays your first image as Image 1, as shown on the left in Figure 11-26.

6. **Press the Multi Selector right to move the highlight box over the Image 2 area of the screen.**

7. **Press OK, select the second image, and press OK again.**

   You see both images in the Image Overlay screen, with the combined result appearing in the Preview area, as shown on the right in Figure 11-26.

8. **Press the Multi Selector right to move the yellow selection box over the Preview thumbnail.**

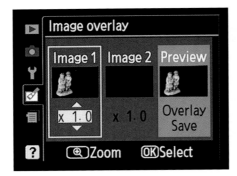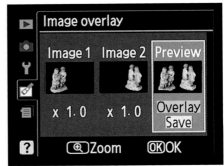

Figure 11-26: After selecting both photos, highlight the Preview thumbnail and press the Zoom In button to preview the results.

9. **Press the Zoom In button to get a full-frame view of the merged image.**

   Or highlight Overlay and press OK to see the preview.

   If you aren't happy with the result, press the Zoom Out button to exit the preview. Then adjust the gain setting underneath the image thumbnails to manipulate the combined image. Press the Multi Selector right or left to highlight Image 1 or Image 2, and then press up or down to adjust the gain for that image.

10. **To save the merged image, highlight Save (in the Preview thumbnail area, as shown on the right in Figure 11-26) and press OK.**

Index

• G •

• H •

• Z •